1910

Fig. 1. Arnold Schoenberg, *The Red Gaze*, 1910, oil. Courtesy Arnold Schoenberg Institute, Los Angeles.

1910

The Emancipation of Dissonance

Thomas Harrison

UNIVERSITY OF CALIFORNIA PRESS
Berkeley · Los Angeles · London

University of California Press
Berkeley and Los Angeles, California

University of California Press
London, England

Copyright © 1996 by
The Regents of the University of California

Library of Congress Cataloging-in-Publication Data

Harrison, Thomas J., 1955–
    1910, the emancipation of dissonance / Thomas Harrison.
        p.   cm.
    Includes bibliographical references and index.
    ISBN 0–520–20043–8 (alk. paper)
    1. Aesthetics, Modern—20th century.   2. Michelstaedter, Carlo,
1887–1910.   3. Expressionism.   4. Anxiety.   5. Europe—Intellectual
life—20th century.   6. Philosophy, Modern—20th century.   I. Title.
BH201.H29   1995
111'.85—dc20   95–25990
                                                                         CIP

Printed in the United States of America

1   2   3   4   5   6   7   8   9

The paper used in this publication meets the minimum requirements of
American National Standard for Information Sciences—Permanence
of Paper for Printed Library Materials, ANSI Z39.48–1984 ⊗

To Guido and Remo Aliotti, born in 1912 and 1913, along with Maria and Flavio.

Contents

    Autoscopy   141
    Qualitative Individualism   146
    Subjective Transcendence   149
    Self-Possession   154
    Pictures of Soul   164

4. An Ethics of Misunderstanding   182
    Ethical and Aesthetic Transcendence   184
    Spiritual Poverty   189
    Tragic Acquiescence   195
    Ecstatic Confessions   202
    Intransitive Love   205
    Ladies of the Unicorn: Structive Art   210

    Afterword and Aftermath   216

    Primary Sources   227

    Secondary Sources   241

    Index   259

Illustrations

Acknowledgments

This book would not have assumed the shape it has without the faith and unflagging support of two remarkable friends: Allen Mandelbaum and Stanley Holwitz. Other early supporters of the work include Charles Bernheimer and Stuart Curran; Alessandro Dal Lago and Thomas Sheehan; Francie Alston, Giuseppe Mazzotta, and Luigi Ballerini; Gregory Lucente and Lucia Re.

As for the idea of this study, my brother Robert claims credit for that. It took place (or would have taken place, for the two of us never remember in quite the same ways) during one of those otiose afternoons in Rome, probably in the summer of 1992, perhaps the same day that we both read from our books for video. After I had held forth for some time about intriguing convergences between Carlo Michelstaedter and other figures of 1910, he convinced me that right there I had my next book. If that is how it happened, I thank him for it, as well as for many other seasons of intellectual exchange.

Then there are those whose lives, or rather, whose understandings of them, have inevitably found a place in these pages: my father, Robert Pogue Harrison, deceased when I was eleven; my sister Sandy; Livio and other members of my "Levantine" Aliotti family; Nanette and Paul Barrutia. I also wish to thank a long list of scholars whose intellectual rigor and research have provided me with models; they have not been cited as often as they deserve in this study: Bini, Cacciari, Campailla, Comini, Lillian Feder, Kallir, Le Rider, Magris, Perloff, Perniola, Pieri, Burton Pike, Pullega, Schorske, Vattimo, and Wohl.

Valuable expressionist collections and personal expertise have been put at my disposal by Drs. Otello Silvestri and Antonella Gallarotti of the Fondo Carlo Michelstaedter; by the Robert Gore Rifkind Center for German Expressionist Studies; by the Arnold Schoenberg Institute; by Stephen Hinton (on Schoenberg), Vivian Endicott Barnett (on Kandinsky), Agnes Heller (on Lukács), and Eric Williams (on Trakl).

Introduction

1910, that is indeed the year when all scaffolds began to crack.

—*Gottfried Benn*

Swollen red eyes, their cavities spreading out through the flesh as if under an order not to sleep. Pupils dilated to the point where they seem to transmit rather than receive perceptions, like a knowing gaze of a fish long dead. The redness of these eyes marks a painful and ghastly emanation out of what seems to have once been a person. This face is being reclaimed, its features giving way to the miasma with which it is stricken. If there is any victory here it is only one of recognition. Arnold Schoenberg: *The Red Gaze* of May 1910.

What is the affliction from which his face suffers? Is it personal or communal in nature? Does it stem from the year 1908, when Schoenberg's wife abandoned him for Richard Gerstl, the expressionist painter, who then took his own life when, at the urging of their friend Anton Webern, Mathilde returned to her husband? Or does it look forward to the collective catastrophe of World War I? Or is it something in its present that it fears and finds all but impossible to bear? Had Schoenberg been able to answer these questions he would not have needed to paint such a painting. Here, as in other canvases of 1910, he expresses something that neither his music nor his writings can convey. Yet we, in front of the painting, still seek words, and in a way that rarely happens before an impressionist or a cubist work. There is something about the rawness, the emotional extremity—the "expressionism"—of its style that calls for an explanation. We want to know the concern of this unsettling art and why it arose at precisely this moment in time.

1

On May 17, 1910, Halley's comet shatters the peace of Europe's skies. As tends to happen at such moments of cosmic disturbance, the event evokes deep-seated anxieties, articulated in newspaper editorials on doom and degeneration. For each collective concern there are thousands of personal ones. Two weeks before the comet, on May 2, Anna Pulitzer, the close friend of the Triestine writer Scipio Slataper, makes her way home from a botched tryst with her friend and shoots herself in front of the mirror. Apparently she has lost some life-sustaining faith. Two weeks earlier, on April 19, and not far from Anna's own home in Trieste, Sigmund Freud and his Vienna Psychoanalytic Society are so vexed by the rise of suicide among the Austro-Hungarian youth that they hold a conference to determine its motivations. Among Italians, the most remarkable young suicide is not Anna Pulitzer but the student Carlo Michelstaedter. Not in Trieste this time but Gorizia, another city on the outskirts of Austria-Hungary, on October 17, 1910, this twenty-three-year-old artist, philosopher, and poet is so determined to end his life that he shoots himself not once but twice with his revolver. It happens on the birthday and in the home of his mother, following an argument with this, her youngest son (the older one had died a year earlier, allegedly also from suicide).

Is there any "idea" at work in these deaths? Two days after Michelstaedter's gesture Sabina Spielrein, the schizophrenic patient and lover of Carl Jung, jots down in her journal an intuition that now, four years before the Great War, is beginning to assume collective proportions. "Secretly," she notes on October 19, "my new study, 'On the Death Instinct,' is taking shape within me."[1] Her completed study, published by Freud in 1912, expresses a thesis that Freud will sign his own name to eight years later, in *Beyond the Pleasure Principle*—to the effect that love cannot be disengaged from its opposite, or from the impulse toward violence, negation, and destruction. On the same day that Spielrein records her secret, researchers who believe that personal behavior is always a function of larger, communal patterns meet for the First Conference of the German Society for Sociology (October 19–22). Present among the sociologists are Max Weber, Martin Buber, and Georg Simmel.

---

1. Throughout this study, titles of books and essays are rendered in English regardless of their original language of publication. For original titles (at least where I know of no English translations) please consult the two lists of sources at the end of this book. Citations from non-English texts appear in my own translations or in slightly modified versions of those listed.

None of these events can be directly tied to Schoenberg's painting. They occur in widely disparate places, among people whose sexes, nationalities, and cultural formations have little in common. And yet they partake in a strange commonality of atmosphere, a wordless similarity of concern. This concern or mood, this knowledge or perception, is the subject of this book. Called nihilism in philosophy and expressionism in the arts, it comprises a vision of history as nightmare, an obsession with mortality and decay, a sense of human marginalization from the autonomous developments of culture, and the responses they spur. Its protagonists are the student Michelstaedter and a set of his intellectual peers: Georg Trakl, Dino Campana, and Rainer Maria Rilke; Vasily Kandinsky, Egon Schiele, and Oskar Kokoschka; Georg Lukács, Martin Buber, and Georg Simmel; Arnold Schoenberg, Scipio Slataper, and Wilhelm Worringer. Other figures occupy either side of the year in question: Giovanni Gentile, Otto Weininger, and Ludwig Wittgenstein. Like Michelstaedter, many were Jewish and citizens of the Austro-Hungarian Empire. Many also died young, sometimes, like Michelstaedter, by their own hand. Nearly all had as precarious a grasp on their intentions as the age on its course.

Michelstaedter's suicide occurs the same day he completes one of the most unusual works of the early twentieth century: a university dissertation called *Persuasion and Rhetoric*. In a sense, however, the real act of completion lies in the suicide itself, for the work on which he had labored so intensely over the course of the year tolerates no breach between theory and practice. Whether the suicide is to be interpreted as an expression or a refutation of the "moral health" described in *Persuasion and Rhetoric*, as scholars still hotly debate, it cannot be separated from the thinking that it ends. For one and the same thing is at work in both, something strangely redolent of the voiceless anxiety of Schoenberg's painting.

Nineteen ten is also the date on the most anguished self-portraits of Egon Schiele and Oskar Kokoschka, the younger compatriots of Gustave Klimt. In Germany rather than Austria three occurrences definitively announce the advent of a new and expressionist art: (1) the schism among the artists of the Berlin Secession, giving rise to the New Secession, (2) the transition between the founding of the Munich New Artists' Alliance in 1909 and the inception of *The Blue Rider* almanac in 1911, (3) the inauguration of the most lasting organ of literary expressionism, the weekly periodical *Der Sturm*. In this year—when Freud makes his first written mention of the Oedipus complex (Freud 1910d) and Carl Schmitt publishes *On Guilt and Types of Guilt*—Georg Simmel supplements his cultural sociology with "The Metaphysics of Death." The Italian Giovanni Boine counters modernity with religion in the Florentine journal *La Voce*. The young Austrian drug addict Georg Trakl begins to write the most disquieting poetry of the first half of our century. Simultaneously, south of the Alps, his counterpart Dino Campana lays the foundations for his *Orphic Songs*, eventually rewritten from memory and published in 1914. Committed to correctional institutions throughout his life, Campana is permanently confined to an asylum in 1918, at age thirty-three. Trakl, incestuously attached to his younger sister, takes his life before reaching his thirties. Schiele, born three years after Boine, dies a year later, in 1918, at the age of twenty-eight. The first artist ever to be imprisoned in Austria for "offenses against public morality," he finds the first model for his tormented nudes in his fourteen-year-old sister Gerti.

In 1910 we also witness a resurgence—perhaps the final great resurgence—of the traditional European ideal to liberate human spirit from the pressures of material reality. It is the moment when the leader of the German lodges of the Theosophical Society, Rudolf Steiner, writes his outline of *Occult Science* and discovers the principles of anthroposophy; when Arthur Edward Waite publishes his *Key to the Tarot* and P. D. Ouspensky furnishes "the key to the enigmas of the world" in his *Tertium Organum*. Italian philosophy, at the same time, experiences the more studied idealism of Benedetto Croce and Giovanni Gentile. Most decisively perhaps, the year signals the astonishing revolution of abstraction in art. Three years earlier the art historian Wilhelm Worringer had linked symbolic and non-figurative art to a "spiritual space-phobia" in the cultural psyche. By 1910 he has perceived the phobia in the age at hand, an age described by Vasily Kandinsky in the first and still most philosophical manifesto for abstract art, *On the Spiritual in Art*. What was at stake for Worringer and Kandinsky alike was the relation between soul and form, or between intuited truth and its figurative articulation. The most thorough study of such a relation can be found in a book published that year under the very same title: *Soul and Form* by the twenty-five-year-old Hungarian, Georg Lukács. In a "mood of permanent despair over the state of the world," as he later characterizes this period of his life in *Theory of the Novel*, Lukács writes yet another essay to include in the book's German edition of 1911: "The Metaphysics of Tragedy." Over the course of that year he sees tragedy as encompassing every effort of the soul not only to reach form but also to act ethically. The good, claims Lukács in "On Poverty of Spirit" (1911), eludes every rule of morality.

As for the forms at the disposal of this "soul," the years preceding the Great War of 1914 see them successively splintered. In one sense the avant-garde destruction of conventional modes of expression follows quite naturally on the liquidation of the word by such poets as Paul Valéry and Hugo van Hoffmansthal. But in 1910 still others are bent on distinguishing between meaning and nonsense, especially in that Habsburg empire to which Michelstaedter himself belonged: the philosophers Fritz Mauthner and Adolph Stöhr, the essayist Karl Kraus, and, as early as 1912, Ludwig Wittgenstein. Kraus and Wittgenstein see the expressive content of language as depending less on the conscious intentions of speakers than on the ethics they inherit from their community; and how fallen ethics seem to be at this moment in time can be gauged by a treasured reading of not only Wittgenstein and Kraus but their entire generation: the best-selling *Sex and Character* (1903) by Otto Weininger. He, too, a suicide at age twenty-three, Weininger argued that no woman or Jew had the spiritual constitution necessary for moral behavior. Action in accordance with the noblest possibilities of being was beyond the reach of all but the most gifted of men.

Of course, the fact that Kraus and Wittgenstein were of Jewish origin did not stop them from subscribing to Weininger's views any more than it did Italo Svevo or Arnold Schoenberg. After all, Weininger was himself a Jew and, if we are to believe the thesis of Theodor Lessing, at this moment in history Jewish self-hatred was a matter of pride. The Jewish anti-Semite Max Steiner suggested as much when in 1910 he also took his life. Countless thinkers of the prewar years were all too prepared to assume responsibility for the guilt described by Weininger. His Jew was in essence an ideal type, a spiritual outsider in normative, Christian culture, without firm roots or faith, reluctant to accept any principle of belief before examining each letter of its word. Like Adolf Hitler three decades later (himself an "artist" in 1910, though rejected by the same Vienna Academy of Fine Arts that accepted Egon Schiele) Weininger would have spied such "Judaism" in the guiding ambitions of each figure of this study—to build certainty and ethics *ex nihilo* (Michelstaedter), to articulate singular visions of exceptional individuals (Schiele, Kokoschka, and Trakl), to offer pure representations of soul (Kandinsky, Schoenberg, and the young Lukács), to give systematic order to intuitions one does not consider one's own (Wittgenstein, by his own admission). To Weininger the work of each of these figures would have smacked of the elucubrations of the Jew in exile, wandering through a desert laid bare by the spiritual diaspora of history.

In truth, a good number of Weininger's themes had already been announced by the cultural critics of the turn of the century: a brooding sense of the "Dusk of the Nations" (Max Nordau, in *Degeneration*), of the utter exhaustion of Western values, of physiological and psychological deterioration that called for the most surgical of operations. Anti-Semitism itself was just a channel for the fear of moral dissolution which such self-styled opponents of decadence as Houston Stewart Chamberlain and Julius Langbehn had inspired in the intellectual classes of Europe. As dozens of sold-out editions of *Sex and Character* convinced them that "being oneself" was far from an innocent matter, an even more notorious thinker was amassing evidence for the spiritual vacuity of the age. His name was Oswald Spengler and his findings were published in 1918 as volume one of *The Decline of the West*.

By 1910 the nihilistic visions of Europe begin to worry observers as distant as America:

> Every reader of the French and German newspapers knows that not a day passes without producing some uneasy discussion of supposed social decrepitude; falling off of the birthrate;—decline of rural population,—lowering of army standards;—multiplication of suicides;—increase of insanity or idiocy;—of cancer;—of tuberculosis;—signs of nervous exhaustion,—of enfeebled vitality,—'habits' of alcoholism and drugs,—failure of eyesight in the young,—and so on, without end.

The words belong to Henry Adams, addressed to historians in February 1910. Indeed, it is historians who are most alarmed, for at the moment of which Adams speaks, events that might otherwise appear incidental take on the dimensions of portentous omens: Military Plan 19 of Czarist Russia, to open hostilities on two simultaneous fronts against Austria and Germany; the total solar eclipse; the "calculated insult" to the Austrian monarchy of the Adolf Loos House, constructed across the square from the Habsburg palace in Vienna. In 1910 these occurrences are read as revelations, as warnings, as a call to arms.

The true call to arms, four years later, had been anticipated in the dramatic account of a German attack on Western Europe called *The Invasion of 1910* (1906). If the English novelist William Le Queux was "prescient" in staging his war in 1910, it is because this moment best formulates a dialectic that was to inform so many decisions of the belligerent powers of 1914–1918. It was a dialectic that rooted all creation in destruction, all knowledge in blindness, all hope in despair, and attributed value to situations that appeared utterly futile. In the prewar work of Michelstaedter, Kandinsky, Lukács, and Buber, the dialectic is still a luminous one, thinking through its own principle of reversal. By 1914 it has grown darkly literal, fueling the unstudied conviction that conflagration is a means of cauterization, and that razing all life to the ground will purge it of its infections. Did thinkers of 1910 suspect that their own dialectic would fall prey to the negativity it strove to overcome? There is little reason to say yes, and yet something brought Michelstaedter and Trakl to suicide and Campana and others to madness. Nor can we dismiss the fact that unprecedented numbers of young men went mad or took their own lives in the years immediately preceding the First World War—that is, before being able to be conscripted into service. We do not possess a sufficiently sophisticated cognitive science to investigate such an issue, but the syndrome returns, especially before World War II. Nineteen ten is the spiritual prefiguration of an unspeakably tragic fatality, heard in the tones of the audacious and the anguished, the deviant and the desperate, in the art of a youth grown precociously old, awaiting a war it had long suffered in spirit.

Here prescience can be felt in the suffering itself. To those who mistrusted all political leaders, and all practical responses to things not intellectually digested, a belligerent reaction such as war to vague fears of dissolution could only be the disease masquerading as cure. This is not to say that intellectuals rallied to oppose the war; most, in fact, did not. Here the testimony of Rainer Maria Rilke is only one among many: "In the first days of August," he reports in a letter of November 6, 1914, "the spectacle of the war, of the war-god, seized me." Disaster and affliction, he reflects, are not presently more widespread than ever before; they are simply more tangible, more active, more apparent:

> For the affliction in which mankind has daily lived from the very beginning can't be really increased no matter what the circumstances. Insight into man's unspeakable misery does increase however, and perhaps this is what everything is leading to today; so great a downfall—as though new risings were seeking clearance and room for launching!

The thinking and art of 1910 sought precisely such clearance for risings and launchings—but in the context of so *articulate* a misery, so philosophical and metaphysical a sense of bereavement, that it could hardly be redressed by political solutions. In fact, if what strikes us most today is precisely the nihilism of the prewar period—the gruesomeness of so much of its painting, music, and writing—it is because in it we perceive an alarm reaching beyond every local concern.

In 1910 the first decade of the last century of a dying millennium comes to a close. In the seven years to either side of it we see some of the most startling changes in modern history: drastic reshufflings of nations, economies, societies, and psyches; artistic, scientific, and political revolutions; the aggressive platforms of Georges Sorel and rebelling minorities throughout the continent. Nothing, in 1910, is definitively over and nothing definitively begun. Every attempted beginning is also an end, every end a hidden beginning. The "degeneracy" and "decadence" once identified in its present and its past name phenomena that would inevitably inherit its future. The prewar years were a workshop of *futurisme* and *passéisme* alike, testing every concern of a simultaneously old and new Europe: the borders of its personal, sexual and social identities, the solidity of its moral and theoretical foundations, the effects of technology and urbanization, the value and methods of its human sciences (reflected in the rise of phenomenology, psychology, sociology, and language-philosophy, not to mention theosophy, anthroposophy, and other, less tangible pursuits). Ten years into the century both a death and a birth seemed to have taken too long in coming.

Can we distinguish any "determining marks" in such a complex, transitional era? To a large extent the distinctions are already made in the very process of research. One chooses, for one reason or another, to investigate a particular series of texts and then notes the questions they raise. One forms a preliminary hunch and goes on to test other documents in its light. One refines and revises the hunch, finally becoming convinced that one has laid hold of something solid. My own method has not been different. I began to conceive of the possibility of this study when I was certain that in the year 1910 a particular set of problems was addressed more singlemindedly than ever before.

My selection of problems was also facilitated by the central role that Carlo Michelstaedter has played in this study from the start. Research into the contexts in which he lived and thought—to illuminate a study of him alone—soon yielded the realization that he was not alone at all: that his nihilistic idealism was an outcome of a quite traditional quest; that his most radical intuitions found support in other,

Fig. 2. Carlo Michelstaedter in the Boboli Garden, Florence, 1907. Courtesy Gorizia Civic Library, Gorizia.

contemporaneous thinkers; that his drawings and paintings belonged solidly to a family of art in that part of the world we call Mitteleuropa; that countless perplexing patterns in prewar art and behavior made sense within the framework of a thinking he made explicit.

Fig. 3. Carlo Michelstaedter, *Demon,* possibly 1903, watercolor and pencil. Courtesy Gorizia Civic Library, Gorizia.

What has ultimately resulted, then, is not a study of Michelstaedter so much as a symptomatology of the age to which he belonged, traced in a cross section of intellectual, artistic, and historical events. And this means that it is not a story of what *happened* in 1910 so much as of what some of these happenings expressed, an account preserving its own individual slant, perhaps in the manner of an expressionist protrait, which does not offer the objective characteristics of a face so much as an imaginative reinscription. Its concern is not "history," but a history of symbols. Yet a history of symbols is history as it is traditionally read, constructed out of such critical years as 1492 or 1776, great transoceanic voyages, world-changing technological inventions, revolutionary events like the fall of the Berlin Wall. Many real cities besides Berlin have been forcibly divided between two states without joining the annals of history, or turning into symbols. One is Michelstaedter's hometown of Gorizia, now split between Italy and the Republic of Slovenia, split before that with Yugoslavia, and in Austrian hands before 1918 (see figs. 4 and 5). And in this city, as in countless others, people and thoughts have come and gone without leaving any trace in memory. For things are historical not merely by happening, but by finding a home in consciousness, in the manner of an Ottoman tower in Bosnia or the flag of Macedonia. This study intends precisely to create such a space in consciousness—for products of a moment which never became symbolic, even though they crystallized developments in the making for centuries. Accompanying this moment are also places—Trieste, Budapest, and Munich, overshadowed by strong memories of contemporary Paris and Moscow. Accompanying the places are a host of "secondary" cultural figures, overshadowed by the more towering icons of Picasso, Einstein, Freud, and Lenin.

What emerges from this twining of texts and strands of texts is a story of notes in the margins of better-known tales in the history of politics, economics, and psychology. It is an admittedly dissonant narrative: at moments jumping rapidly from one unit of coherence to another, at others plodding slowly through the subtleties of a single theoretical point. It sketches only a thumbnail of a complex cultural body, not the hand or the arm or the heart—a blossom, not the branch or the root. And as for the "trunk" that we sometimes believe underlies such a blossom—as if it were some fundamental, historical condition of which thinking and art are offshoots—it is no less symbolic an entity than what it might seem to produce, both constructed out of numberless processes, not one of which can be fully described, even where the blossom one attempts to understand is a single person or a single line of poetry. There is simply too much to synthesize to describe such a "trunk," too much to coerce into intellectual order without adequate means, with no explanation for why *just this* blossom proved necessary or took the shape that it did. Here, thirst for the Why? is better slaked by the What?—or by patient observation of evidence. Recognition of connections, crossings, and analogies in the What may be the only means we have of approaching the Why.

The "blossoms" in this study are works of philosophy, sociology, painting, music, and poetry, as well as existential and ethical gestures like suicide and madness. If Michelstaedter remains the "proper noun" for this flourishing it is because—as philosopher, poet, painter, and moralist—he contains the greatest number of its features. Its common noun is expressionism.

Expressionism is typically conceived of as an artistic current that begins with the banding together of a group of Dresden painters in 1905 to form the *Brücke* (Bridge) and ends around 1924 or 1925. In 1910–1911 a more decisive wave of expressionism is set into motion by Vasily Kandinsky and his associates in Munich. Still a third gets under way at the same moment in Berlin, centered around the journals *Der*

Sturm and *Die Aktion*. These journals draw Austrians as well into the expressionist fold, particularly Oskar Kokoschka, Arnold Schoenberg, and Egon Schiele, who had been operating independently in Vienna. A confluence of developments in painting, theater, and poetry, expressionism is thus traditionally considered indigenous to Germanic culture. Rarely is it said to have practitioners in Italy, England, or France.

There is another critical line, however, which maintains that expressionism is not a style of its own, but merely a label for the Germanic chapter of avant-garde art, whose innovations receive names such as fauvism, cubism, futurism, orphism, and vorticism elsewhere. Still others claim quite the contrary, to the effect that expressionistic art has clear and distinct features, but that ultimately they overreach geographic, generic, and temporal boundaries, encompassing disciplines as different as philosophy, politics, and dance as well as artists as distant in time as Rabelais and Lucan. This, the most dominant direction in criticism today, is also the one that I will follow, seeking the tones of expressionism in a dissonant, international chorus—in Italy as well as Germany, in sociology as well as painting, in the logic of actions as well as arguments. Radical though it may sound to speak of Georg Simmel, the "impressionistic sociologist," or of Georg Lukács, the "anti-modernist," in the context of expressionism, the provocation disappears the moment we ask what they were trying to achieve in the prewar years. What exactly were the concerns of their work? And how different were these concerns from those of the poets and artists? Was it not Freud who spoke of psychoanalysis as aiming to unveil the "most intimate" of a person's secrets (in 1910 and again in 1912)? As based on the recognition of "psychic conflict"? As viewing civilization as the implacable enemy of the individual? When we inquire into such issues of intention and method, intersections between paths so different in direction become rather more clear.

We need not broaden the definition of expressionism to trace these points of convergence. On the contrary, we can narrow it down to a few salient traits. The expressionism at stake in 1910 is more theoretical than artistic in character. Concerned though it is with art, it thrusts its roots even more deeply into metaphysics, sociology, and ethics. As the term itself suggests, expressionism is interested in the nature, the function, and the credibility of human expression. Artistic procedures always furnish some answer to these "other" types of issues: the conditions at work in the creative process, what kind of person pursues it, on behalf of what and with what probability of success. As I see it, expressionism is a paradoxical undertaking: It manifests both absolute faith and absolute disbelief in the most venerable preconceptions fueling the very project of artistic expression, including beauty, order, understanding, and truth. In intellectual history it signals the end of a Western, humanistic tradition, the termination, as it were, of its guiding objective. Indeed, in one reading, this simultaneous culmination and negation of a project to give form to universally comprehensible knowledge is precisely what enables so many of the theoretical and artistic changes that succeed this radical juncture: the formal license of avant-garde art, no longer held to common standards; the new objectivist literature of the twenties, returning from the world of potential to that of things; abstract expressionism; the historicizing ontology of Martin Heidegger; the turn of intellectuals in the postwar years toward political and social engagement.

Nineteen ten belongs squarely to the first of the two or three phases into which the expressionist current is typically divided. In this period, its theories and techniques are still fully in process of formation—more tentative than doctrinaire, more daring than programmatic. Art is still considered to be a vehicle for ethical and metaphysical research, not a proven methodology or style. With sympathies more anarchic than socialistic, expressionist thought has not yet assumed stable ideological direction. The prophets of the "New Man" have yet to finish mourning the old one. Agony, at this moment, is stronger than hope, and subjective isolation makes the "brotherhood of man" a still dubious notion. More particularly, in 1910 four expressionist characteristics come clearly into view.

The first is a battle between adversaries that seem incapable of resolving their differences: order and chaos, vitality and death, ecstasy and despair, individuality and solidarity. Whether in concept or form, each arises only in the presence of the other, and struggles in vain to break free. Expressionist art does not offer the centripetal visions of naturalistic or impressionistic works, not even the coherent compositions of cubism or futurism. It heeds no written or unwritten rules about what it should represent or how to go about it. Instead it thrives on what Schoenberg calls the emancipation of dissonance: a willful disruption of harmonic order. Of course this is not to say that expressionist works are not instantly recognizable. They are, but as the scene of a racked vision, of an articulated turmoil unprecedented in the history of art. Matter, in expressionist painting, comes to exude an explosive and brutal power, cohesive and destructive at once, binding as well as loosening all natural relations. Human surroundings undergo sudden and stunning convulsions, bursting with menacing, apocalyptic power. Obvious examples lie in Ludwig Meidner's *Apocalyptic Landscapes* of 1912–1913, more subtle ones in the paintings of Kandinsky and Franz Marc. In fact, it is partially the mad and transcendent animation of this cosmic condition that makes it "ex-pressionistic," as though the outside world willfully encroached on the space of all interpreting subjects, storming humanity with illegible intent. And this is probably what Marc had in mind when he spoke of the "space and soul-shattering" intent of his paintings. In expressionism a dynamic and conflictual universe addresses a consternated subject, including the subject observing the work. Here spirit and object, essence and appearance, and many other metaphysical oppositions enter into such irresolvable contradictions that they signal the need for a radical revision of the understanding.

The second expressionistic characteristic involves virtual despair over the "negative" element in the contending pair: sickness rather than health, estrangement rather than solidarity, disintegration rather than wholeness. In fact, in a certain perspective the battle of opposites appears to represent disintegration pure and simple, especially in the light of the political realities to which artists find themselves responding. Recognizable in their lurid depiction of the nullifying dimensions of human existence, expressionist works do have their own subject after all: the psychological and metaphysical drama of mere dwelling in the world. And this dwelling is indelibly marked by the ecstasy and suffering of the body. Indeed, to find artists confronting the pressures of the flesh with such intensity one must return to the Gothic. In 1910 the classical, humanist harmony between body and soul has been all but broken. The body itself has become irremediably duplicitous. The only true locus of soul—or of Henri Bergson's *élan vital*—it is also the catatonic, irrational form with which that soul contends.

To the subjects of early twentieth-century monarchy the moral and economic structures of everyday life are as materiality to the inner life that it traps: namely, agents of oppression, forces to assail and destroy. No art of the time, including futurism, performs this assault more radically than expressionism. Moreover, its attack on these forces of cultural "rhetoric" is hardly an experiment in form. Rather, it is an anguished *critique* of form, of form as minister of deformation. The investigation of mortality and disintegration, the resistance to social conventions, and the rebellion against the inadequacies of formal expression—these three reactions to a perceived negativity of being—all lead to the third expressionist move, the envisioned "solution" to this soulless, dehumanizing deficiency, identified with the discovery and liberation of subjective vitality.

"In or about December, 1910," claims Virginia Woolf, "human character changed." In truth, however, what changed was not character itself but the way it was viewed. At the end of King Edward's reign, as Woolf argues in this essay from the twenties, people suddenly became conscious of needs they never knew that they had. Up until 1910, artists had considered the needs of human nature to be adequately reflected by the material and historical conditions in which it was rooted. But at the end of the first decade external situations appeared to have lost their revelatory power, their complicity, as it were, with inner intention. Scientists and philosophers began to wonder whether the most well-established truths were nothing more than matters of impression and mood, of perspective and judgment. Positivism, realism, and naturalism appeared to have forsaken the subject they first intended to serve, but of which they had never really spoken: the human subject, the psyche, self, or however one wished to call it—the innermost truth of subjective experience—which was improperly reflected by historical events.

"When religion, science, and morality are shaken," writes Kandinsky at the time Woolf describes, "and when the outer supports threaten to fall, man turns his gaze from externals in on to himself." Painters and thinkers focus their efforts on freeing Michelstaedter's "persuasion" from "rhetoric," subjective necessity from contingent, objective externals. In one way or another, all expressionists seek to ferret out a naked human essence from under its lifeless qualities. They strive to give voice to what history has not endowed with words: the broad passions and aspirations of this hidden "essence."

The portraits of Schiele and Kokoschka, the atonal music of Schoenberg, the idealism of Michelstaedter and Lukács take the inward turn more sharply than even Woolf imagined, questioning not only the improperly reflected self, but its entire set of operational procedures. Here all efforts are geared to the liberation of "soul," as though it were the seat of all living experience. And thus surface new

visions of the artist-seer, the idea of a messianic restoration of the
true nature of life through the redemptive power of the courageous
social exception. But more often than not, the project results in the
"savior's" own self-immolation, and the savior ends up discovering
that what is ostensibly "authentic" and "true" and "inner" never lies
within the realm of the speakable, and may ultimately be just as rhetorical a construct as all it opposes.

This ethical stance represents the fourth expressionist trait, bringing a romantic project to its final culmination and dissolution. At the
moment in time when artists make the most exasperated call for the
inward turn, they also discover its dire and inevitable consequence:
the obliteration, in the attack on rhetoric, of the basis for even those
interiorized narratives that Woolf imagined. Indeed, the commitment
to subjective experience in 1910 marks more of an end than a beginning of a tradition, which reaches an impasse at the very moment that
it becomes most extreme, giving rise to the suspicion that all seemingly
self-expressive persons are silenced by the idioms they use. While collective group history may offer no counterimages for interiority, interiority is also forced to admit that this history still governs everything
it can do and say. Subjectivity has no voice but that which speaks by
contorting the same terms it wishes to escape. The avant-garde arts of
France and England do not explicitly face up to this problem. They
sidestep the project of individual "persuasion" and celebrate instead
the incoherent and aleatory rule of rhetoric, as though in it the subject
might discover a means of deeper self-certainty. The Italian, Germanic,
and Slavic expressionists, by contrast, still cling to the project and its
accompanying problem, reassessing persuasion to be at best an inter-
mediate condition between the transcendence of "soul" and its historical oppression. Such a condition is as visible in Emil Nolde's paintings
anticipating the emaciated victims of wars that have not yet occurred
as in the outright rejection of material reality by Kandinsky. These artists of an era where human nature changes by recognizing that it is already and *inevitably* changed by living discover that if "expression of
self" is not to degenerate into a nostalgic fantasy it must consist of an
immanent transformation of the constrictions to which it is destined.
Here the resolution of Rilke's protagonist in *The Notebooks of Malte
Laurids Brigge*—"to be the heavy heart of all that is indistinguishable"—remains the only true ethos of art: an art of the greatest subjective pathos on the one hand, and of the most brutalizing objectivity on
the other. And thus the project of self-realization is thrown back on

the experience of self-loss from which it springs. The fourth expressionist trait circles back to the first, revealing that an ethics has always spurred its dissonant, expressionist aesthetic—an ethics of misunderstanding, where no eloquence can be achieved except in its absence and no expression can be more than a form for pregnant but impregnable contents.

CHAPTER ONE

The Emancipation of Dissonance

The middle road is the only one which does not lead to Rome.
                                        —*Schoenberg*

Tertium non datur.
                    —*Michelstaedter*

At the end of his treatise on harmony Arnold Schoenberg makes a wry but revealing admission: *Mit mir nur rat ich, red ich zu dir* (In speaking with you, I am merely deliberating with myself). This entire *Theory of Harmony*, completed on July 1, 1911, is presented as though it were nothing more than an internal conversation. This "teacher" is a pupil pursuing his own instruction, perhaps grappling with problems that do not even allow for a solution. If he voices his uncertainties publicly, it is certainly not in order to persuade anyone. It is to put others in a similar situation. His method, he notes, is like shaking a box to get three tubes of differing diameters to rest inside each other. One does it in the belief that "movement alone can succeed where deliberation fails." And the same applies to learning of every type. "Only activity, movement is productive." The teacher's first task "is to shake up the pupil thoroughly." His internal unrest must infect his students, "then they will search as he does" (Schoenberg 1911a: 417 and 2–3).

What goes for the teacher also goes for the artist. In Schoenberg's own phrase, the music he composes in the years surrounding the *Theory of Harmony* "emancipates dissonance" from the rule of consonance (Schoenberg 1926, 1941). Consonance, a pleasing resolution of clashing tones, is like comfort. It avoids movement; it "does not take up the search." Schoenberg's compositions have more faith in disquiet than rest, uncertainty than knowledge, difficulty than ease. This type of art—and all good art, in Schoenberg's view—plays out an unfinished, intellectual quest. Aiming only "to make things clear to himself," the artist pursues clarity in open confusion. Here there is no intention of "provoking" an audience with such dissonant compositions, as many might think. The artist simply "comes to terms with himself and the public listens; for the people know: it concerns them" (Schoenberg 1911a: 2 and 417).

What Schoenberg describes in the *Theory of Harmony* is a singularly unsettled new art of the prewar years: an art of perceptual struggle, of willing contention, of dynamic and irresolvable tension. Its newness consists in the manifestation of a plight, the transcription of a quandary. Similar claims are advanced by other artists in the years that Schoenberg turned from classical harmonic structures to atonality. The harmony of the age, writes Vasily Kandinsky, can only be one of "opposites and contradictions." "Clashing discords, loss of equilibrium, 'principles' overthrown, unexpected drumbeats, great questionings, apparently purposeless strivings, stress and longing . . . this is our *harmony*." What might strike the audience as a lack of artistic cohesion, notes the painter, is actually the proper form for a much deeper, though not immediately perceivable, unity. Wilhelm Worringer, the art historian, generalizes the same principle to art of all ages: "The imaginative life of mankind," he writes in *Form Problems of the Gothic* (1910), "obeys a very simple law; it lives on antithesis." Two years later the painter August Macke declares that "the form of art, its style, is a result of tension" (Kandinsky 1909–11: 193 and 209; Worringer 1910: 28; Macke 1912: 85).

Macke's, Worringer's, and Kandinsky's statements are not descriptions of the timeless nature of art, even if they are meant as such. They are fruits of a moment, deductions and generalizations on the basis of a contemporary, historical scenario. Other artists and thinkers offer comparable accounts at nearly the same time.[1] Moreover, their statements ultimately say less about art in itself than about the foundations on which it rests. Antitheses and contradictions are that which art *brings into* harmony (Kandinsky); the imagination *lives on* antithesis (Worringer); art *results* from tension (Macke). And these tense, antithetical foundations involve a whole world of experience—political as well as

---

1. Marc Chagall's fluctuations from "sordid reality to a supreme beauty," writes Kamensky, give shape to a fundamental "alliance of anguish and joy, of disquiet and exaltation" (1989: 22 and 77). The "cold romanticism" of Paul Klee entails a "concept of contraries, embracing the entire Universe, in which out of their action one upon the other all creativity arises" (Comte 1989: 44). The theories and art of Piet Mondrian are grounded in "a system of opposites such as male-female, light-dark, mind-matter" (Tuchman 1986: 36).

existential, ideological as well as psychological. Before the Great War a call is sounded for art to speak of unity by way of difference or not speak at all.

Why such a call? Why such dissonance in music? Such jarring and clashing forms in painting? Such dark and unreconciled tragedies in plays, novels, and poetry? Do they have counterparts in the social and institutional realms? And what might be "emancipating" about this ordering of disorder? The question Why? cannot be laid to rest by portraying the historical grounds of the issue at stake. As Aristotle explained it, Why? seeks not only material causes but also final ones— the objectives of the phenomenon in question. While art always responds to historical conditions, it also aims to reveal something these conditions themselves do not express. In the process it complicates the understanding with which we started, redefining our sense of the "causes" by the nature of its response. When we identify circumstances and experiences that help nourish a creative act, we have only offered the first turn in a circle, a circle not completed until we return to those experiences with the new understanding that is provided by the act in question. And this changes our initial view, starting the circle all over. No understanding of circumstances "determining" a work of art is of much use unless it is directly determined by the work itself. And this gives us as many understandings as there are readings. At this moment the question Why? cedes its priority to the questions What? and How? (circular though they also prove to be). What are the issues that a work strives to define? And how are they formed by the terms in which they are said? Here the question Why? breaks into a series of reciprocally determining relations, ramifications of social, ideological, and psychic experience which might not even share a common foundation. At this point one turns to the relations, hoping that their Why? might become clear in their What? and their How?

GORIZIA, JUDAIC INDETERMINACY AND TRIESTINE ART

To many keen minds in Europe, experience in 1910 appears racked by contradiction. The continent stands on the brink of the First World War. And in one perspective the war already bespeaks the dissonance whose unity the artists seek: a struggle between union and division, nationalism and internationalism, aristocracy and bourgeoisie, ethnic specificity and imperial anonymity. The European frame of mind in the years preceding the war is also the effect of concrete struggles: the un-balancing of power by the Triple Entente in 1907, the annexation of Bosnia-Herzegovina by Austria in 1908, the Moroccan and Ulster crises, the Turco-Italian clash, the Baltic Wars, the conflicting allegiances of Czechs, Serbs, Magyars and other amalgamated groups of the Otto-man and Austro-Hungarian empires. Social ideology finds itself in-creasingly polarized between the Radical and the Conservative, the Left and the Right, Man and Woman, the Young and the Old.[2] For Freud it is time to reckon with the fact that even the psyche is an "arena and battle-ground for mutually opposing purposes or, to put it non-dynamically, that it consists of contradictions and pairs of con-traries" (Freud 1915–17: 76–77). Psychoanalysis tells a story in which the conscious mind vies with its unconscious counterpart, the licit with the illicit impulses, the wishes with the needs, whose cooperation will never be less than strained. The conflict, as the sociologists Max Weber and Georg Simmel argue, extends out from the self to its social rela-tions. The health of the ego relies, psychologically as well as sociologi-cally, partially on acceding to the demands of others, partially on re-sisting those same demands.

Since the late nineteenth century, European thinkers had diagnosed two radically antithetical syndromes in both psyches and civilizations: ascendancy and decline, sanity and sickness, vitality and degeneration.

2. Good studies of the social, ideological, and political conflicts of Europe in the early twentieth century include Angelo Ara and Claudio Magris, eds., *Trieste: Un'identità di frontiera* (Turin: Einaudi, 1982); R. J. B. Bosworth, *Italy and the Approach of the First World War* (London: Macmillan, 1983); Modris Eksteins, *Rites of Spring: The Great War and the Birth of the Modern Age* (New York: Doubleday, 1990); the three studies by Peter Gay, (a) *Freud, Jews and Other Germans: Masters and Victims in Modernist Culture* (London: Oxford University Press, 1978), (b) *The Tender Passion: The Bourgeois Experience, Victoria to Freud*, vol. 2 (New York and London: Norton, 1986), and (c) *The Cultivation of Hatred: The Bourgeois Experience, Victoria to Freud*, vol. 3 (New York and London: Norton, 1993); Eric J. Hobsbawm's two studies, *The Age of Empire, 1875–1914* (New York: Vintage, 1989), and *Nations and Nationalism Since 1870: Programme, Myth, Reality*, 2d ed. (Cambridge: Cambridge University Press, 1993); H. Stuart Hughes, *Consciousness and Society* (New York: Vintage Books, 1958); Allan Janik and Stephen Toulmin, *Wittgenstein's Vienna* (New York: Simon and Schuster, 1973); William Johnston, *The Austrian Mind: An Intellectual and Social History 1848–1938* (Berkeley: University of California Press, 1972); James Joll, *The Origins of the First World War* (London and New York: Longman, 1984); Jacques Le Rider, *Modernity and Crises of Identity*, trans. Rosemary Morris (New York: Continuum, 1993); William J. McGrath, *Dionysian Art and Populist Politics in Austria* (New Haven: Yale University Press, 1974); Frederic Morton, *Thunder at Twilight: Vienna 1913/1914* (New York: Macmillan, 1989); George L. Mosse, *The Crisis of German Ideology: Intellectual Ori-gins of the Third Reich* (New York: Grosset & Dunlap, 1964); Carl E. Schorske, *Fin-de-siècle Vienna: Politics and Culture* (New York: Random House, 1981); Robert Wohl, *The Generation of 1914* (Cambridge, Mass.: Harvard University Press, 1979).

By the early twentieth century, *Lebensphilosophen* (life philosophers) and pragmatists have reduced the conflict to a fundamental opposition between exuberant will and petrifying reason, or soul and spirit. Phenomenologists and language philosophers have separated signs from their meanings, and apparently self-evident facts from values. All this plays a part in the dissonance artists felt called on to harmonize in 1910.

Were these conflicts more "real" or more "tragic" than others in previous eras? For example, did the youth of Italy or Austria-Hungary suffer more deeply from sexual repression in 1910 than the youth of a century earlier, as has frequently been suggested? Whatever facts might answer such questions are not as important as the way these facts themselves are perceived. Repression, the process by which a psyche defends itself against an unacceptable impulse, was one of the new perceptions of the age. "It was a novelty, and nothing like it had ever before been recognized in mental life" (Freud 1925: 18). Moral and psychological repression was no doubt even stronger in earlier ages; but it was not identified in that way before the turn of the twentieth century. Something similar applies to the notions of conflict, struggle, and tragedy. If tragedy relies on the perception—not the fact—that experience is hounded by painfully irreconcilable oppositions, then the years preceding the First World War were among the most tragic in Europe. Miguel de Unamuno spoke on behalf not only of Spain but of the whole continent when he described *The Tragic Sense of Life* in 1913: "Since we only live in and by contradictions, since life is tragedy and tragedy is perpetual struggle, without victory or the hope of victory, life is contradiction" (Unamuno 1913: 14).[3] By 1910 the philosophies of Arthur Schopenhauer and Friedrich Nietzsche had pervaded even the middlebrow culture of Europe. Georg Simmel goes so far as to describe tragedy as fundamental not only to culture but to the organic unfolding of life (in "The Metaphysics of Death" of 1910 and "On the Concept and the Tragedy of Culture" of 1911). Georg Lukács views tragedy as the essential form of human experience which surfaces at all moments of decisive historical transition. It is of his own historical age that he is thinking when he notes that tragedy structures the modes of collective understanding in each "heroic age of decadence,"

3. For a list of many theories of the tragic in Europe between 1890 and 1920 see Michele Cometa, "La tragedia tra mistica ed utopia: Note sulla *Metaphysik der Tragödie* di György Lukács," *Rivista di Estetica* 10 (1982): 28–29.

as new sentiments and institutions surge up to battle old ones. The "profound ethical and ideological conflict [from which] tragedies draw their origins" has one of two consequences: "either the soul of old humans is lacerated by the irreducible dissonance between the old and the new, or the new feelings are destroyed by the weight and still vital force of the old institutions" (Lukács 1911b: 56–57).

This strife-ridden conception of human experience is hardly alleviated by the historical conditions into which many artists of this moment were born. In Austria-Hungary, to take one example, the situation was fairly complex. "There has never been anything like it in history," writes Oskar Kokoschka.

> When I think back to my schooling I have the feeling that it was a reflection of the whole history of Austria. Many peoples were joined together in the old Austrian Empire, each retaining its individuality, its particular aptitude. . . . In my class there were boys from the Alpine countries, Hungarians, Slavs, Jews, Triestines, Sudeten Germans. A real gathering of peoples. And every second master came from a different country, and had brought with him some unmistakable national element, a colouring in his voice, his manner, his way of thought. In this sense, school was a preparation for my later life, in which I became a wanderer. (Kokoschka 1974: 17)

The wanderer that Kokoschka became was partially what the state had already forced him to be; a situation which might have seemed like a complex organic unity was actually a sprawling mélange of ethnic and political rivalries that "made most people aware of themselves as minorities" (Gordon 1987: 133). How could issues such as dissonance, difference, and conflict not come to the fore when they were already experienced in the daily travails of cohabitation? The problems were endemic to multicultural states, faced with the task of managing the interests of their increasingly differentiated and self-conscious citizens. In 1908, the particular year that Kokoschka recalls, a similar awareness arises across the Alps, where a group of young men found an eclectic Florentine weekly called *La Voce*. A forum on sexuality, politics, psychoanalysis, the arts, Catholicism, American pragmatism, and the urgency of collective moral direction, *La Voce* is bent on the "cultural renovation" of Italy. What it concludes, however, is that renovation requires an "affirmation of peripheral identities against the central one" (Asor Rosa 1985: 45).

If the tensions of cultural heterogeneity are stronger in Austria-Hungary than in other empires of Europe, it is because it incorporates so many peripheral identities in its dozens of ill-defined parts—like the one Florentines seek to liberate from their northern neighbors, the Italian regions of Friuli and Venezia-Giulia. Their symbol is the city of Trieste, harangued for capitulating to the Austrians by the futurist F. T. Marinetti in March, 1909. But Marinetti knew less about Trieste than his fellow Italian, Scipio Slataper, and it came as a surprise to many readers of *La Voce* that this author of the five "Letters on Trieste" (1909) was not as concerned with the political disenfranchisement of Italians in Trieste as with the city's own lack of identity. The first of the letters carried its theme in its title: "Trieste Has No Cultural Traditions." What is distinct about this city without traditions, claimed Slataper, is that it consists in an unprecedented distillation of three different cultures: Italian, Germanic, and Slavic. Certainly a "Triestine type" has developed out of this comixture; with the blood of three races coursing through his veins, Slataper himself is a perfect example. Yet the intellectual task still facing Triestines is to make this confluence productive. They must now learn, explains Slataper, to "transform the harm of this contact into an advantage." What awaits the living products of this extraordinary cultural amalgam is a *formalization* of the singular blend—a "Triestine art," one which could re-create "this fitful and anxious life of ours in the joy of clear expression" (Slataper 1909: 44 and 46).[4]

Extended beyond the borders of a single city, Triestine art means international art, not traceable to a pure and single root. Triestine art is one that would present the varied, irrepeatable contingencies of a complex place and time as productive, proper, and necessary. And this is in part the ambition of what we call modernism in art, as least the modernism of the early twentieth century, visible no less in the medieval recuperations of the poet Ezra Pound than in the Oceanic and African inspirations of French painters and sculptors. The most explicitly internationalist art, however, took place not in Florence or Paris but in Munich, where Kandinsky had immigrated in 1896 and where, be-

---

4. "Like all souls in transformation," continues Slataper, "we [Triestines] search for ourselves and turn into the slaves of others. We know German. We could dominate all of Nordic literature. But instead, indolent, we are overwhelmed by it. Or, stupid, we despise it. We must defend ourselves from the Slovenes: but what if we strengthened ourselves with the Slavic genius and enthusiasm? Our soul could be enlarged if it accepted them as new powers and used them to recondition and fortify its energy. . . . Trieste does not yet know itself. . . . Where else is life such a terrible torment of antithetical powers and self-exhausting longings, cruel struggles and renunciations? . . . This is Trieste. Composed of tragedy. Something that by sacrificing limpid life obtains its own anxious originality. One must sacrifice peace to express it" (Slataper 1909: 44–46). For background on Slataper in English see Cary 1993 and Adamson 1993.

tween 1910 and 1912, he compiled an almanac of art considered to be the epitome of this transcontinental and transhistorical aesthetic, not to mention the very manifesto of expressionism: *Der Blaue Reiter* (The Blue Rider). In fact, it was for their "unGermanness" that Kandinsky's group was condemned—and not only by the Nazi *Degenerate Art* exhibit of 1937, but already in the critical polemics of 1910–1911.[5] In our century, purist nationalism has always been up against a more palpable development whose symbol is Trieste, one dissonant locus in the hyphenated empire of Austria-Hungary. This, too, is the soil of art in 1910.

On the same soil, forty-four kilometers northwest of Slataper's Trieste, is a city known to Austrians as Görz, to the Italians as Gorizia, and to Slovenes as Gorica. Carlo Michelstaedter's family had emigrated to its vicinity from the German city of Michelstadt, near Darmstadt, in the 1700s, upon hearing that the province offered working opportunities for Jews. By the end of the nineteenth century, these Michelstaedters were firmly Italian, even if educated, like most citizens of the empire, primarily in German. Italian for themselves and Austrians for the state, they were primarily Jews for others. On such disinherited fringes of states, questions of identity are not a choice but a painful fatality.[6]

Gorizia passed from Austrian to Italian rule at the end of World War I. Twenty-seven years later, after the signing of the armistice of World War II, the city of Gorizia was overrun by the Yugoslav troops of General Tito. A full month passed before the Allies responded to Italian appeals for help. No doubt the delay could be attributed to the fact that, in part, Tito was an ally and Italy in part a vanquished power. Whatever the explanation, Tito's claims to the territory took hold. No better way was found to settle the contentions between Italians and Slavs than by running the national frontier right through the

5. The polemic began after the second exhibition, in September, 1910, of the group over which Kandinsky then presided, the Neue Kunstler-Vereinigung, Munchen (Munich New Artists' Alliance, or NKVM), and was mounted by Carl Vinnen and conservative artists in a publication called *Ein Protest deutscher Künstler,* ed. Carl Vinnen (Jena: Diederichs, 1911). Kandinsky, Franz Marc, Worringer and others swiftly responded with *Im Kampf um die Kunst: Die Antwort auf den Protest. Mit Beiträgen deutscher Künstler, Galerieleiter, Sammler und Schriftsteller* (Munich: Piper, 1911). On the Nazi response to Kandinsky, Nolde, and other modernist artists, see *"Degenerate Art": The Fate of the Avant-Garde in Nazi Germany,* ed. Stephanie Barron (Los Angeles: Los Angeles County Museum of Art, 1991).

6. On Michelstaedter and the Jewish community in Gorizia, see Orietta Altieri, "La famiglia Michelstaedter e l'ebraismo goriziano," *Dialoghi intorno a Michelstaedter,* ed. Sergio Campailla (Gorizia: Biblioteca Statale Isontina, 1988): 35–41.

Fig. 4. Map of East Central Europe in 1910.

Fig. 5. Map of East Central Europe in 1992.

city. Nearly fifty years later, an iron barrier still separates one side of Gorizia from the other, causing streets to come to dead-ends, as in former Berlin. A fourth of one *piazza* is in Italy, three-fourths in a country later transformed, in 1991, into the Republic of Slovenia. To walk from one side of town to another you must cross border patrol. And still, as in Michelstaedter's day, Italians and Slovenes inhabit both parts of the city, alongside rare Austrians who adorn their houses with photographs of the emperor Franz Joseph, deceased in 1914. Only the Jews are gone, Michelstaedter's eighty-nine-year-old mother and sister among them, deported by the Germans to Auschwitz in 1943, the population reduced from nearly three hundred to fewer than ten.[7] Consistently marginalized from the states to which it has belonged, Gorizia—like Trieste—means less to Italy today than it once did to Austria. To make the irony even more bitter, the cemetery of those Jews who embraced the Italian cause against Austria—the one where Michelstaedter and his family are buried—lies neither in Italy nor in Austria, but in a country that none of them knew. Here, too, the home of all is the home of none.

Mitteleuropean scholarship has a name for this syndrome: the experience of the Jew, an emblem of not belonging, of the failure of ethnic, social, ethical, and psychological integration. It did not take Otto Weininger to posit this link, forging connections between Judaic experience and a spirit of indirection, opposition, and disintegration. The main steps had already been taken by the tradition to which he belonged. By the beginning of the twentieth century dozens of thinkers had associated Judaism with all that threatened firm cultural identity: skepticism, reflection, materialism, egotism, and indifference to conventional belief. At one point or another, historians of culture had laid the responsibility for such ills as rationalism, empiricism, and individualism all at the door of the Jews. In the most extreme reading, the alleged propensity of Jews for speculative thinking was traceable to an inbred perversion. They were "anti-nature," instinctively opposed to the productive and self-evident forms of a natural life. In a milder reading,

---

7. According to the annals of Gorizia's *Gymnasium* in the mid-nineteenth century, two-thirds of registered students were Slovene, a third Italian or Friulian, and very few Austrian. By 1914 the number of Italians enrolled in all the schools of Gorizia was 2,953, Slovenes, 3,400. See Marco Waltritsch, "Le istituzioni scolastiche e culturali slovene a Gorizia sino alla prima guerra mondiale," *La scuola, la stampa, le istituzioni culturali a Gorizia e nel suo territorio dalla metà del Settecento al 1915* (Gorizia: Istituto per gli Incontri Culturali Mitteleuropei, 1983): 33 and 41. On the once sizable Jewish population of Gorizia see Chiara Lesizza Budin, "La scuola ebraica goriziana dalle origini all'anno 1800" and other articles in the collection *Ha-tkiva', La speranza: Attraverso l'ebraismo goriziano* (Gorizia: Edizioni della Laguna, 1991).

advanced in the forties by Jean-Paul Sartre, the talent of Jews for abstraction, speculation and calculation appeared rather to be the consequence—not the cause—of an ill, and one for which they were not
responsible. It was a reaction to their forcible exclusion from the traditions and opportunities of the cultures they inhabited.[8] In addition
to these essentialist or historical arguments, there were ideological reasons that were adduced to explain differences between Christians and
Jews. Judaism was a private, paradoxical creed, less grounded in rit-
ual than Christianity. It encouraged its subjects to develop their reflective and analytical skills. Not fettered by the accumulated history of a
Church, Jews were more likely to explore the paths of free thinking.

Weininger gave metaphysical reasons for the Jewish type, not biological or historical ones. The Jew, he declared, is essentially a "dis-
believer," a person who believes in nothing. Judaism and nihilism are
thus synonymous, inclining people to place their immediate and practical interests above all else. What happens, asks Weininger, when a person "has no ultimate goal, a foundation on which the psychologist's
probe strikes with a definitive sound?" Anything and everything. The
psychic contents of the Jew are "all affected by a duality or plurality;
from this ambiguity, duplicity, indeed multiplicity, he can never liberate himself" (Weininger 1903: 27). Bereaved of that "psychic simplic-
ity" which flowers into unquestioning devotion to a spontaneous moral
tradition (obviously the Christian tradition), the Jew is a creature of
masks, speculative in more senses than one: given to restructure reality
in thought as well as to mirror the beliefs of others, irrespective of
whether they are true or false.[9]

8. Jean-Paul Sartre, *Réflexions sur la Question Juive,* trans. George J. Becker as
Anti-Semite and Jew (New York: Schocken Books, 1948). For critical reflections on the
Jewish question, including the "self-hatred" they have so often appeared to embody, see
Sander Gilman, *Jewish Self-Hatred: Anti-Semitism and the Hidden Language of the
Jews* (Baltimore: Johns Hopkins University Press, 1986); Allan Janik, "Viennese Culture
and the Jewish Self-Hatred Hypothesis: A Critique," *Jews, Antisemitism and Culture in
Vienna,* ed. Ivar Oxaal, Michael Pollak and Gerhard Botz (London and New York:
Routledge & Kegan Paul, 1987): 75–88; Theodor Lessing, *Jüdischer Selbsthass* (Berlin:
Jüdischer Verlag, 1930); Kurt Lewin, "Self-Hatred Among Jews," in *Resolving Social
Conflicts: Selected Papers on Group Dynamics,* ed. Gertrud Weiss Lewin (New York:
Harper and Row, 1948), 186–200; Quirino Principe, ed., *Ebrei e Mitteleuropa* (Brescia:
Shakespeare & Co., 1984); Alexander Ringer, *Arnold Schoenberg: The Composer as
Jew* (Oxford: Clarendon Press, 1993).
9. In a particularly self-doubting moment Ludwig Wittgenstein reproduces a similar idea: "It could be said (rightly or wrongly) that the Jewish mind does not have the
power to produce the tiniest flower or blade of grass; its way is rather to make a drawing of the flower or blade of grass that has grown in another's spirit and to put it into a
comprehensive picture. . . . It is typical of a Jewish spirit to understand someone else's

Almost a century after the publication of Weininger's *Sex and Character,* the ambiguity, duplicity, "indeed multiplicity" that he would have liked to erase from human behavior have come to be seen as fundamental traits of modernist culture. In fact, it is not by chance that today, at the end of the century, we search Central and Eastern Europe, the historical soil of this Jewish experience, for insight into our own postmodern future. The vanished Jew of Mitteleuropa is just the most dramatic casualty of a breakdown of political and psychological integrity that has marked the last hundred years. Others include the "mad" groups of wandering artists. Karl Lueger, the anti-Semitic mayor of Vienna from 1887 to 1910, made it clear how extensive the Jew-concept could be when he declared, "I decide who is a Jew" (cited in Eksteins 1990: 319). Authority defines even those it excludes, not just as dissonant to the rule, but as intrinsically anarchic.

This is not to say that in 1910 Jews or descendants of Jews like Schoenberg, Michelstaedter, Buber, Wittgenstein, Lukács, and Simmel suffered the type of persecution that awaited them after the First World War. According to Schoenberg at least, the racial theories at the beginning of the century had more influence on Jews than Gentiles:

> There were only small groups, among students mostly, which were subdued by them. And all the great Jewish thinkers, scientists, artists, writers and innovators . . . had as many admirers, followers and pupils, corresponding to their work, without any regard for their Jewish origin. And from my own experience I can tell you that the number of my Aryan pupils and followers was very much larger than I could have expected. . . . Indeed, I personally found myself far more appreciated by Aryans than by Jews. . . . The latter, deprived of their racial self-confidence, doubted a Jew's creative capacity more than the Aryans did. (Schoenberg 1934–35: 504)[10]

---

work better than he understands it himself." In his characteristically quizzical style, Wittgenstein notes that "the Jewish 'genius' is only a holy man. Even the greatest of Jewish thinkers is only a talent. (Me, for instance.) I think there is some truth in my idea that I really only think reproductively. I don't believe I have ever *invented* a line of thinking; on the contrary, it has always been given to me by someone else. I have merely seized upon it immediately in a passion for my own activity of clarification. That is how Boltzmann, Hertz, Schopenhauer, Frege, Russell, Kraus, Loos, Weininger, Spengler, Sraffa have influenced me. Can one take the case of Breuer and Freud as an example of Jewish reproductiveness?" (Wittgenstein 1977: 18–19; note dated 1931; trans. slightly modified).

On problems confronting Jewish writers in the first half of this century, see Klara Pomeranz Carmely, *Das Identitätsproblem jüdischer Autoren im deutschen Sprachraum: Von der Jahrhundertwende bis zu Hitler* (Königstein/Ts: Scriptor Carmely, 1981) and Solomon Liptzin, *Germany's Stepchildren* (New York: World Publishing Company, 1944). On Wittgenstein and Judaism see Steven S. Schwarzschild, "Wittgenstein as Alienated Jew," *Telos* 40 (Summer 1979): 150–160.

10. Of course, not everyone in Schoenberg's time agreed with his assessment—for example Arthur Schnitzler, who notes in 1912 that in the future "it will perhaps no

Nor is it to deny that a wide spectrum of differences separates Wittgenstein's Protestant upbringing from Buber's defense of the Hasidic tradition (a spectrum actually crossed by Schoenberg: born into a Jewish family, he converted to Protestantism in 1898 but in the face of Hitler, in 1933, reverted back to Judaism). It is simply to say that the Jewish question loomed inevitably over each of these figures—in a sense as the question of all questions, for it epitomized the antagonism between convention and difference, normalcy and abnormalcy, consonance and dissonance, belief and unbelief that marked the whole era. It pointed to the problem of ideological, psychological, and cultural disunity; but it also raised the suspicion that what lurked beneath such issues of unity and identity was a problem of indeterminate foundations, of personal and ontological non-knowledge.

The rival allegiances of groups, a growing distance between individual and public spheres, a feeling that one's innermost identity was inadequately anchored to political and ideological institutions: these factors form a general phenomenology to which art in 1910 feels compelled to respond. In responding, however, it also reconstitutes the phenomenology, furnishing perspectives for reinterpreting and reassessing its nature. Indeed, this feedback from interpretation to "originary" datum is what Schoenberg associates with the artistic process, thriving on displacing the expectations of audiences rather than on reaffirming received ideas. Few artists in 1910 are interested in articulating the "historical foundations" of their art. Such an operation could be performed just as well without any help from art. No artist in this study aims merely to reflect their social or political conditions (where "aesthetic chaos" would mirror the reality of fractured experience). That function can be performed by much lesser artists. If anything, the artistic "chaos" of 1910 seeks an order that is *missing* from historical experience: new modes of comprehension transcending the traditional and stubborn dualities (cause/effect, male and female, consonance/dissonance, Aryan/Jew, belonging/not belonging). This, if anything, is the "final cause" of the antagonisms of 1910.

---

longer be possible to gain a correct impression (at least I hope so) of the importance, spiritually almost more than politically and socially, that was assigned to the so-called Jewish question when these lines were written. It was not possible, especially not for a Jew in public life, to ignore the fact that he was a Jew; nobody else was doing so, not the Gentiles and even less the Jews. You had the choice of being counted as insensitive, obtrusive and fresh; or of being oversensitive, shy and suffering from feelings of persecution. And even if you managed somehow to conduct yourself so that nothing showed, it was impossible to remain completely untouched" (cited in Ringer 1979: 16–17).

Kandinsky's "harmony of contradiction," for example, envisions the possibility of more flexible interpretive acts than those mechanically refracting the world, ones decongealing these oppositions and allowing them to turn productive. Years after the First World War, when Schoenberg hears a rumor that Kandinsky has become anti-Semitic, he addresses his onetime friend in the most unanswerable of terms. He notes that the real Kandinsky, the artist and genius of 1910, the Kandinsky that Schoenberg loved, could not possibly have thought in such terms (Schoenberg and Kandinsky 1984: 78–83). To emancipate dissonance is not only to recognize, suffer, or reflect such dissonance. It is to make it the basis for a new type of art. To borrow a phrase from Massimo Cacciari (1993: 106), the prewar aesthetics of Schoenberg and Kandinsky wish to promote the "functional multiplicity of languages" over and beyond their reduction into one. The suspicion that anarchy might be the only true ground for meaning confronts art, not with the liberty of license, but with the most stringent of formal tasks.

THE CHIMERA

Two years after Schoenberg's *Theory of Harmony* a restless bohemian called Dino Campana presents a comparable scenario for contemporary art. His own art of poetry is the fruit of travels by foot throughout Italy and Europe, each ending in a clash with the law and a forced return to his hometown of Maradi, north of Florence. The pattern is repeated dozens of times, even as far away as Argentina. And each time Campana is charged with mental alienation; finally he is committed to an asylum for the last fourteen years of his life (1918–1932).

Orphic Songs (Canti Orfici, 1914), his only collection of poems, opens not by commemorating a lyrical experience, advancing a symbol, or evoking a love, but by describing a situation that Campana calls "The Night":

> Ricordo una vecchia città, rossa di mura e turrita, arsa su la pianura sterminata nell'Agosto torrido, con il lontano refrigerio di colline verdi e molli sullo sfondo. Archi enormemente vuoti di ponti sul fiume impaludato in magre stagnazioni plumbee: sagome nere di zingari mobili e silenziose sulla riva: tra il barbaglio lontano di un canneto lontane forme ignude di adolescenti e il profilo e la barba giudaica di un vecchio: e a un tratto dal mezzo dell'acqua morta le zingare e un canto, da la palude afona una nenia primordiale monotona e irritante: e del tempo fu sospeso il corso. (Campana 1914: 83)

[I recall an old city, red-walled and turreted, parched on the boundless lowlands in scorching August, with the distant coolness of green and wet hills in the background. Enormously empty arches of bridges over the river swamped in meager leaden stagnations: black molds of mobile and silent gypsies on the banks: in the distant glare of a cane field, the distant nude forms of adolescents and the profile and Judaic beard of an old man: and suddenly from out of the dead water the gypsy women and a song, from the voiceless marsh a primordial, monotonous, and irritating dirge: and the course of time was arrested.]

In this lurid conglomeration of images, everything contends with everything: red with green, youth with age, motion with immobility, closeness with distance, brightness with darkness. Above the torrid and burnt out plains the hills are a "frigidarium." The flowing river has become stagnant. The arches of the bridges are "enormously empty," constructed not of their stone, but of the spaces they frame. Two shapes can be made out in the dazzle of the dark scene, bound only by contrast: the distant naked forms of adolescents and the Judaic "profile and beard" of an elderly man. The first image is general and indistinct, the other magnified and detailed. From the soundless swamp a song emerges. Time, which typically runs, has come to a halt. The rest of this opening poem only confirms the pattern, elaborating a simile of paradox, a hallucinatory narrative of sensual and imaginative deviance.

The second poem of the *Orphic Songs,* perhaps the earliest to be written, gives a name to this perplexing experience: "Chimera." Mythologically, a chimera is a fire-breathing monster with a lion's head, a goat's body, and a serpent's tail. Figuratively, she is a creature of the imagination, as inexplicable as she is unattainable. In the field of genetics, a chimera is an organism possessing the tissues of two sexes or species. In each case she is a hybrid phenomenon, an anomalous event, a possibility as alluring as she is rare. Addressing his Chimera directly, Campana does not mask his confusion:

> Non so se tra roccie il tuo pallido
> Viso m'apparve, o sorriso
> Di lontanze ignote
> Fosti, la china eburnea
> Fronte fulgente o giovine
> Suora de la Gioconda:
> O delle primavere
> Spente, per i tuoi mitici pallori
> O Regina o Regina adolescente:
> . . .

Non so se la fiamma pallida
Fu dei capelli il vivente
Segno del suo pallore,
Non so se fu un dolce vapore,
Dolce sul mio dolore,
Sorriso di un volto notturno:
Guardo le bianche rocce le mute fonti dei venti
E l'immobilità dei firmamenti
E i gonfii rivi che vanno piangenti
E l'ombre del lavoro umano curve là sui poggi algenti
E ancora per teneri cieli lontane chiare ombre correnti
E ancora ti chiamo ti chiamo Chimera.
(Campana 1914: 105–106)

[I do not know if among rocks
Your pallid face appeared to me, or if
You were the smile of unknown distances,
Your slanted ivory brow refulgent
Oh young sister of La Gioconda:
Oh for your mythical pallor
Of dead springs,
Oh Queen oh adolescent Queen:
. . .
I do not know if the pale flame
Of her hair was the living sign of her pallor,
I do not know whether it was a sweet haze,
Sweet to my grief,
Smile of a face in the night:
I look at the white rocks the mute sources of winds
And the immobility of the firmaments
And the swollen streams that go weeping
And the shadows of human labor curved there on frozen hills
And still distant bright shadows running through soft skies
And still I call you I call you Chimera.]

No attempt to identify this Chimera can diminish her sway over Campana's entire literary production. She names no living woman, no momentary sensation, no haunting vision of the poet—indeed, no identity at all—but rather historical experience pure and simple, experience that unhinges the witnessing mind, generating confusion in its agent. In turn this agent—this poet—can find no significance but in articulating that same confusion. Like Schoenberg's dissonance, the Chimera names an art that emancipates the confusion built into experience, revealing it, transmitting it, making it appear to have its own order. Campana's poem is organized around one chronically repeated statement, "I do not know," as if to say, "I can give you nothing but the Chimera I see, sweet to my grief." By the time of T. S. Eliot, Eugenio Montale, and other poets of the twenties, such confessed ignorance is commonplace; in Campana and in 1910, it stems from a naked confrontation with the disorientation at work in the imagination.

To get to the bottom of his concern, Campana seeks out the clarity of the night:

> Ma per il tuo ignoto poema
> Di voluttà e di dolore
> Musica fanciulla esangue,
> Segnato di linea di sangue
> Nel cerchio delle labbra sinuose,
> Regina della melodia:
> Ma per il vergine capo
> Reclino, io poeta notturno
> Vegliai le stelle vivide nei pelaghi del cielo,
> Io per il tuo dolce mistero
> Io per il tuo divenir taciturno.
> (Campana 1914: 105)

> [But for your unknown poem
> Of voluptuousness and grief
> Ashen-faced musical girl
> Marked with a line of blood
> Circling in sinuous lips,
> Queen of melody:
> But for your virgin head,
> Reclined, I nocturnal poet
> Kept watch of the bright stars in the seas of the sky.
> I for your sweet mystery
> I for your taciturn becoming.]

Straining to understand the Chimera's poem, the nocturnal poet presents his bewilderment as the product of a specular world. His benighted intelligence spirals into a battle between vitality and death, between darkness and stars. On the adolescent and virginal Queen lies a pallor of dead springs. A line of blood marks her bloodless face, signaling her lips. Her flaming hair is the single "living sign" of what is otherwise closer to a corpse. The unknowable, chimerical poem announces an inextricable union of presence and absence in voluptuous pain, to the point where the poet cannot say whether this gruesomely lovely face ever appeared at all or whether he just felt it as a smile of "unknown distance." The origin of both the experience and its voice in art is as taciturn as the mute source of winds, testament to unfathomably duplicitous conditions. "At night in the deserted square," Campana writes later in his collection, "I, under the sad electric light, felt my infinite solitude" (Campana 1914: 161–162). This poem, called

"Dualism," finds the poet suspended between two unreconcilable worlds: one manifested by love for a real, historical woman and the other by the appeal of an abstract, unknowable one, whose name must remain "Oblivion" (Campana 1914: 164).

Some elements of Campana's style are familiar to us from French symbolist poetry, so much so that scholarly emphasis on this lineage has obscured a proper view of the more raw, "Teutonic," expressionistic dimensions of his verse. Symbolism and expressionism are both interested in relations between things dissimilar on the surface, in the junctures and recesses implied by the very tying of meanings together, in the possibility of awakening some invisible world by means of different and unusual ties. Both stress the intellectual confusion between sensory and theoretical perception. The difference between the arts, however, lies in the nature of their respective achievements. Symbolism valorizes consciousness at the very edge of perception. It suspects that there may be some unifying ground of signs and surface appearances. Expressionism is more concerned with the disorientation already at work in perceptual and conceptual understanding, the disjunction between "alternative" and "everyday" modes of vision. Where the earlier nineteenth-century poets discover invisible links among discordant phenomena, the later ones heighten the phenomenon of discord itself, suggesting that harmony can be discovered only in these structures of tension, not beyond or behind them. Here artistic revelations of "another world" beyond the apparent one become all but impossible. The surfaces of perceptible experience fail to become symbols of intuitable wholes. Rather, these surfaces appear "unnaturally" natural, eluding the meanings one might like to assign them, while yielding no others. And this is the "demonic" dimension of expressionistic writing, entrusting itself to the space between the visible and the invisible, the natural and the transcendent, the "will" and the power.

An example lies in a story called "The Perfecting of a Love" (Die Vollendung eine Liebe, 1910), written during the short-lived expressionist phase of the Austrian writer Robert Musil. The task Musil sets himself in this masterpiece of expressionist prose—in this story "formed by disgust with storytelling," as he puts it (Musil 1911b: 10)—is to externalize the psychic unrest of a woman on the verge of betraying her husband. Most of this psychic externalization occurs through mind-stretching analogies between things pertaining to entirely different orders of being, as if to suggest that rational or discursive commentary cannot come near to explaining the inner movements of human subjectivity:

> There was something gay and light about it all, a dilation as when walls open out—something loosened and unburdened and full of tenderness. And from her own body too the gentle weight was now lifted, leaving in her ears a sensation as of melting snow, gradually passing over into a ceaseless, light, loose tinkling. She felt as if with her husband she were living in the world as in a foaming sphere full of beads and bubbles and little feathery rustling clouds. (Musil 1910–11: 133)

As Musil explains it in a sketch for a foreword to *Unions* (1911), the volume in which "The Perfecting of a Love" appeared, the objective of this writing is to penetrate to a deeper sphere of the psyche than one revealing honest characters to have "specks of rascality [and] rascals specks of honesty. . . . A little deeper still, and people dissolve into futility." One takes this deeper sphere seriously "not from the futility, but from the tragic enthusiasm it engenders" (Musil 1911b: 9). And it is for this reason that Musil constructs his floating network of concomitant images and values: to articulate what concepts cannot: "the wandering point of fixation, the *dis*unity in disparate phenomena." This, he claims, is "*inner* understanding: a being confounded" (Musil 1912: 14–15).

Nevertheless, at the rare moments when the narrator *does* try to explain (discursively or rationally) the internal turmoil of his protagonist Claudine, we sense the extent to which her turbulence involves the dissociation of the realm of appearances from all ideal requirements of meaning. Latent in Claudine, notes the narrator, is an intuition that something is grotesquely inappropriate about the shapes that external experience assumes. What struck her most as she gazed around her

> was the random nature of her surroundings: not the fact that everything looked the way it did, but that this appearance persisted, adhering to things as if it were part of them, perversely holding on to them as with claws. It was like an expression that has remained on a face long after the emotion has gone. And oddly—as though a link had snapped in the silently unwinding chain of events and swiveled out of its true position, jutting out of its dimension—all the people and all the things grew rigid in the attitude of that chance moment, combining, squarely and solidly, to form another, abnormal order. Only she herself went sliding on, her swaying senses outspread among these faces and things—sliding downwards—away. (Musil 1910–11: 163)

What bothers Claudine is not simply that this aspect of things is arbitrary, but that it "persists," resisting the fluidity of temporal change. Chance forms seem to operate independently of all inner intention, holding onto things "as with claws." This aggressive situation never allows a thing to be what it is, to act and signify as it might deem fit. At moments like these all natural phenomena appear irremediably unnatural. And in contrast to the tenacity of this inessential objective world, the subjectivity of Claudine goes "sliding on . . . sliding downwards—away."

Perceived reality is never estranged to this point in consonant, reciprocal, symbolist worlds. If there are any reciprocal relations in Musil's passage, they are only those of mutual and insoluble oppositions. Just as the appearance of a thing comes loose from its essence, so the moment becomes dissociated from eternity, the contingent from the necessary, the perception from thing perceived, the volatility of inner subjective life from the heavy immobility of objective fact. Expressionist writing does inherit the symbolistic tendency to transform the structure of everyday experience in such a way as to make meaning transcend all appearance; but this "meaning" is now far too transcendent to seize. To make matters worse, such transcendence of meaning is never so autonomous or complete as to transubstantiate or cancel its natural point of departure (the physical world). All that remains sure is the *disjunction* between an appearance or sign and its possible significance. Imaginative knowledge is impossible to extricate from its world of contorted forms.

Expressionism finds its path between symbolism and the other aesthetic that it inherits: naturalism, or the "crude" and "overly realistic" depiction of positive, historical life. Just as expressionism naturalizes the domain of the symbol by tying it to everything it wishes to transcend, it also makes the natural symbolic. Only now the natural is symbolic of no more than its own discordant, dynamic, and insufficiently expressive energy. Campana is only one point of transition. Each one of his images struggles to become a symbol, but few succeed. And when they do, they are forced. What is not forced—and this may have to do with Campana's own mental imbalance, the "natural logic" of his madness, as it were—is the reciprocal clash of these images, each striving to become a symbol, but also failing to receive cohesive, significant organization.

The expressionism of Campana also appears in the recurring and insuperable confrontation, in his verse, between a suffering ego and a deliriating cosmos. *The Tragedy of the Last German in Italy*: thus reads the subtitle of the *Orphic Songs*. The collection also ends with a colophon, a paraphrase of Walt Whitman: "They were all cover'd with the boy's blood." This ending of the volume turns the issue away from the subject of the tragedy—the last German in Italy—to the responsible agents. Campana explains from his asylum what he meant by the last German. He is the "idealistic and imperialistic" barbarian of the Middle Ages, who met his end in Italy through "moral purity." The boy of the Whitman passage is similar: an innocent victim of corrupt assassins' hands. Both images reinforce the collection's governing figure of the poet as a mythical Orpheus torn limb from limb by hysterical Maenads. The artist as a martyr done in by his own attempt to charm the jungle finds more resonance in the Teutonic, expressionist company of Kokoschka, Schiele, and Trakl than in the Gaulic and symbolist one of Arthur Rimbaud, Paul Verlaine, and Stéphane Mallarmé.[11]

Only a handful of prewar poets depict experience in such violent and conflictual terms—Georg Heym, Jakob van Hoddis, and Gottfried Benn among them. A few others, like Sergio Corazzini and Else Lasker-Schüler, the premier woman expressionist (married from 1901 to 1911 to the expressionist impressario Herwarth Walden), make language oscillate between opposites that eventually come to settle their differences:

11. Campana's gloss on the subtitle of *Canti Orfici* can be found in Campana 1978 and Campana 1914: 14–18, where, discussing these same issues, the editor Ceragioli cites an interesting letter from Campana to the futurist writer (and cofounder of *La Voce*) Giovanni Papini: "I am indifferent—I, who live at the foot of innumerable Calvaries. Everyone has spit on me since I was fourteen; I hope that somebody will finally want to run me through [*infilarmi*]. Know, though, that you will not be running through a sack of pus, but the supreme alchemist, who has created blood out of pain. Hurrah! In my hate for sacks of pus encased by futurism, I wish either to run through [others] or be run through" (Campana 1914: 16).

Studies of Campana include Giovanni Bonalumi, *Cultura e poesia di Campana* (Florence: Vallecchi, 1953); Gabriel Cacho Millet, *Dino Campana fuorilegge* (Palermo: Novecento, 1985); Mario Costanzo, *Studi critici: Rebora, Boine, Sbarbaro, Campana* (Rome: Giovanni Bardi, 1955); Maura Del Serra, *L'immagine aperta: Poetica e stilistica dei Canti Orfici* (Florence: La Nuova Italia, 1973); Enrico Falqui, *Per una cronistoria dei Canti Orfici* (Florence: Vallecchi, 1960); Teresa Ferri, *Dino Campana: L'infinito del sogno* (Roma: Bulzoni, 1985); Jonathan Galassi, "A Hymn of Non-Attainment: Dino Campana," *Conversant Essays: Contemporary Poets on Poetry*, ed. James McCorkle (Detroit: Wayne State University Press, 1990); Cesare Galimberti, *Dino Campana* (Milan: Mursia, 1967); Ida Li Vigni, *Orfismo e poesia in Dino Campana* (Genova: Il Melangolo, 1983); Maria Maggi, "La 'fatale' chimera campaniana," *Esperienze letterarie* 13, no. 3 (July–Sept. 1988): 95–106; Francesca Bernardini Napoletano, ed., *Dino Campana nel Novecento: Il progetto e l'opera* (Roma: Officina Edizioni, 1992); Romolo Rossi, "Dino Campana: Nostalgia e sublimazione nella tendenza al suicidio," *Il Ponte* 45, no. 1 (Jan.–Feb. 1989): 139–144.

Komm, wir wollen uns näher verbergen . . .
Das Leben liegt in aller Herzen
Wie in Särgen.

Du! Wir wollen uns tief küssen—
Es pocht eine Sehnsucht an die Welt,
An der wir sterben müssen.

[Come, let's go sneaking off then . . .
In everybody's heart life lies
As in a coffin.

Ah! Let's kiss deeply, you and I—
A longing's knocking at the world
From which we'll surely die.]
(Lasker-Schüler 1982: 130–131)[12]

The most radical oscillation, however, occurs neither in Campana nor
Lasker-Schüler, but in her friend Georg Trakl, the most ambivalent poet
of the twentieth century.

POETIC DUPLICITY

It is impossible to imagine a writer more sensitive to the spiritual
indefiniteness resulting from two millennia of opposition between the
sacred and the secular than Trakl. This poet charges his understanding
with the elementary power of almost every antithesis with which European thinking has struggled from the start: life and death, innocence
and guilt, sanity and madness, fertility and sterility, nature and law, divinity and evil, relevation and benightedness. In Trakl the conflicting
pull of these forces has finally become unbearable. Whatever one would
like to keep separate here commingles incestuously, contaminating the
nature of its other. Was it Trakl's own psyche, so frequently investigated
by scholars and psychologists, that made him so prone to paradox?

Born of Austrian parents in 1887, two years after Campana—in the
same year as Michelstaedter and Giovanni Boine (Kokoschka, Schiele,
Lukács, Slataper and Wittgenstein were similarly born between 1885
and 1890)—Trakl had an even more tormented life than the Italian
poet. As a child he was pathologically shy, subject, like Michelstaedter,
to fits of rage. To avoid having to face passengers in trains, he would
travel standing in the aisles outside compartments. He was given to sui-

12. For an analysis of the "bipolar structure of Else Lasker-Schüler's mode of being"
see Hans W. Cohn, *Else Lasker-Schüler: The Broken World* (Cambridge: Cambridge
University Press, 1974): 37–152. On Sergio Corazzini and his place in twentieth-century
art see Stefano Jacomuzzi, *Sergio Corazzini* (Milan: Mursia, 1963).

cidal acts from a very young age—throwing himself in front of a moving train, leaping in front of a skittish horse, walking into a pond until he disappeared underneath the water, leaving only his hat to mark the place for his rescuers. Ridiculed by his family for writing poetry, Trakl grew increasingly introverted. His father was at best indifferent, at worst insensitive, to him and his five siblings. His mother (whom he hated and once said that he would have liked to murder) was cold, uncaring, and drug-addicted. By age fifteen, Trakl, too, was regularly equipped with chloroform. The drugs that he used to "keep himself in life," as he put it, for the next twelve years, included opium, morphine, Veronal, and cocaine.[13]

Not surprisingly, Trakl became a chemist. Unable to keep a job, he volunteered for the war in 1914. Left to tend for ninety wounded men, with scarce medications, on the treacherous eastern front of the Austrian campaign, Trakl had as gruesome an experience as any in the war, witnessing men not only in incurable pain but hanging themselves from trees. The poet cracked, and attempted to take his own life. Apprehended before succeeding, he tried to desert, was apprehended again, and committed to medical supervision. The diagnosis was dementia praecox. Three weeks later, toward the end of 1914, he died from an overdose of cocaine.

Among his few close friends, and amid long periods of silence, Trakl would speak erratically of spiritual degeneracy. No doubt he shared more of these reflections with his younger sister, Grete, to whom it seems he was incestuously attached. And the closeness was reciprocal: in 1917, less than three years after his death, she repeated Georg's gesture, shooting herself at a party with Herwarth Walden.

---

13. My account of Trakl's life and poetry is indebted to a long list of useful studies: Massimo Cacciari, "La Vienna di Wittgenstein," *Nuova Corrente* 72/73 (1977): 59–106; Margherita Caput and Maria Carolina Foi, Introduction to Trakl 1983: ix–xxii; Richard Detsch, *Georg Trakl's Poetry: Toward a Union of Opposites* (University Park and London: Pennsylvania State University Press, 1983); Robert Firmage, Introduction to Trakl 1988: vii–xxix; Martin Heidegger, "Language in the Poem: A Discussion on Georg Trakl's Poetic Work," in *On the Way to Language*, trans. Peter D. Hertz (New York: Harper & Row, 1971), 159–198; Hans-Georg Kemper, *Georg Trakls Entwürfe: Aspeckte zu ihren Verständnis* (Tübingen: Niemeyer, 1970); Hans-Georg Kemper, "Georg Trakl and his Poetic Persona: On the Relationship Between Author and Work," in Williams, ed. 1991: 24–37; Walther Killy, *Über Georg Trakl*, 3d ed. (Göttingen: Vandenhoeck & Ruprecht, 1967); Erasmo Leiva-Merikakis, *The Blossoming Thorn: Georg Trakl's Poetry of Atonement* (Lewisburg, Pa.: Bucknell University Press, 1987); Sharp 1981; Sokel 1959; Theodor Spoerri, *Georg Trakl: Strukturen in Persönlichkeit und Werk* (Bern: Francke, 1954); Eric Williams, *The Mirror and the Word: Modernism, Literary Theory, and Trakl* (Lincoln and London: University of Nebraska Press, 1993).

So many themes of Trakl's poetry replicate those of his life—especially incest, derangement, and persecution—that scholars may be right to approach his poetry as a series of carefully crafted disguises for feelings, experiences, and phobias from which he actually suffered. And yet such transformations of personal experience are common to every poet. What else is at work in Trakl's cryptic language, distorted to the point where it all but erases its historical referents? What is actually wrought by his linguistic transcriptions? From the very start, contentions so rack his perception and grammar that nothing seems to remain but questions:

Nachtlied
Des Unbewegten Odem. Ein Tiergesicht
Erstarrt vor Bläue, ihrer Heiligkeit.
Gewaltig ist das Schweigen im Stein;

Die Maske eines nächtlichen Vogels. Sanfter Dreiklang
Verklingt in einem. Elai! dein Antlitz
Beugt sich sprachlos über bläuliche Wasser.

O! ihr stillen Spiegel der Wahrheit.
An des Einsamen elfenbeinerner Schläfe
Erscheint der Abglanz gefallener Engel.

[*Night Song*
The breath of the Unmoved. An animal face
Grows stiff with blue, with its holiness.
Mighty is the stillness in the stone,

The mask of a nightbird. A gentle triad
Ebbs into unity. Elai! your countenance
Bows speechlessly above the bluish water.

O you silent mirrors of truth!
On the ivory temples of the lonely one
Appears the reflection of fallen angels.]
(Trakl 1969: 68, 1988: 29)

If elemental forces speak louder here than visible, semantic intentions, it is because of their internal alignment and reinforcement in analogical chains ("something unmoved," "the stillness of stone," "a speechless countenance," "the silent mirrors of truth," and so on). So opaque are these figures of speech that whatever significance they promise retreats to the penumbras of unintelligibility. All faces stiffen into a mask, every presence into an absence. Here all one can recognize—as Ludwig Wittgenstein did, when making the anonymous gift of a large family inheritance to Trakl—is an unmistakable Trakl "tone," a tone of still, bright darkness, in which all things are veils of incomprehension.[14]

The tone is sounded by a recurring situation. In a lunar or sylvan setting, a subject suddenly witnesses an unnatural encounter or signal. It is sometimes a sight, sometimes a communicating animal, sometimes the voice of one deceased. But never is the protagonist, the action, or context endowed with a precise or stable identity. Everything oversteps its own nature. Within one and the same poem, words such as "blue," "animal," and "brother" take on mutually exclusive connotations; Trakl replaces them from draft to draft with words that mean their opposite. To make matters worse, he twists and breaks syntax— the regulating structures of comprehension—into all so many shards of sense. Frequently it is impossible to decide whether to read a word as an adjective modifying a noun or an adverb describing the action. As subjects are estranged from their surroundings, characteristics are attributed to phenomena ill-equipped to carry them ("stillness" as "mighty," for example). Recognizable elements of the historical world turn polymorphous, bereaved of a proper name, their internal and external relations uncertain. Descriptions break off into invocations. Speaking becomes a form of listening. Indeed, there comes a point (as noted by Sokel, Saas, and Firmage) where phenomenal reality is subjected to such a process of abstraction that movements, colors, and motifs assume the free-floating independence that they have in Kandinsky. A "new dimension of spiritual space" is opened up by Trakl's poems, notes Rainer Maria Rilke (1950: 527). And it undermines everything definite and well-defined, everything systematically structured by the moral and intellectual understanding.

The structural dissonances entail thematic ones:

> *Klage*
> Schlaf und Tod, die düstern Adler
> Umrauschen nachtlang dieses Haupt:
> Des Menschen goldnes Bildnis
> Verschlänge die eisige Woge
> Der Ewigkeit. An schaurigen Riffen
> Zerschellt der purpurne Leib
> Und es klagt die dunkle Stimme
> Über dem Meer.

14. See the article by Ludwig Ficker, the editor of *Der Brenner,* to whom Wittgenstein made his contribution, "Rilke und der unbekannte Freund," *Der Brenner* 18 (1954): 234–248.

Schwester stürmischer Schwermut
Sieh ein ängstlicher Kahn versinkt
Unter Sternen,
Dem schweigenden Antlitz der Nacht.

[*Lament*
Sleep and death, the somber eagles,
Rush all night about this head:
May the icy surge of eternity
Engulf the golden image
Of man. The crimson body
Shatters on the horrid reefs,
And a dark voice weeps
Above the sea.
Sister of stormy melancholy,
Look, an anxious vessel sinks
Beneath the stars,
The silent countenance of night.]

Untergang
Über den weißen Weiher
Sind die wilden Vögel fortgezogen.
Am Abend weht von unsern Sternen ein eisiger
Wind.

Über unsere Gräber
Beugt sich die zerbrochene Stirne der Nacht.
Unter Eichen schaukeln wir auf einem silbernen
Kahn.

Immer klingen die weißen Mauern der Stadt.
Unter Dornenbogen
O mein Bruder klimmen wir blinde Zeiger gen
Mitternacht.

[*Decline*
Above the white pond
The wild birds have flown away.
An icy wind blows from our stars at evening.

Above our graves
The shattered brow of night is bowed.
We rock beneath the oaktrees in a silver skiff.

The white walls of the city ring forever.
Beneath thorn arches,
O my brother we blind hands climb toward midnight.]
(Trakl 1969: 166 and 116, 1988: 121 and 69)

Each of these poems is articulated around groups of antithetical phenomena. On one side stand blindness, midnight, thorn arches, a shat-

tered brow, and a grave. On the other, a white pond, stars, white walls, a silver skiff, and an icy wind. In "Lament" we find not only sleep, death, a dark voice, and a body shattering on reefs, but also alternative images for what may be the same things: stars, the sea, a surge of eternity, and the golden image of man. Both poems insert a subjective "we" into a lifelessly impersonal setting, a dialogue of "brothers" and "sisters" into disembodied communicative acts. All interpretation is directed to the semantic tensions embodying the voice of this "stormy melancholy," even on the level of preposition (tensions between "above" and "under," "toward" and "from," not to mention the verbs generated from them: *umrauschen*, *fortgezogen*, and so on). "It is," writes the poet, "a nameless unhappiness when one's world breaks in two" (Trakl 1969: 530). Here the "two" are the disparate realms in which the Western vocabulary has traditionally cast its experience. In every object of vision Trakl perceives both: the luminous and the shadowy, the inner and the outer, the spiritual and the material. His images fluctuate between a Christian theology of all-unifying love (the "gentle triad" of "Night Song") and pagan violence. Everything that rises sinks, everything that sinks rises up again. His murderers are his victims, his saints his sinners, and those who are "deranged" clairvoyant. Subjective and objective experience is caught in a perpetual transit; the "from where" and "to where," however, remain unclear.

If there is a "unity" in Trakl's poetic experience it consists in intellectual agony: in the breaking apart of one's world at the moment one struggles to bring it into order. It is the tragic and sacred pain of philosophers both ancient and modern, of Heraclitus and Nietzsche, rooted in the soil of paradox. Trakl knows none of the intuitive serenity of symbolist and late nineteenth-century poets. Or if he does, it is simultaneously accompanied by upheaval, bearing witness to the aporetic nature of all articulated truths and feelings. The unity is also present in the coherence of tone and imagery, in the tragic quality of the situations depicted, in the state of mind they evoke with their threats and their risks and their confusion. An inexplicable "project" is in process in Trakl's poetry, the investigation of a dark autumnal fate. What is even more astonishing in all this is the musical order into which Trakl succeeds in organizing his delirium. His poems tend to fall into three or four parts, each composed of four evenly lengthed lines of three to five feet. The rhythms are iambic and dactylic. Alliteration and vowel consonance present the rarest of phonetic combinations ("Schwester stürmischer Schwermut," "weißen Weiher . . . wilden Vögel . . . ein eisiger Wind"). From 1909 to 1911 he frequently even rhymes his verse. Only after 1912 does he complicate this musical coherence with uneven meters and stanzas, bringing forth the formal forests of his late prose poems.

Music tames the wildest of passions. Versified disorder is disorder controlled. For Trakl this control proves necessary: His semantic and syntactic dissonance would overwhelm his readers were it not for the unity of sound in which it is bound, where each poem is a voice or a variation in a type of larger, choral composition, unfolded in repetitive patterns over the course of his collections. Able to speak only in dissonant ways, Trakl found harmony in song. He entrusted his meanings to music.

It is much more difficult to identify "content" in music than poetry. Without lyrics coupled to tones, we "make sense" of musical compositions, not by seeking a meaning, but by relating them to some prior world of sound, experience, and feeling with which we are already familiar. The result is imponderable enough as it goes—with indescribable impressions, muscular and nervous energies, vague waves of association solicited anew each time a piece of music is heard. Something like this made the philosopher Schopenhauer describe music as a pure voice of the will—or of that kernel of subjectivity which desires and suffers even before it knows how or why. It could be that this is as close as we can get to describing the content of music: a set of feelings coherently presented in form. And the coherence is pleasing, even when saddening, making one think that music is *by definition* sound arranged in melodious and harmonic patterns. Or so it would seem until Schoenberg's compositions of 1908–1913. For these expressionist pieces reject even that sonorous consonance on which such dissonant poets as Trakl relied. Here even that aesthetic coherence of sound which mitigated the loss of semantic clarity is broken. Schoenberg dares do, in the most instinctively appeasing of aesthetic media, what Trakl does on the verbal and conceptual plane. Indeed, he goes further, bringing more elements of his art into opposition.

DECENTRALIZED MUSIC

If the premise is right that feeling, will, or subjective interiority are the "content" of music (though the claim can be debated), and if these are also the raw material of Schoenberg's music, then we must note at least this: Here the spectrum of feeling becomes extraordinarily vast—

unpatterned and self-estranged. It is no longer spurred by an "outer occasion" (a military victory, a devotional creed, a gurgling fountain or peaceful landscape). Even where there is a text that accompanies the music (a "program" so to speak), Schoenberg's compositions divorce themselves from it, freeing themselves from all content but that of their own formal relations.[15] The content of this new, expressionist music, developed before the war and elaborated in original ways by Schoenberg's pupils Anton Webern and Alban Berg, is form unhinged from all content whatsoever—forms of pure sound in its unmitigated and alien materiality. If they have any emotional purpose, it is certainly not solace, consolation, joy, or reassurance. It is something closer to the unsettled, inexplicable emotions of turmoil, agitation, and unease. Here Apollo, the clarifying god of consonant harmony, gives way to the frenzied Dionysus.[16]

15. There is not sufficient space in this study to examine the interesting relationship between Schoenberg and the Triestine composer and pianist Ferruccio Busoni, who operated in Berlin between 1905 and 1914 and whose theory of "absolute music" in *Sketch of a New Esthetic of Music* (published in Trieste in 1907 and dedicated to Rainer Maria Rilke) found resonance in Schoenberg. Suffice it to note that when Busoni defends the self-sufficiency of musical form in late 1910 he immediately thinks of Schoenberg: "I shall have to revise my little Esthetic, in which not everything seems to have been expressed with sufficient clarity. I am a worshiper of form!! This is a matter about which I am hypersensitive. . . . But I reject *traditional* and *unalterable forms* and feel that every idea, every motif, every object demands its *own* form, related to that idea, to that motif, to that object. In nature this is so: the *bud* already contains the fully grown plant. Although I could write in great detail, these words will convey my meaning to you. I would like to draw your attention to a little piece by *Arnold Schoenberg*, reshaped for piano by myself, which has just been published (Piano piece, op. 11, no. 2). . . . You will find it hateful, particularly the sound of its harmonies, but it has its own individual feeling and seems to be perfect in *its* form" (Busoni 1987: 115). On the ties between Schoenberg and Busoni, see their exchange of letters between 1903 and 1919 in this same volume as well as Busoni 1957 and Daniel M. Raessler, "Schoenberg and Busoni: Aspects of Their Relationship," *Journal of the Arnold Schoenberg Institute* 7, no. 1 (June 1983): 7–28.

As with Trakl, the analysis of Schoenberg that follows is indebted to dozens of studies, including Adorno 1985; Cacciari 1980 and 1982; Crawford 1993; Carl Dahlhaus, *Schoenberg and the New Music: Essays*, trans. D. Puffett and A. Clayton (Cambridge and New York: Cambridge University Press, 1987); Hailey 1993; Hermand 1991; Jan Maegaard, *Studien zur Entwicklung des dodekaphonen Satzes bei Arnold Schoenberg* (Copenhagen: Wilhelm Hansen, 1972); Luigi Rognoni, *Espressionismo e dodecafonia* (Turin: Einaudi, 1954); Rosen 1975; Schorske 1981; Joan Allen Smith, *Schoenberg and His Circle: A Viennese Portrait* (New York: Schirmer Books, 1986); H. H. Stuckenschmidt, *Arnold Schoenberg: His Life, World and Work*, trans. Humphrey Searle (London: John Calder, 1977); William Thomson, *Schoenberg's Error* (Philadelphia: University of Pennsylvania Press, 1991); Tiessen 1928.

16. Indeed, theoretical inspiration for Schoenberg's atonal innovations was provided by the Dionysian aesthetics described in Friedrich Nietzsche's *The Birth of Tragedy out of the Spirit of Music*. One senses that Schoenberg was particularly struck by section 24, where Nietzsche equates dissonance with primordial, artistic power. How can we explain

In the centuries leading up to Schoenberg, European composition had been governed by certain stabilizing structural elements: (1) a tonal center, or key, recognizable soon after a piece began, (2) a resolution of the piece into no less definitive a key (usually, but not necessarily, the same one with which it began), (3) a fixed scale of tones on which a melody could be constructed (major, minor, modal), (4) a harmonization of the melody in chords built out of privileged combinations of tones in the scale (from the Baroque period onward, the 1–3–5 intervals of the major triad chord). Variations on these patterns were naturally permitted within the composition, even serving to produce rich and surprising effects; but they were eventually expected to settle back into the consonant pattern from which they had veered. Dissonance was the name for these momentary deviations from an established harmonic order.

Schoenberg's innovation consisted in nothing less than a valediction to this framework for composition. Hesitantly in 1908, and more decisively in *Erwartung* of 1909, he confided his melodic and harmonic lines to a formal language bereft of conventional resolutions, resting in no order that could be deduced from the tones of a scale. This was a logical, not a random development. The dissonance freed by Schoenberg between the last movement of the *Second String Quartet* (1907–08) and *Die glückliche Hand* (1910–13) is the end point of a musical itinerary prepared by the withering away of triadic harmony in nineteenth-century music. The decisive move here lay in the chromaticism of Richard Wagner, which no longer subordinated dissonance to modulations from one key to another, but made it an inherent struc-

---

the enigma by which "that which is ugly and disharmonic" is represented so often in music, asks Nietzsche? "Surely, a higher pleasure must be perceived in all this." The enigma can be explained by the tragic experience of heroic suffering, which makes us see "that even the ugly and disharmonic are part of an artistic game that the will in the eternal amplitude of its pleasure plays with itself. . . . The joy aroused by the tragic myth has the same origin as the joyous sensation of dissonance in music."

Moreover, even Nietzsche's explanation for the purpose of dissonance in this section of *The Birth of Tragedy* is replicated in Schoenberg (as will become clear later). The suffering hero's wish to achieve tragic knowledge and simultaneously *to overcome* such knowledge, he writes, is analogous to the problem of musical dissonance: It makes us "desire to hear and at the same time long to get beyond all hearing." Dissonant, Dionysian art arises among those who have been compelled "to see at the same time that they also longed to transcend all seeing." The terms are similar to those in Schoenberg's aphorism, discussed later in this chapter, on expressionist art—the product of those who open their eyes wide "to tackle what has to be tackled," but who also simultaneously shut them. See Friedrich Nietzsche, *Basic Writings,* ed. and trans. Walter Kaufmann (New York: Modern Library, 1968): 139–143. I am grateful to my brother Robert for bringing Nietzsche's comments on dissonance to my attention.

tural component of the composition, a formal correlative, as it were, of empirical fluidity and movement. In Wagner's wake, Richard Strauss, Aleksander Scriabin, Claude Debussy, and Gustave Mahler elaborated dissonance to the point where the only step not yet taken was the *complete* and *categorical* liberation of dissonance from all dependence on tonal resolution. This was the leap of Schoenberg, determined, as he put it, to do away with the bad faith of composers who ventured to the farthest reaches of tonal experimentation only to end their pieces by obediently reaffirming the harmonies expected by their audience.

Dissonance is radicalized when it is presented as the universal and exclusive substance of harmonic order. On one level Schoenberg's compositions from 1908–1913 seem to be entirely ruled by negativity and contradiction. They sound "atonal" and "athematic," contemptuous of all "natural" aural laws, replacing the virtually divine providence of the triadic chord with a pandemonium of clashing sonorities. What once were moments of passing harshness now pervade the entire fabric of the works, causing unrelieved anguish in listeners. Indeed, one sometimes wonders whether these musical contortions, like the figural ones of expressionist painting, do not intend primarily to disrupt the whole notion of an enjoyable "aesthetic experience," scoffing at the call for beauty, order, and the regulation of feeling. These musical anti-forms seem to be based on a contention that an easily recognizable arrangement of pitch, rhythm, and harmony means an unnecessary concession to psychic comfort. The voices of Schoenberg's compositions move independently; musical syntax loses its binding power; paratactical collisions seem not to be means to an end, but ends in themselves.

On further study, however, it appears that a new compositional method is at work in the dark disorder of this free atonal music, even if it is not easy to hear, and even if it is exercised differently by each work. The question Schoenberg raises at this critical moment in his art is whether one can establish unity among elements of a work which do not seem to share any preestablished "sympathy"—irreconcilable musical intervals, for example, or strident orchestrations. Can unity be found in strife itself? Ordinarily one tolerates the conflict between one thing and another because of some larger whole to which they contribute, where their immediate differences appear superseded, if not reconciled. But what if we do not "rationalize" these differences by reference to a larger, abstract system in which they participate? What if one tries to find unity within the actual and immediately present relations of sound? The question, in other words, is whether what has been traditionally called dissonance cannot be seen as revealing its own consonance.[17] If the answer is yes, then this will mean that each work will have its own individual unity, not furnished by an external and abstract scale or by a habitual harmonic procedure.[18]

This is the paradoxical unity that Schoenberg seeks as he tries to make each composition enact its own inexorable logic, revealing formal possibilities that contemporary audiences hardly suspected that music had. The relative unimportance of pitch (or the position of notes on a scale) in these compositions is compensated for by greater sensitivity to the dynamics with which these pitches are sounded. Harmony becomes a function of volatile and interrelating tone timbres and colors known as *Klangfarben*. So exacting was Schoenberg on this issue of the execution of his tone colors that he believed that his music was not appreciated simply because instrumentalists had not acquired the necessary sensitivity to perform it. "My music is not modern," he is reported to have said, "it is just badly played" (Rosen 1975: 50). In the cold and rarefied songs of *Pierrot Lunaire* (1912) the dynamics of the vocal line vary from whisper to shriek. Their texture, too, is unstable. Neither a singing nor a speaking, it is in between: *Sprechstimme*, a pitched declamation, an unprecedented hybrid of tone and word. The unorthodox orchestrations of the chamber ensemble require instruments to be used in unlikely ways and registers. With the voices of the soprano and the instruments almost never coinciding, it becomes "impossible for the mind to draw from the work's unfolding a sense of general law or pattern being observed, as one can when listening to tonal or twelve-tone music" (Wuorinen 1975).

The new effect of this prewar music does not rest exclusively on surprising dynamics of timbre and color. It also involves the dramatic power of sonorous simultaneity, the supersaturation, as it were, of musical texture in an instant of time. Traditional, thematic organizations of melodies in larger, harmonized units give way to motivic constructions of short, independent sequences of notes. Not immersed in homol-

17. On the history of Schoenberg's notion of the emancipation of dissonance see Robert Falck, "Emancipation of the Dissonance," *Journal of the Arnold Schoenberg Institute* 6, no. 1 (June 1982): 106–111. For a good analysis and overview of Schoenberg's music as an aesthetic of strident oppositions one should read Robert Fleisher's "Dualism in the Music of Arnold Schoenberg," *Journal of the Arnold Schoenberg Institute* 12, no. 1 (June 1989): 22–42. Fleisher further argues that Schoenberg's tendency to aesthetically re-create the world in antithetical terms is possibly rooted in the principles of Jewish mysticism.

18. "Now, I like to imagine a species of art-praxis wherein each case should be a new one, an exception!" (Busoni 1907: 41).

ogous and homogeneous contexts, the motifs appear abandoned and naked. No "accompaniment" makes their journey a destiny. Taken in their community of solitude, however, these divergent motifs and voices shape a fluid, contextual harmony so responsive to its own components that it alters with each newcomer. This may be most evident in the monodrama *Erwartung,* where, as Anton Webern remarks, the musical components follow each other in "an uninterrupted, ever-changing stream of sounds which have never been heard before. There is not a single bar in this score which does not display a completely new tonal picture. The instruments are treated as soloists throughout" (cited in Schoenberg 1991). Once constructed in vertical layers of chords, harmony is now generated by the horizontal divagations of crossing lines. Musical repetition gives way to multiplicity, uniqueness, and difference.

Parts once subordinated to wholes and "signs" once serving pre-established meanings now become so autonomous and self-contained that they produce the briefest musical miniatures in history. The best examples probably lie in the works of Anton Webern, particularly his *Six Bagatelles* (1911–13), five of which last less than a minute, and his earlier *Six Pieces for Large Orchestra* (1909), ranging in length from fifty seconds to five and a half minutes. But none of Schoenberg's *Five Orchestral Pieces* (1909) is longer. The thirty-six songs of his *Book of the Hanging Gardens* (1908) add up to only twenty-five minutes. In such a terse environment, overarching, synthetic wholes become as impossible as "natural," organic progressions. If music once illustrated feeling extensively, in broad narrative lines, it now does the opposite, compressing the expression to an instant. The thirty minutes of *Erwartung,* for example, are devoted to a single second of emotion in which a woman discovers her lover killed by the edge of a wood. The strident miniatures, too, are interested in the transitional density of immediate time, including its quotient of silence, as though wishing to say that when faced with the inherent "expressions" of a moment's contending forces, all "impressions" received from the outside grow dumb. As registers, colors, and lines are developed in such a way as to let no note drown out any other, "a unity of sound is created, in spite of everything" (Webern, cited in Schoenberg 1991). For the very first time in music, all notes seem capable of coexisting with each other. "The tonal relations, clusters, and rhythms expand and contract 'like a gas'" (Schorske 1981: 351). And this makes for a type of resolution after all.

While theorizing new forms of musical harmony, Schoenberg was also exploring other avenues of artistic expression. One was painting. Of his sixty-five canvases, two-thirds were painted between 1908 and 1910 and his first exhibit was held in Vienna on October 8, 1910.[19] In the same period Schoenberg also experiments with stage productions and trenchant aphorisms. The formal restlessness of his career bears out the principle already explicit in the *Theory of Harmony*, to the effect that there is no single or fixed procedure by which to express an artistic intention. No abstract method can fully formalize or finalize the energy that sets it in motion. Every form is a provisional response to provisional problems in time. Historical, existential, and moral as these problems are, they necessitate a constant transmutation and overspilling of form, an exploration of numerous expressive genres, a form for the "formlessness" of every novel intention. Schoenberg's multiple forms of art perhaps ultimately finalize the "non-finality" of artistic content—or the fact that this "content" can only be that which a form enables it to be. And this is why Schoenberg speaks of a dynamic circularity in the relationship between art and experience, art and audience, art and idea.

SPIRITUALITY AND MATERIALISM

At the moment Schoenberg found himself turning to painting, the painter Vasily Kandinsky sought inspiration in music. What Kandinsky was attracted to in music was its nonrepresentational nature. In it he sought a model by which to break the representative constrictions of visual art. Just as Schoenberg developed tone color to the point where textures of sound have the formal autonomy of an abstract tableau, so

---

19. Only three days later, on October 11, 1910, the futurist Francesco Balilla Pratella—whose principles have sometimes been compared to those of Schoenberg—issues a *Manifesto dei Musicisti Futuristi* in Milan. The tenth principle is the most amusing: "We must deprecate ballads in the manner of Tosti and the loathsome Neapolitan songs, as well as sacred music which has no reason to exist now that the decline of religious faith is complete." Pratella does not spell out the futurist technical platform until five months later, on March 11, 1911: "We, the Futurists, proclaim that the traditional modes derived from major, minor, augmented, and diminished intervals, and even the novel scales of whole tones, are merely special cases of the harmonic and atonal chromatic scale. We also declare as invalid the concepts of consonance and dissonance." Balilla predicts that eventually even the chromatic atonal mode will be overcome by an "enharmonic" mode, which, "by incorporating small subdivisions of tones, offers to our renewed sensibilities a maximum of determinable combinatorial sounds and novel relations of chords and timbres. . . . We, Futurists, have for a long time cherished these enharmonic intervals found only in the natural dissonances of orchestral instruments which are differently tuned and in the spontaneous songs of people sung without preoccupation with art." Both manifestos are printed in Slonimsky 1971: 1294–1298.

Kandinsky attempted to liberate the signifying possibilities of painting
from all reliance on a depicted objective world. After attending a concert by Schoenberg on the first day of 1911, Kandinsky received confirmation of the direction he himself had been taking throughout the
previous year. Recognizing the analogous efforts of Schoenberg to construct new principles of formal harmony, he immediately contacted the
musician, establishing an alliance that proved to be one of the most
productive in twentieth-century art. These proponents of atonal music
and abstract painting were both determined to articulate tensions that
had hitherto received no legitimate form. The turning point in Kandinsky's thinking, he recounts in 1913, came when, standing in front of
Monet's painting the *Haystack,* he failed to see what subject it represented. At that moment he realized that this absence of recognizable
content made no difference whatsoever in the painting's effect. On the
contrary, what suddenly became clear was the absolutely "unsuspected
power of the palette, previously concealed from me, which exceeded all
my dreams" (Kandinsky 1913: 363). This was the thought that developed into abstract art, so analogous to the new forms of Schoenberg's
music.

The year preceding Schoenberg's concert in Munich, 1910, is the
one in which Kandinsky reaps the implications of his intuition. It is
the transitional moment of his career, during which he works out his
conceptual rationale for abstract art. As yet, however, he has not taken
the plunge into full abstraction. He has not abandoned the depiction
of natural, empirical forms. In 1910 he stands at the *juncture* of two
imaginative worlds, two different conceptions of art, two "warring
forces" in the history of European thinking. And what Kandinsky's
great paintings of the prewar years show is precisely the meeting of the
worlds. At this moment he conceives of harmony as residing in their
clash, a clash that he sees as both the origin and the end of artistic
expression.[20]

20. Studies of Kandinsky from which my analysis has profited are Lothar-Günther
Buchheim, *Der blaue Reiter und die "Neue Künstlervereinigung München"* (Felda-
fing: Buchheim Verlag, 1959); Magdalena Bushart, *Der Geist der Gotik und die expres-
sionistische Kunst: Kunstgeschichte und Kunsttheorie, 1911–1925* (Munich: Silke
Schreiber, 1990); Will Grohmann, *Kandinsky: His Life and Work* (New York: Harry N.
Abrams, 1958); Jelena Hahl-Koch, *Kandinsky* (New York: Rizzoli, 1993); Klaus Lankheit, "A History of the Almanac," in *The Blaue Reiter Almanac,* ed. Klaus Lankheit,
trans. H. Falkenstein, M. Terzian, and G. Hinderlie (London: Thames & Hudson/New
York: Viking, 1974); Long 1980; Sixten Ringbom, *The Sounding Cosmos: A Study in
the Spiritualism of Kandinsky and the Genesis of Abstract Painting* (Åbo: Åbo Aka-
demi, 1970); the essays by Ringbom and Long in Tuchman, ed., 1986: 201–217 and

Written mainly in 1909–1910 and published at the end of 1911, Kandinsky's study *On the Spiritual in Art* calls the two warring forces materialism and spirituality. At the beginning of the twentieth century, it claims, the two are contending for the control of Europe. Materialism has held the upper hand for centuries. Its knowledge is based on the procedures of science and statistical computation, assuring us that truth can be observed, tested, and communicated in clear and unequivocal form. Its ethic is consumeristic, hankering after what Søren Kierkegaard calls the "interesting" experience. Its economy legitimates greed and its politics consists in muscling one's neighbors. In decades to come, Max Weber and Martin Heidegger will have something similar in mind when they speak of the totally administered, rationalized world, which reduces all of life to an ensemble of objects. In Kandinsky's view, the art of proper materialism is realism. By the end of the nineteenth century it gives way to naturalism, which in turn dissolves into impressionism. And in this development, Kandinsky claims, we see that the reign of materialism is coming to a close. In impressionism hard, objective facts are presented as functions of something else, not primary but secondary truths, consequences of subjective interpretation.

In the first decade of the new century a spark of inner life has finally begun to pierce the materialistic night. The spirit, writes Kandinsky, has begun to awaken, even if not surely enough to provide cause for celebration. The fledgling "soul" as yet lacks direction and a means of expression. More distressing still, it lies in a precarious state of convalescence, struggling to recover from that debilitating "desperation, unbelief, lack of purpose" with which it has been afflicted for so many centuries. The feeble glimmer of a star in a vast gulf of darkness is at present no more than a beacon of hope, which "the soul scarcely has the courage to perceive, doubtful whether this light might not itself be a dream, and the circle of blackness, reality" (Kandinsky 1909–11: 128). The maturing of soul will depend on whether it succeeds in countering the practical pressures bearing down on it.

Never has the strife between these cosmic forces been as pronounced as in the moment in which Kandinsky is writing. The "modern movement" of culture, claims the painter in 1912, is a conjunction of two related syndromes:

131–153; Mark Roskill, *Klee, Kandinsky, and the Thought of Their Time: A Critical Perspective* (Urbana and Chicago: University of Illinois Press, 1992); Paul Vogt, *Geschichte der deutschen Malerei im 20. Jarhundert* (Cologne: DuMont Schauberg, 1976); Weiss 1979; Armin Zweite, *The Blue Rider in the Lenbachhaus, Munich* (Munich: Prestel, 1989).

1. The destruction of the soulless material life of the nineteenth century, i.e., the collapse of those supports of the material [life] that have firmly been regarded as unique, and the crumbling and the dissolution of the individual components thereof.

2. The building-up of the spiritual-intellectual life of the twentieth century, which we too experience, and which already manifests and embodies itself in powerful, expressive, and definite forms. (Kandinsky 1912a: 256–257)

There is no question in Kandinsky's mind: He intends to promote the second moment, the construction of the spiritual life. This is what he identifies as the avenue to unimagined new meanings in art and knowledge. And yet, at this stage of his career he cannot separate the construction from the destruction to which it is tied. However much theosophists and cultural philosophers might have called out for spiritual regeneration and self-realization at the turn of the century, Kandinsky considers no rebirth to be possible outside the world of hard and fateful constrictions. The spiritual atmosphere is like the air, he writes, "which can either be pure or filled with foreign bodies." What makes up this atmosphere are not only visible and external experiences but also "perfectly secret actions that 'no-one knows about'":

Suicide, murder, violence, unworthy and base thoughts, hate, enmity, egotism, envy, "patriotism," prejudice are all spiritual forms, spiritual entities that go to create the atmosphere. And on the contrary, self-sacrifice, help, pure, high-minded thoughts, love, altruism, delight in the happiness of others, humanity, and justice are also such entities, which can kill the others as the sun kills microbes, and can reconstitute the pure atmosphere. (Kandinsky 1909–11: 192)

In 1910 Kandinsky resolves to bring art into the service of such purification. In fact, this is the decision that causes the rupture between him and the group of artists known as the Munich New Artists' Alliance (NKVM) over which he had presided since 1909.[21] But what is remarkable about this acknowledged pioneer in abstract and formalist art, however, is his insistence that no artistic form has any rationale

21. It was the "excessive spirituality" of Kandinsky's agenda, said some members of the NKVM, that precipitated the final break in 1911, after Kandinsky had contacted Schoenberg and found a sympathizer in Franz Marc. Statements made by the NKVM in *Das Neue Bild* of 1912 hardly veil their reference to Kandinsky: "A picture," writes Otto Fischer, "is not only expression but also representation. It is not a direct expression of the soul but of the soul in the subject. A picture without a subject is meaningless. Half subject and half soul is sheer delusion." When Alexei von Jawlensky and others in the NKVM protested Fischer's statement, the group definitively disbanded (Dube 1990: 100).

whatsoever *outside* of the content that it serves. Even paintings that contain no recognizable figures of the material world, he claims, must be held strictly accountable to the question of *what* they express. Without this accountability they can never amount to anything more than senseless ornament. "*Form,*" writes Kandinsky in "On the Question of Form," "*is the external expression of inner content*" (Kandinsky 1912a: 237). What are we to understand by inner content? At first blush it would seem to be precisely that spirituality which Kandinsky has taken such pains to distinguish from materialism. And this spirituality, in turn, is associated with what, in *On the Spiritual in Art,* he calls the "internal necessity" of the artist, a "secret, inborn power of 'vision,'" the "feeling (to which the talent of the artist is the path)" (Kandinsky 1909–11: 131 and 141). The spirituality that constitutes a work's content appears to be a type of order or knowledge, grasped by emotion and articulated by art, of the invisible structures of historical existence.

And yet, this description of content tells only half the story. If we examine Kandinsky's writings between 1909 and 1911 more closely, we find that the content of art is not *one* of two elements in the cosmic antithesis but *the antithesis itself*. At Kandinsky's last exhibition with the NKVM, in September, 1910, he addresses the question of artistic form and content as follows:

> Cold calculation, patches leaping at random, mathematically exact construction . . . silent, screaming drawing . . . fanfares of colors . . . great, calm, heavy, disintegrating surfaces.
> Is this not form?
> Is this not the *means*?
> Suffering, searching, tormented souls with a deep rift, caused by the collision of the spiritual with the material. . . . The living element of living and "dead" nature. Consolation in the appearances of the world—external, internal. Premonitions of joy. The call. Speaking of the hidden by means of the hidden.
> Is this not content?
> Is this not the conscious or unconscious *purpose* of the compulsive urge to create? (Kandinsky 1910a: 82)

The modern, if not eternal, content of art is the collision of the spiritual and the material, or human experience as a clash of fundamental, ontological difference. Art is concerned with the interconnection of inner and outer, spirit and matter, subject and object. "Our point of departure," Kandinsky claims in 1909,

> is the belief that the artist, apart from those impressions that he receives from the world of external appearances, continually accumulates experi-

Fig. 6. Vasily Kandinsky, *Untitled (First Abstract Watercolor),* 1910 or 1913, pencil, watercolor, and Indian ink. Courtesy Musée National d'Art Moderne, Paris.

ences within his own inner world. We seek artistic forms that should express the reciprocal permeation of all these experiences . . . in short, artistic synthesis. This seems to us a solution that once more today unites in spirit increasing numbers of artists. (Kandinsky 1909–10: 53)

Accordingly, Kandinsky's paintings of these years contain both types of elements: dissolving forms of the material world—mountain peaks, churches, horses, boats, and riders—as well as abstract patterns. Works such as *Untitled (First Abstract Watercolor)* (dated 1910, but more likely from 1913) and *Improvisation XI* (1910) present the derealization of the physical world as an impetus for new and alternative constructions. Colors, structures, and centers of visual energy become every bit as important as the phenomena contextualized within them. Here jagged, linear vectors cut across soft, diffused, and rounded shapes. Bold and primary colors, combined in ways "long considered disharmonious," press up against or bounce off each other in countless directions (Kandinsky 1909–11: 193). The physical depth lost in the two-dimensionality of his canvases is compensated for by deep swirls of temporal and spatial movement onto which the composition opens like a window on cosmic combustion. Pictorial motifs become ciphers of

Fig. 7. Vasily Kandinsky, *Improvisation XI*, 1910, oil. Courtesy Russian Museum, St. Petersburg.

universal forces within a network. Here unions and contrasts are one and the same.

At this junction of materialism and spirituality, Kandinsky describes his language of form and color as constructed out of a series of self-propagating oppositions: warm and cold, light and dark, concentric and eccentric, activity and passivity (Kandinsky 1909–11: 161–195; Cheetham 1991: 76–77). The two poles between which art has always found its place—namely, objective "impression" and subjective "expression"—come to meet at their extremes. "Realism = Abstraction / Abstraction = Realism. *The greatest external dissimilarity becomes the greatest internal similarity*" (Kandinsky 1912a: 245).

The new spiritual order contained in this kind of painting is admittedly not easy to recognize. Many people see it rather as anarchy, the same word they use to characterize music in 1910. For them, observes

Kandinsky, anarchy means "aimless iconoclasm and lack of order." But this is not anarchy; anarchy is rather

> a certain systematicity and order that are created . . . by *one's feeling for what is good*. Thus, here too there are limits . . . [but they] are constantly widened, whereby arises that ever-increasing freedom which, for its part, opens the way for further revelations. (Kandinsky 1912a: 242)

What seems to be disorder, then, is actually the order of a struggle that is at the heart of art: of freedom against constraint, of formative energy against form, of new meanings against the signs in which convention tries to trap them. What looks like anarchy is simply the record of art's inevitable destruction and reconstruction of language. Anarchy is only a disparaging word for artistic *extensions* of formal order, of art's battle against the fossilization of rhetoric on behalf of a "feeling for the good."[22]

What does Kandinsky mean by this feeling for the good? In the same text he likens it to a process of "evolution," "freedom," "progress forward and upward," "revelation," "the inevitable, continual triumph of new values." The feeling for the good is that which is embodied in those "powerful, expressive, and definite forms" that burst the constraints on a soul (Kandinsky 1912a: 236 and 257). Schoenberg describes a comparable energy when he stresses that art cannot be produced by technical ingenuity, but only by spiritual compulsion: "Expressive content wishes to make itself understood; its upheaval produces a form. A volcano erupts . . . a steam-kettle explodes" (Schoenberg 1911b: 367). The same inevitability is at work in the feeling for the good. The feeling for the good is not itself an "expressive content" with a proper, corresponding form of its own. It is rather an *upheaval* of the content in the very effort to make itself understood. Accordingly, the form of this upheaval can only be turbulent, dynamic, and unresolved. This, if anything, is the "expressionism" of Kandinsky's and Schoenberg's art: a "pressing out" of something not necessarily understood in which discovery occurs. Like others of their generation, Kandinsky and Schoenberg were familiar with the theories of the art

22. Schoenberg makes a similar observation about the innovations that led him to atonal compositions and later to dodecaphonic ones: "What I did was neither revolution nor anarchy. I possessed from my very first start a thoroughly developed sense of form and a strong aversion for exaggeration. There is no falling into order, because there was never disorder. There is no falling at all, but on the contrary, there is an ascending to a higher and better order" (letter to Slonimsky, June 3, 1937; Slonimsky 1971: 1316).

historian Alois Riegl to the effect that every artwork manifests an artistic will, or *Kunstwollen*. Here, however, something else is at work. What art ultimately expresses—the "content" it shapes—is actually the struggle for expression. And this struggle is good in itself. It is *itself* the good, a feeling for the good, a wish to understand. This may, indeed, be the only justification for "expression."

The idea is repeated in different terms by August Macke, also, like Schoenberg, a contributor to Kandinsky's *Blue Rider* almanac. Art, writes Macke, exists only where a work reveals the historical, existential, or emotional turbulence out of which it arises: "The joys, the sorrows of man, of nations, lie behind the inscriptions, paintings, temples, cathedrals, and masks, behind the musical compositions, stage spectacles, and dances. If they are not there, if form becomes empty and groundless, then there is no art" (Macke 1912: 89). Joy and sorrow—without which no form can be artistic—are upheavals of spiritual content, destabilizations of a given mental condition. Art is an intellectualization of passion. It is not a manifestation of spiritual content so much as a form revealing the upheaval *of* this content, in joy or sorrow. Dances, cathedrals, paintings, and plays are products of dissonant or ecstatic experience. If they do not reveal this turbulence they amount to nothing. Thus even a certain "formalist" art has its own content, which consists in its own effort at self-definition.

DESTINY AT ODDS WITH ITSELF

If the Munich school of Kandinsky and Marc gives an intellectual, metaphysical face to this self-expressive discord, painters in Vienna, Dresden, and later Berlin are more struck by the toll it takes on the psyche. Schoenberg is as pivotal a figure here as he is in Munich. He studies painting with Richard Gerstl, the pioneer of Viennese expressionist portraiture. A teacher of Webern and Berg, he is a friend of the writers Karl Kraus and Peter Altenberg as well as the architect Adolf Loos. He bridges the arts. Like Kokoschka and the *Brücke* artists from Dresden, he takes his message to Berlin (Kokoschka in 1910, Schoenberg and the others in 1911). While his atonal music is analogous to the abstractions of Munich, his pictorial work is closer to the tortured figural representations produced in other Germanic cities. Indeed, his close-ups of haunted and distorted faces, his "gazes," "stares," or "visions," were disturbing to Kandinsky, as was the work of other painters soon to be called fellow expressionists: Kokoschka, Egon Schiele,

Ernst Ludwig Kirchner, and Erich Heckel. They were too egocentric for Kandinsky's taste, too dramatic and confessional, too subjective (Kallir 1984: 60–61; Vogt 1980: 52). And yet, with his crude and stylized faces, Schoenberg was ultimately more typical of pictorial expressionism than his Russian friend.

The climate of prewar painting, and of expressionism in particular, is created by a rejection of the placid harmonies of impressionism on the one hand, and of naturalistic imitations of physical nature on the other. The main inspirations for expressionism are Vincent van Gogh, Edvard Munch, and Paul Cézanne; sexuality, physical and emotional dynamics; the "primitive directness" of non-European arts. One effect of these interests is enthusiasm for new structures and techniques of pictorial composition, manifested especially by Pablo Picasso, Henri Matisse, Marc Chagall, and the Italian futurists. Another is the questioning, in art, of the very provenance of visions and forms. Once seemingly natural or objective unities have been reinterpreted as impressions or symbols, artists find it increasingly difficult to steer away from the question of the origin of these symbol-impressions. And this question of the provenance of vision is the question of the artist— who might well be a seer, but might just as easily be deranged. It is this analysis of human vision which begins with Munch, van Gogh, and Cézanne. In presenting both the natural and the symbolic grasps of vision as unstable, painting shifts its focus from the object to the subject of vision. Even where the canvas does not show a literal self-portrait of the artist but only a naked, awkward body, as in Cézanne's *Male Model* of 1900, human reality is still the focus of the formative act, as difficult to make graceful as any sensory object. The post-impressionists bequeath to the expressionists the problem of the *link* between natural and symbolic data, between impression and expression, between figures and the many ways they can be envisioned.

Prefigurations of these problems can be found in the works of Munch, which show neither spirit nor matter, but an experience to which both must answer. A lithograph of 1901 called *Sin* presents a beautiful, naked woman staring past the viewer with a hypnotic, malignant gaze. Her shoulders and arms are hidden by disheveled hair flowing down to her waist. The outlines of her waist disappear altogether, as though she mysteriously materialized out of the white-gray background. Munch turns the magnificent woman that his model must have been into a spectral image. Her hair is an unnatural orange, her flesh a colorless white, sparsely shaded with yellow, her eyes lime green.

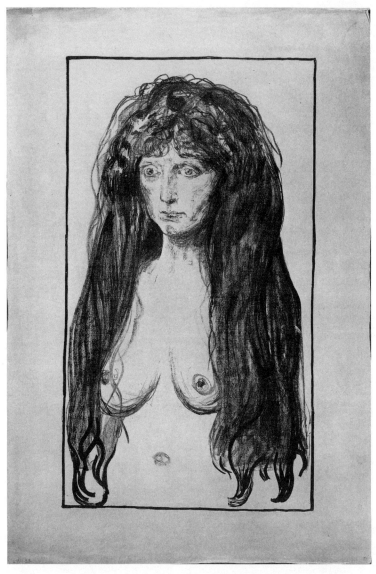

Fig. 8. Edvard Munch, *Sin*, 1901, lithograph. Photo courtesy Munch Museum, Oslo.

What Munch accomplishes here and elsewhere is neither an affirmation nor a rejection of empirical form, but a *critique,* voicing the suspicion that matter may be a conduit for a world of the spirit whose effects are all but terrifying. A "naturalist of the phenomena of soul" (Przybyszewski, cited in Tuchman 1986: 33), Munch reads into and out of such form, not presenting it as an icon for some transcendent meaning in a purely symbolist fashion, but pondering its inherent implications. Instead of "transfiguring" this form he contorts it, boring into it to ask what it says in itself before it says anything else, before yielding some clear identity. And this is the difference between an expressionist depiction of a figure and a realistic one. Expressionism seeks "something else" *within* the figure's appearance—some recess in its surface. It does not believe that it has captured the essence of a face or a phenomenon unless it has also unveiled this "something else," this subjectivity, as it were, of an object, or this objectivity of a subject. Expressionistic revisions of perceptible form are shocking rewritings of the real, translations of everyday experience into chimerical unions of spirit and matter. They estrange the habitual appearances of things, turning their once recognizable features into tokens of something that neither the mind nor the eye can understand. Expressionist art keeps the physical fully real and the transcendent alarmingly distant.

What Munch begins, the artists of 1910 complete, depicting vision, understanding, and artistic activity as motion from body to soul and soul back to body again, from appearance to idea and idea to appearance, the couplings never reducible to one.[23] The inner impinges on the outer, the outer on the inner. In Dresden, Vienna, and Berlin, the duplicitous experience is not as cerebral as it is in Munich. It is more moral, emotional, psychological, re-creating its discomfort in viewers. In Kokoschka, Heckel, Kirchner, Karl Schmidt-Rottluff, Emil Nolde, and others, vision and understanding are firmly planted in existence: in the historical conditions accompanying the aspiration to spiritual transcendence. However much these prewar expressionists may grasp for the true nature of "soul," they end up reaffirming its primordial

---

23. Compare the terms in which Anton Webern and Kandinsky describe the pictorial art of Schoenberg: "What Schoenberg represents in his paintings are not impressions of so-called reality, but its reflections on a higher psychic plane. These paintings are the realization of completely transcendental phenomena made perceptible through outer senses." And Kandinsky: "When Schoenberg paints he does not intend to produce a 'pretty' or an 'attractive' picture. Scorning the objective result, he seeks only to fix his own subjective 'apperception' and therefore needs only such means as appear to him indispensable at the moment" (Slonimsky 1971: 169).

conflict with matter, or that dissonance from which Kandinsky had said that art arises.

Prototypical expressionist depictions of the human figure can be found in the water colors, woodcuts, and oils of the *Brücke*. Schematically speaking, most show human experience transported to arenas it does seem to occupy in habitual and everyday experience—whether the heights of ecstatic elation or the hell of physical oppression. Experience is either the scene of a losing battle or the occasion for a vigorous flight, as in Kirchner's *Bareback Rider* of 1912. Nolde cultivates both extremes, from the exuberant *Dance around the Golden Calf* (1910) to martyric subjects like *Apostle Head V* (1909) and the *Life of Christ* cycle (1912). No less than that of Kandinsky and Marc, this art expresses the efforts of a spirit to *reach* expression—in a gesture or a grimace, in a diffident or a mystified glance, in a signal of unspeakable feeling or, as in Kokoschka's *Portrait of Auguste Forel* (1909), the radiant intellectuality of a face that ignores its own decrepitude.

Even if these artists attempt to break through the rhetoric of material form, they have only this rhetoric with which to work, in which to locate the persuasion of a soul. If the intimacy of the spirit is their subject, as historians of expressionism have traditionally claimed, then this intimacy is paradoxical and schizoid, noble but also fragile, luminous but dark, transcendent but constricted. The paintings of Kirchner and the *Brücke,* Gerstl, Kokoschka, and Schiele give us likenesses of a soul no more than Kandinsky's paintings give us autonomous spirit. If anything, they give us *failures* of likeness, visions of noncorrespondence, as though to suggest that something is operative in human reality which no likeness can convey, something that can only be approached by way of grotesque distortions of the typical conduits of human expression. Against the background of fragmented, supersaturated or empty spaces, among jarring colorations or clashing planes, a face or a figure mysteriously emerges, flattened into two dimensions, bespeaking perception but not understanding. Whatever assumptions the sitters for portraits by these artists might have had about their inner identities, in these works they find them unmasked, and then remasked, recast as essences at odds with their appearances. Offering neither a likeness of a subject nor a transformation of that likeness into a transcendent symbol, expressionistic portraits present allegories of a destiny spent anxiously negotiating the difference—between fact and interpretation or objective and subjective reality, both allegories of a third, estranged condition in which everything is tension, emotion, and drama.

The governing principle of these dramatic portrayals has frequently been called empathy, a process investigated by Theodor Lipps, Max Scheler, and other thinkers in the years between 1890 and 1920.[24] Empathy involves a prodecure whereby one psyche feels itself into another. Now, there is certainly more empathy at work in the art of 1910 than in the art of many earlier moments in Europe, and certainly more in the expressionists of Mitteleuropa than in most French avant-gardists. Nonetheless, the scandalized distance of portraitists like Kokoschka and Schiele from their subjects could hardly be greater. "Whatever has been said about my being a humanist," Kokoschka confesses in his autobiography, "I do not really *love* humanity; I see it as a phenomenon, like a flash of lightning from a clear sky, a serpent in the grass":

> The human soul's propensity for goat-like leaps, its tragedy, its sublimity, and also its triviality and absurdity, attracted me, as a visitor to the zoo is attracted by the idea of observing the life of his own forebears. . . . I could have foretold the future life of any of my sitters at that time, observing, like a sociologist, how environmental conditions modify innate character just as soil and climate affect the growth of a potted plant. (Kokoschka 1974: 36–37)

If anything, what Kokoschka empathizes with is the dehumanization of his subjects, in the same way that Schiele distorts the body he represents to the point of brutalizing it. In both, the line between empathy and aggression is hard to fix.

To empathize with one's fellow creatures means to imagine their experience so vividly that one comes to feel it oneself. However, to step out of one's self-enclosure in this way is not merely to be receptive to external impressions. It is to project one's own self-understanding *onto* the other, to go through the process of imagining how *I* might feel if I

---

24. An overview of theories of art as empathy can be found in Wilhelm Perpeet, "Historisches und Systematisches zur Einfühlungsästhetik," *Zeitschrift für Aesthetik und allgemeine Kunstwissenschaft* 77 (1966): 193–216. For a description of expressionism as an empathetic art (involving subjective uses of color and an endeavor to elicit emotional rather than cerebral responses to a work of art) see Jost Hermand, "Expressionism and Music," in Pickar and Webb, eds., 1979: 58–73. The watershed for this empathetic, "expressive" turn in painting lies in Henri Matisse's influential essay, "Notes of a Painter" of 1908: "What I pursue above all," writes Matisse, "is expression." The technical means of a painter (which are best when simplest, he adds) "must derive almost necessarily from his temperament." Five years later he illustrates the issue more clearly. "Take this table," he says to an interviewer. "What I paint is not the literal table but the emotion it produces in me." If impressionists are interested in rendering "fugitive impressions," others such as Matisse consider the impression to be "nearly deceptive [*presque comme mensongère*]." They wish to grasp "a truer and more essential character" beneath the surface impression (Matisse 1908: 42, 51, 47, 45).

were in that person's shoes. If empathy binds two selves, it does so on the basis of their difference. It finds the place for its experience and vision in that space between inner and outer, between fact and projection, which Kandinsky identifies as the realm of art.

The duplicity of this space is captured by the most striking characterization there is of expressionist art. In an aphorism from 1909–1910, Schoenberg describes this "empathetic" type of art as (1) a spiritual outburst, (2) a quest for understanding, (3) a moral battle, (4) an echo of the inexpressible tension out of which these first three features arise:

> Art is the cry for help of those who experience in themselves the fate of humanity. Who wrestle with it instead of accommodating themselves to it. Who do not bluntly serve the engine of "dark powers," but who plunge into the running machinery to grasp its construction. Who do not avert their eyes to protect themselves from emotion, but rather open them wide to tackle what has to be tackled. But who frequently shut their eyes to perceive what the senses do not convey, to behold within what only seemingly takes place outside. And within, inside them, is the agitation of the world; what breaks through to the outside is only its echo: the work of art. (Schoenberg 1910a: 12)

Art is a cry for help or need (*Notschrei*)—a cry for harmony, resolution, and peace. And it arises only as a consequence of grappling with fate (*Schicksal*). Art may thus be understood as a search for clarity and understanding in the face of a destined human struggle that calls for courage, clear-sightedness, and stamina. And yet, to see this fate one must also sometimes close one's eyes to its deceptive empirical forms. Only then does it reveal itself in its pure and naked form as the movement, agitation, or commotion [*Bewegung*] of the world. This, if anything, is the "content" of art, encountered in both inward and outward experience. Whatever a work's ostensible topic might be (a nocturnal, chimerical face or an abstract truth), this is its true substance and interest. Art is no more than its echo.

AN ONTOLOGY OF OPPOSITION

Is there a general metaphysics or ideology that explains art's need to give form to dissonance at this moment in time? There is none that is immediately apparent, and yet countless indications reveal that by 1910 duplicity has become the overriding issue for the reflective mind. The work of Campana, Trakl, Schoenberg, and the painters bears witness to a situation in which thinking no longer understands how to reintegrate those antitheses out of which it had always attempted to construct its knowledge: the one and the many, the ego and the world, fact and value, freedom and possibility. In the period stretching from the Renaissance humanists to the German idealists, philosophers had generally found a way to tease these oppositions into a cooperative scheme. But by the end of the nineteenth century these terms have lost their flexibility. Every seeming integration of opposites appears only to mask a more primordial principle from which the integration arises: *polemos panten pater,* strife is the father of all things.

The manifestations of this strife are so notable by the late nineteenth century that Wilhelm Dilthey feels the need to defend the *Geisteswissenschaften,* or the spiritual sciences, against the natural and empirical ones. The increasing domination of science over all issues of truth make it necessary to legitimate more intuitive, more amorphous, and less systematic approaches to knowledge. Before Dilthey, Nietzsche had already maintained that the hard and fast facts of science were themselves just methodical lies. But the full-fledged battle comes later, between 1900 and 1920, when virtually every thinker, scientist, and psychologist in Europe is forced to sort out the conflicting claims of objective material evidence and the interpretive imagination *in which* this evidence comes to count as evidence. At this moment of history there appears to be little point in saying anything at all before settling this crisis in understanding.

On one side of the divide stand thinkers who assert the purely theoretical (rather than the referentially reliable) status of scientific truths and facts. Before taking his own life in Duino, near Trieste, in 1906, the eminent physicist Ludwig Boltzmann shakes the foundations of science by arguing that two mutually exclusive explanations of natural occurrences can be equally valid. In *The Philosophy of "As If"* of 1911, Hans Vaihinger reduces materialistic accounts of experience to imaginative schemes. Between 1903 and 1907 Henri Bergson argues that intuition, not sensory perception, is the primal conduit of knowledge. The theosophists Besant, Leadbeater, and Steiner describe knowledge as a response to the auras and thought-forms of a nonrational world soul. Giovanni Gentile sees history as the unfolding of pure idea. Sharing premises with these "idealists" and "intuitionists" are phenomenologists, vitalists, and a variety of cultural moralists, a short list of whom would include Ludwig Klages, Georg Simmel, Edmund Husserl, Miguel de Unamuno, Ortega y Gasset, Martin Buber, and Max Scheler.

The same period sees the beginning of a new type of cultural sociology (partially represented by Simmel, Lukács, Max Weber, and Vilfredo Pareto) that traces the deleterious effects on social organization of any purely pragmatic understanding of experience as a manipulable totality of facts.

On the other side of the divide stand defenders of hard and practical knowledge. One group, meeting for the first time in a Viennese café in 1910, achieves fame under the rubric of neopositivists or logical empiricists (Otto Neurath, Philipp Frank, and Hans Hahn). Another, composed of historical materialists, makes its classic attack on idealism and "impressionistic" philosophers in Vladimir Lenin's *Materialism and Empirio-criticism* (1909). Others include behaviorists, experimental psychologists, sociologists, and psychoanalysts, though each group will have its defectors (Carl Jung, for one). Representatives of either side of the debate will try to discredit their antagonists' position or reinterpret it as a bad version of their own. Idealists will describe scientific materialism as a possible worldview among many, while neopositivists will claim that idealism is no more than a linguistic misunderstanding.

Between these two positions lie various attempts to synthesize perceptible and conceptual experience into a unitary picture of reality (the phenomenism of Ernst Mach, the pragmatism of William James, the "fourth dimension" of P. D. Ouspensky). But these monistic aspirations only confirm the original suspicion—that never since the Greeks has the mind been so racked by a spirit of antithesis. When Kandinsky asserts that the harmony of the age must necessarily be a harmony of opposition and contrast, it is because the ostensibly single world has broken into two.

This is the climate for the most antithetical conception of experience to be advanced since Nietzsche's *The Birth of Tragedy*. It is Carlo Michelstaedter's dissertation, *Persuasion and Rhetoric,* completed on October 17, 1910 and published posthumously.[25] Indeed, it is more

25. The best study of Michelstaedter's work as a whole—that is, not only of *Persuasion and Rhetoric,* but also of his drawings, paintings, poetry, and dialogues—is Bini 1992. To understand Michelstaedter's place in intellectual history one must also read Cristina Benussi, *Negazione e integrazione nella dialettica di Carlo Michelstaedter* (Rome: Edizioni dell'Ateneo & Bizarri, 1980) and the four studies by Campailla (1973, 1980a, 1980b, 1981). Links between Michelstaedter and contemporary expressionists, examined most at length by Bini, have also been noted by Campailla; Marco Cerruti, *Carlo Michelstaedter* (Milan: Mursia, 1967); Fulvio Monai, "Michelstaedter anticipatore in arte dell'espressionismo," in Campailla, ed. 1988: 159–175; and Folco Portinari, "Michelstaedter: Deserto con poesia," *La Stampa. Tutto libri* (October 3, 1987). Other studies of Michelstaedter include Gabriella Bianco, *La hermenéutica del devenir en Carlo Michel-*

polarized a conception than Nietzsche's, for Nietzsche at least tried to overcome the Platonic division of all life into essence and appearance, being and becoming, identity and difference. Michelstaedter instead accepts these classical oppositions of Western thought, pushing them to the point where they must either be explicitly rejected, as Heidegger does in the late twenties, or redefined in only the most paradoxical of ways.

On the surface Michelstaedter belongs to the first group of contending thinkers: the humanists, idealists, vitalists, or irrationalists (misleading though these labels may be). The single intention of Michelstaedter's writing, sketches, and existential decisions is to repair that rift between theory and practice from which he considers the West to have suffered since Plato and Aristotle. When, in 1905, the eighteen-year-old Michelstaedter moves to Florence instead of Vienna (where he had decided to study engineering), his decision seems to be based on two main factors: faith in the humanizing potential of figurative art, epitomized by the traditions of Renaissance Florence, and a desire to discover the spiritual homeland which his upbringing in Austria-Hungary had never afforded: Italy, his cultural soil, the all-unifying mother tongue.

Michelstaedter spends his first years in Florence studying classical figure drawing, as though in the hope that art could achieve that unity of theory and practice and body and soul which he sought. However, as his intellectual curiosity prevails over the technical study of art, Michelstaedter enrolls in the University of Florence. His interests take him to the theoretical roots of humanism itself. By 1909 he has decided to write a thesis on the concepts of persuasion and rhetoric in Plato and Aristotle. His dissertation and creative writings thus show the same objective as his figurative art, and precisely the one he finds increasingly rare in contemporary culture: integration of intention and

staedter (Buenos Aires: Torres Agüero, 1993); Giorgio Brianese, L'arco e il destino: Interpretazione di Michelstaedter (Padua: Francisci Editore, 1985); Cacciari 1992; Giacomo Debenedetti, "Michelstaedter," in Saggi critici: Prima serie (Milano: Marsilio, 1989), 39–50; Francesco Fratta, Il dovere dell'essere: Critica della metafisica e istanza etica in Carlo Michelstaedter (Milan: UNICOPLI, 1986); Claudio La Rocca, Nichilismo e retorica: Il pensiero di Carlo Michelstaedter (Pisa: Biblioteca di "Teoria," 1983); Francesco Muzzioli, Michelstaedter (Lecce: Milella, 1987), which also contains the most complete bibliography of writings on Michelstaedter up to 1987; Perniola 1989; Piero Pieri, La differenza ebraica: Ebraismo e grecità in Michelstaedter (Bologna: Cappelli, 1984) and his more recent La scienza del tragico: Saggio su Carlo Michelstaedter (Bologna: Cappelli, 1989); and Antonio Verri, Michelstaedter e il suo tempo (Ravenna: Alfio Longo, 1969).

expression. This Jewish Italian Austrian, who wrote nearly as fluently in Greek and Latin as in German and Italian, sought a single language for human comportment. Indeed, if by language we mean a medium through which meanings and judgments are transmitted, the language he sought would not even be a language at all. It would be the un- mediated voice of experience itself.

From the start Michelstaedter's dissertation on persuasion and rhet- oric sets itself the most difficult of tasks: to overcome the rift that the West has opened up between being and becoming, permanence and change, soulful repose and anxious desire. And yet, the procedure he follows in attempting to do so only makes the bind tighter, for he ends up defending the first set of terms against the second. Being, permanence, and peace are allied with "persuasion," by which Michelstaedter means passionate commitment and singleminded intention. People are com- mitted, persuaded, or convinced of their action only when they recog- nize and practice the truth of their being. Persuasion means resisting the shifty appeal of rhetorical illusion. However, the problem for Mi- chelstaedter is that this persuasion is all but impossible to achieve in the world as we know it, which is exhausted by the second set of terms: turbulent becoming; change, anxiety and desire; the mediation of lan- guage and signs; the coercions of external necessity. Rhetoric is the name for this second set of terms, and it pervades every aspect of histori- cal behavior, whether theoretical or practical, human or animal (for animals, too, have their illusions about life, "rhetorical" strategies for coping with change). Persuaded though a creature may be of its goals or ideals, it can hardly avoid operating rhetorically, or by following pragmatic, self-interested ends on the basis of interpretive activities. To make matters worse, the very distinctions on which Michelstaedter's argument relies—being vs. becoming, oneness vs. multiplicity, persuasion vs. rhetoric—are themselves rhetorical ones, phantasms of language. Mi- chelstaedter is thus faced with the seemingly impossible task of repair- ing a rift apparently inhabiting the very nature of the understanding.

The first lines of his dissertation set forth the condition in which such tension arises:

> *I know that I want and do not have what I want.* A weight hangs on a hook and in hanging suffers that it cannot descend: it cannot get off the hook for, being a weight, it pends and in pending depends.
>
> We want to give it satisfaction: we free it from its dependence; we let it go, so that it may satisfy its hunger for lower spots and independently de- scend as far down as it wants to descend.—But it is not happy to stop at any spot that it reaches and would like to keep descending, for the next

spot is even lower than the one it occupies at any moment. And no future spot will ever be one that will please it and be necessary to its life, so long as a lower one awaits it . . . every time it is presented each spot will have been rendered void of attraction, not being still lower; so that *at every spot it lacks lower spots,* and these attract it all the more: it is always in the throes of the same hunger for what is lower, and its will to descend stays infinite.—

For if everything were finished at a given point, and if at a single point it could *possess* the infinite descent of the infinite future—at that point it would no longer be what it is: *a weight.*

Its life is this lack of its life. If it ever lacked nothing—but were finished and perfect—if it possessed itself, it would have ceased to exist.—The weight is its own impediment to possessing its life, and its inability to satisfy itself depends on itself alone. *The weight can never be persuaded.* (Michelstaedter 1910: 39–40)

The paradox of the weight is that in order to be what it is it must wish to be *other* than it is, to exist in some other situation of space and time. The "mistake" of the weight is that it is internally obsessed with things external to its nature. It imagines that it can be released from its own inbred anxiety by a change in its historical conditions (a notion nourished in turn by the fantasy that the weight *could* be reconciled to a particular condition, which is false). The weight is bewitched by the doctrine that life is elsewhere. It suffers from a rhetorical illusion. (And the "rhetoric" of Michelstaedter's own parable, anthropomorphizing a lifeless object, is perfectly expressionistic, making the external and the internal, the inanimate and the animate impinge on each other in ways that cannot be undone.) If the weight had self-knowledge it would acknowledge that it will always and necessarily suffer the seduction of things outside it. It fails to see that, in an existence where everything is activity and change, if ever it "possessed itself . . . it would have ceased to exist." Thus the weight is its own obstacle to the fulfillment of its life. Until it changes its way of thinking, it will never appreciate its present.

And the same can be said for organic life as a whole, ceaselessly hankering for what it is not, pursuing not life but a vision of life, a future project, whose productivity and creativity is only an offshoot of self-destructive anxiety. As all fullness proves empty and all emptiness full, experience amounts only to "mortal pain" (Michelstaedter 1910: 47). Wanting things today (even in the literal sense of "wanting" as lacking), we make some plan for tomorrow. And tomorrow we continue in kind.

There are more contradictions to life than this. Michelstaedter notes, for example, that things might be themselves if ever they could succeed in being identical at any two moments. "*Life would be,*" he writes, "if time did not constantly defer its being into the next instant." Life "would be *one, immobile, and formless* if it could consist in a *single point*" (Michelstaedter 1910: 43). However, no sooner does a creature achieve a condition in time than it finds itself in another, subsequent time, making the life of the present no life at all, but just a succession of different moments, without duration or extension. *Praesens nullum habet spatium,* St. Augustine had said in *The Confessions* (XI, 15 [20]): the present occupies no space. Such experience is not "being," but flux and becoming, eternal variance and impermanence. In historical time, as Schopenhauer had argued a century earlier, all things are ruled by a craving or will. They ceaselessly desire more than they ever possess and further their "life" in a fear of death.

In the presence of others each one of these "subjects" is instantly transmuted into an object, a thing for those others to manipulate as they will. "Everything *has* insofar as it *is had*" (Michelstaedter 1910: 44). Nothing has any being except "*in relation to a consciousness,*" namely, the consciousness of someone or something else for which this subject is not itself, but an object (Michelstaedter 1910: 45). All "identity" is thus a function of difference, just as the "now" is a function of a "before" and an "after." Knowledge, by consequence, is an ingrained error, a self-interested conviction of an individual viewing the world from some particular situation of time and space.

The average person never faces up to this error and tends to think simply

> "this is," rather than "this is, according to me." He says "this is good" instead of "I like this"; for the I according to which a thing is, or is good, is indeed his own *consciousness, his pleasure,* his *current condition,* which for him is absolutely firm outside of time. . . . And things *are* good or bad, useful or harmful [insofar as] his current condition has, in pleasure (or displeasure), *organized a forecast* of whatever is suited to the continuation of his organism. (Michelstaedter 1910: 52)

Everyday experience is conducted on the basis of deceptive deductions, working schemes, "useful" and self-furthering orientations.

The word "orientation" is not Michelstaedter's, but Martin Buber's. In the year that *Persuasion and Rhetoric* was first published (1913), the Austrian philosopher speaks of orientation as the typical manner of establishing some order between those two great "polarities," being and counter-being, which govern the contingency and differentiation of all things in the world. Because we fail to discover truthful and permanent stability in a world of contraries, we resort to a rhetoric of orientation: strategies for masking these differences in coherent relations. Instead of recognizing the value of things in their singularity, we subject them to conceptual and practical schemes, superficial and facile correlations. "Orientation installs all happening in formulas, rules, connections" (Buber 1913a: 94). People become pragmatically yoked to

> the multiplicity of their aims, their means, their knowledge—everything is conditioned by everything, everything is decided out of everything, everything is related to everything, and over all there rules the security of orientation that has information. (Buber 1913a: 77)

The result of this rhetorical orientation is not persuasion, or a firm and reliable language, but pure "commotion." Buber objects to this commotion on the same grounds as Michelstaedter; for each thing it substitutes a sign, for every meaning a formula—all in the interests of a self that is no self.

Michelstaedter and Buber are both moral thinkers, concerned, above all, with the question of how experience should be conducted in a dissonant, rhetorical world. Once one recognizes the "commotion" for what it is, two avenues seem to open up for the reflective person. Either one continues to seek "meaning," "identity," and "being" in another setting—namely, outside the domain of language, and more particularly in the unutterable persuasion of inner experience—or else one seeks a more *communicative* system of signs, allowing one to achieve that integrated understanding which is lacking in "orientation." The first would appear to be the choice of the ethical self, the second of the artist.

The first implies ascetic self-ensconcement. Here everything that does not appear to be inherently connected to the innermost essence of an I is reduced to the status of a mere illusion. The second route makes the I itself look like the illusion, no more than a sum of what it is not, a fictitious unity of the myriad things and beliefs by which it is filled. If the self, like the weight, is thoroughly occupied by its objects of orientation, and these are all external, then it never assumes any direction of its own. The first of these avenues entails militancy towards things in which one loses oneself (everyday experience, the society of others, the tyrannical instincts of nature, the habits and thoughts one inherits from culture). The second entails a dissolution of the I in the cosmos, in which subjectivity gives itself over to the ebb and flow of objective becoming.

At first glance Michelstaedter's idea of persuasion seems closer to
the first solution. It names that ideal of "being oneself" whose most
ancient advocate is Socrates and whose most recent version would
have been familiar to Michelstaedter in the Nietzschean notion of the
Übermensch. When Michelstaedter speaks of persuasion, the word is
usually synonymous with self-determination. Recognizing that there
are no valid external reasons for doing one thing rather than another,
persuaded persons act on the basis of inner conviction. They withstand the suasive, chimerical lure of fashion, the opinions of others,
the speciousness of reasons and religious appeals. Persuasion begins in
the knowledge that one can never rely on others for personal direction.
The I must thus embrace self-rule. In this light, persuasion, like Kandinsky's spirituality, is the force that breaks the external constraints on
a soul, allowing it to produce its own forms. No signposts or proverbs
or storehouse of wisdom can lend it guidance:

> There is no accomplished thing, no prepared way, no achieved method or
> work by which you can reach life; there are no words that can give you
> life: for life consists wholly in creating everything by oneself, in not adapt-
> ing to any way: there is no language, but you must create it, you must cre-
> ate the world, create each thing: in order to possess your life as your own.
> (Michelstaedter 1910: 103)

Yet to create the world in this way is also to have no world, for,
where everything is flux and becoming, it is neither the same river one
steps into twice nor the same person who does so. To be oneself in this
manner is also to be no one. The two avenues that open up upon the
recognition of the rhetoric of everyday action—narcissistic solipsism
and ecstatic externality—may thus be two extremes that meet. If the
essential desire of an I always consists in something *else* that it must
covet, resist, or subdue, then the distance between an I and another is
also an absolute proximity. Here subject and object, identity and difference, dissonance and consonance, pain and joy, dissolve into each
other.

Indeed, Michelstaedter reduces the entire panoply of human emotions to variations of pain and joy, *dolore* and *gioia.* Even emotions
such as anger, remorse, envy, and boredom are only covers for these
two basic responses to having and not having, being and not being, accomplishing and failing. The best description of the dissonant life of
this I-that-is-no-I probably lies in the *Fragments* (Frammenti, 1915) of
Michelstaedter's contemporary, Giovanni Boine, he too, like Slataper,
a writer for *La Voce*:

35) A blindman who loses his staff, I have discarded each one of your forms of logic. A leaf in the wind, a boat bobbing on the surf, I do not reach for the tiller.

36) I say that there is no rudder. Will and passion—empty words.

37) Passion and will are entirely in the joy of today, and entirely in the pain of the present.

38) I am desperately joyful and hopelessly sad. I believe violently in Hell and am *de facto* certain of a Paradise.

39) For my life is not constructed on the basis of a project, piece by piece, like buildings made of stone, and I run toward no goal like a horse to the finish. I have no future for I have no past. Lacking memory, I even lack hope.

40) My desire is the blaze of a furnace, and my annihilation like the abyss of the night. I know only how to rejoice, only how to suffer. I have no shelter from pain, nor temper my joy with reflection. (Boine 1915: 263)

Not only would Michelstaedter have endorsed these fragments of his fellow Italian expressionist; he would also have understood the fluctuant condition of Boine's protagonist at the end of the novel *Sin* (Il peccato, 1913):

> He undulated in this abundant, tragic-joyful conception of the world as though in a bursting torrent; a violent and barbaric jubilation where limits are limitless, as though in a music whose melody is born from clashing disharmony . . . he undulated between this Bacchic exultation and an attentive, sharp control of the soul, a nearly stingy, always conscious effort of order. (Boine 1913: 71)[26]

Here we find a tumultuous coexistence of two seemingly opposite things: ecstatic unity with the outside world and rational control on the part of an estranged individuality, both facets of a single metaphysics of tragic-joyful strife. Alone and at odds with all things, the I of both Boine and Michelstaedter is at the same time only a function of these things, a "moment" in a formless torrent. And this transforms the first conception of persuasion—as autonomy and self-possession—into the second—ecstatic dissolution.

26. For introductions to Boine, who has not been translated into English, see Giorgio Bertone, *Il lavoro e la scrittura: Saggio in due tempi su Giovanni Boine* (Genoa: Il Melangolo, 1987); Renato Minore, *Giovanni Boine* (Florence: La Nuova Italia, 1975); Concettina Pizzuti, "'Plausi e botte' al romanzo del primo novecento," *L'Anello che non tiene* 2, no. 1 (Spring 1990): 29–46.

To be persuaded ultimately means to live out the paradoxical junction of these two extremes. One might say that persuasion is the conscious knowledge of the solitary I in this single, duplicitous condition, where no subject exists but in objects, no being but in becoming, and no permanence but in change. Once rhetorical distinctions have lost their power of persuasion, there is no sure way to distinguish between self-affirmation and self-abnegation, or between victory and defeat. Indeed, Michelstaedter's examples of persuaded selves are philosophers, martyrs, prophets, and artists who found their homes in the world only by feeling they did *not* belong: characters such as Heraclitus, Pergolesi, Leopardi, Beethoven, Tolstoy, Ibsen, Socrates, and Christ.

Images of such characters reconciled to the dissonance of the world return repeatedly in the first years of the century. They are what Michelstaedter and his fellow Italians Giovanni Gentile and Julius Evola call instances of the *individuo assoluto* (the absolute individual), who must lose life before being able to gain it. Thus Oskar Kokoschka, in a poster for *Der Sturm* (*Self-Portrait,* 1910, fig. 23), depicts himself bare-chested, with no hair on his head, grimacing and pointing with his finger to a bloody wound in his breast. To master the splitness of life is to be a type of Christ: an absolute being in a relative world. Christ represents the transcendent mystery "of the divine incarnate in the Son of Man," writes Kokoschka. And the story of his passion

> is the eternal story of man. Even the miracle of the Resurrection can be understood in human terms, if it is grasped as a truth of the inner life: one does not become human once and for all just by being born. One must be resurrected as a human being every day. (Kokoschka 1974: 25–26)

In a similar vein, "Whoever wants to possess his own life," writes Michelstaedter, "must not consider himself born, and alive, just because he was born" (Michelstaedter 1910: 70). Or in Buber's words, whoever "lives life in genuine, realizing knowledge must perpetually begin anew, perpetually risk all anew; thus his truth is not a having but a becoming" (Buber 1913a: 90). The image returns in Schiele's self-portrait as the martyr Saint Sebastian, shot through with arrows, as well as in the poems that Schoenberg chooses to set to music, whose subjects are fate-contending selves, fools, and alienated artists.[27] By the end of *Pierrot Lunaire,* after the poet and the fool of its songs have

---

27. On the artist as victim in Kokoschka and Schoenberg, with particular reference to the Christ image, see Schorske 1981: 354–358 and Kallir 1984. On the same conceit in Schiele, see Kallir 1994 and Comini 1974.

jointly ventured into drunkenness, idiocy, violence, and martyrdom, the bitter lunar setting makes way for a sun-drenched return to the fullness of day.

This conjunction of moon and sun, of dying and rebirth, is all that remains after the formal orientations of rhetoric have lost their force. But so strange is such a conjunction that Michelstaedter is unable to devote more than thirty of the one hundred fifty pages of his *Persuasion and Rhetoric* to it. To acquire a broader sense of what Michelstaedter means by persuasion we must return to Buber and to a text that he too wrote in 1910.

PERSUASIVE LIFE-EXPERIENCE

In "The Way of the Tao" Buber describes almost the very thing that Michelstaedter means by persuasion as "fulfillment" or "perfection." In a world racked by struggle and fragmentation, he claims, the primary responsibility of a thinking person is self-perfection. This is the basic teaching not only of Taoism but also of early Christianity. The essence of Christianity, claims Buber, "is not concerned with the unity of God, but with the likeness of the unified man to God." The Christian conception of God

> is there, so to speak, only for the sake of the necessary. And the same holds with the teaching of the Tao, where all that is said of the "path" of the world points to the path of the perfected person, and receives from it its verification and fulfillment. (Buber 1910a: 38)

Buber also calls the perfection of the path "direction." Not waylaid by the seductive calculations of rhetoric, people achieve direction in the form of "purposeful undividedness: as the unifying force that overcomes all straying away from the ground of life" (Buber 1910a: 50). If "straying" is orientation, the "ground" from which we stray is opposition, contradiction, absurdity, and risk. For this is what rhetoric masks by means of its identities, theories, and systems. One returns to the ground by accepting its disorder as a fundamental and insuperable condition. One returns to the ground by establishing direction upon it.

Unlike orientation, direction arises only in recognition of the "thousand-named, nameless polarity of all being," or in acknowledgment of the tension

> between piece and piece of the world, between thing and thing, between image and being, between world and you, in the very heart of yourself, at all places, with its swinging tensions and its streaming reciprocity. Know

the sign of the primal being in it. And know that here is your task: to create
unity out of your and all duality, to establish unity in the world. (Buber
1913a: 98)

A persuasive realization of the unity of being comes with the knowledge that there is no method for achieving such unity. As with Kandinsky's "anarchy," the apparently incoherent forms of historical experience come to be seen as the only "material" of spiritual construction.
Only this seeming incoherence originates that direction which truly
"realizes" the world, making it real for the very first time (Buber
1913a: 71). The persuaded person, in Michelstaedter, "must take the
responsibility for his life on himself, for how he must live it in order to
reach life . . . he must create himself and the world, which does not
exist before him." He "must make his own legs for walking—and make
a path where there is no road." Such a person "*is alone in the midst
of the desert*" (Michelstaedter 1910: 73 and 70). One embraces such
a desert by appropriating that spiritual indeterminacy, that internal
multiplicity and lack of identity, which belies the unifying illusions of
rhetoric. And in this speechlessly indeterminate condition, claim Buber
and Michelstaedter, the unbearable emptiness of presence gives way to
fullness and elation (Michelstaedter 1910: 86). All things that once
seemed intolerably "different," contingent, and relative now appear to
be unconditionally what they are. The lack of existential finality begins
to look like a final and permanent state. Things dead return to life. And
while insatiable, rhetorical lust "accelerates time in its continuous anxiety for the future," the persuaded, self-directed person "occupies infinite time in the present. . . . Each of his moments is a century in the
life of others" (Michelstaedter 1910: 89).

Michelstaedter's persuasion and Buber's direction are not subjective
qualities imposed upon a world of experience. They are the "primal
tension" of experience itself, moving one "to choose and realize this and
no other out of the infinity of possibilities." In this primal tension the
soul strips off "the net of space and of time, of causes and of ends, of
subjects and of objects . . . it goes forth to meet the whirlpool, enters
into the whirlpool. And such is its power that it charms it, magically
charms it, so that it stands naked in the naked and is not destroyed"
(Buber 1913a: 56–57). From the most manifold, incommensurable experiences now opens a "gate of the one." "All that is scattered, fleeting, and fragmentary grows together into unity" (Buber 1913a: 39).
This unity is not an inner, psychological condition or a mystical union
of outside experience. It is the unity of complex, contingent, and finite

relations into which all things enter at any moment in time, the manifold dimensions of a "life-experience" in which subjects and objects historically participate. This life-experience is not something outside us, an empirical "material" that we form and that can be detached from the manners in which we form it (Buber 1913a: 66). Nor is it a screen that changes with our perspectives and mental projections. Rather, it is our immersion in the dynamics of time and space. Life-experience allows no self to be detached from things outside it, no things to be detached from a self. The only I of which we can speak in this historical experience is "the I of a tension. . . . No pole, no force, no thing—only polarity, only stream, only unification" (Buber 1913a: 142). Direction, realization, perfection, and persuasion only exist in act. They are forms of experience, or better, the actual *formation* at work in experience.

In persuasion, the non-finality of form is final—unique in its insuperable limitations, properly evanescent, elusive of explanation and categorical description. Finite and "meaningless" things no longer require the aid of something transcendent—a religion or a system of knowledge—to redeem their existence. If anything, these things are redeemed precisely by the fact that there is *nothing* transcendent about them, or by the fact, as Rainer Maria Rilke puts it in the elegies that he begins in 1911, they occur

> *Once* and no more. And we too,
> *once*. And never again. But this
> *once* to have been, if only this *once*:
> to have been of the earth seems beyond reckoning.
> (Rilke 1911–23: 65)[28]

This once and once only is what makes these events transcendent—transcending themselves in the moment. In rhetorical, orientative hours "the many overshadow and weaken the one," writes Buber. In persuasive direction, on the contrary, such hours make way for moments "in which the one shines in the undiminished fullness of its splendor, because it is related to nothing other than itself" (Buber 1913a: 69). And this is what restores the "sacredness" of being, the only sacredness there is in a world of becoming. Out of the godless depths of disorder and despair "holy countenances" start to radiate in faces that previously could only, and barely, be fixed in memory. Here nothing is related to

---

28. Valuable elaborations of this philosophy of finitude, inspired by the art and philosophy of this same period of history, can be found in Cacciari 1980 and 1982.

anything but the horizon of its own historical presence, offering itself
as a "sign of the eternal." This kingdom "of danger and of risk, of
eternal beginning and of eternal becoming" is the only true kingdom
of god, for Michelstaedter as well as Buber, "the kingdom of holy insecurity" (Buber 1913a: 68, 94, 95). The very fact that "depths" and
"meanings" are always withheld from the surfaces of the world is that
which revives the notion of the sacred.

This is also the "holiness" of experience that Trakl's duplicitous
vision cannot separate from the fallenness of the world, as though it
were the consequence of *not* being able to give a literal reading of
experience: holiness as the product of the eternal risks of misunderstanding. A similar paradox can be found in Georg Lukács's *Soul
and Form*, which sets itself the task of understanding how "soul"—the
very antagonist of all shifting, deceptive, historical forms—can only
be expressed in form. The last essay of his collection makes the paradox clear: The basis for the formal realization of experience is tragic
disunity. If mysticism lies in "suffering the All," or in dissolving one's
"identity" into the outer, objective world, then tragic experience lies in
"creating" the All (Lukács 1910–11a: 160). Mysticism consists only in
passive submission to one side of life's polarity; tragedy means active
engagement *in* the polarity. A similar development unfolds in Rilke's
The Notebooks of Malte Laurids Brigge. Throughout the first half of
his stay in Paris, the fictional author of these notebooks despairs over
the insubstantial nature of experience and the ways it is typically understood. What he discovers later, however, is that this feeling of meaningless oppression is the only true birthplace of joy, love, and artistic
understanding.

This mention of Rilke, Lukács, and Trakl brings artistic activity into
the arena of what in Michelstaedter and Buber would appear to be
purely a matter of lived experience. The link between living one's life
and forming it only becomes stronger when we think of Schoenberg
and Kandinsky. Kandinsky speaks of his art as harmonizing contradiction. As we have seen, the very substance of such an art is the war of
opposites, the contradictory "ground" from which no one can stray
without falling into rhetoric. The "spirituality" that Kandinsky and
Schoenberg identify as the content of art and harmony is ultimately
the *Bewegung der Welt,* the grappling with destiny of which Buber
and Michelstaedter speak and which art can only echo. While it is easy
to characterize the aesthetic, ethical, and epistemological forms of "materialism" (in realism, consumerism, science, and so on), Kandinsky

cannot do the same for the forms of spirituality which he sees awakening in 1910. For by definition, spirituality is the very principle of
formative generation, a process which is not exhausted by any mere
form. It is volatile and self-transforming, changing with the nature of
time. The *institution* of language, it has no metalanguage or method to
which it can answer. As with Schoenberg's open and restless new harmonies, persuasive generations of form always "yield possibilities in
excess of those that have actually been realized" (Schoenberg 1911a:
11).

Nonetheless, a question still remains when Michelstaedter and Buber are placed back to back with these other artists. Kandinsky and
Schoenberg conceive of the harmony of dissonance as an achievement
of aesthetics, not of immediate, historical experience. Michelstaedter
and Buber, by contrast, say that this dissonant harmony can only be
lived, and lived with the commitment of the entirety of one's being,
not merely depicted, theorized, or imagined. How can we reconcile
these positions? One way might be to observe that what Michelstaedter and Buber say, they say in *books*. To make their own arguments
persuasive, they illustrate them with images, figures, and legends. For
example, Buber likens the sense of reality which arises from dissonant
but unified life-experience to the "heightened meaning" of a word in a
poem (Buber 1913a: 67). In a poem, a word means more than it says
and more than any other word can say about it. If ever there was a
place where rhetoric is transmuted into persuasion, or dissonance into
harmony, or depths conveyed by a surface, it is here, in a work of art.
In rejecting his life, did not Michelstaedter confess that his sacred, persuasive harmonization could not be equated with a given historical
form? That there was a rift between it and his life? Trakl, also a suicide, spends more time depicting the dark than the luminous dimensions of holy experience. Campana ends his days among the insane.
Schoenberg never outgrows his polemical bearing toward his own epoch,
upholding to the end the estranged and maligned independence of the
creative artist. As a current in art and thought, expressionism at large
is certainly more taken by the (rhetorical) deficiencies of being than
by any of its self-justifying persuasions. If anything, its affirmations of
negativity, discord, and dissonance present a better fit for the main
model for these artists—the tragic, Dionysian philosopher Nietzsche—
than for their own achievements. And he, too, went mad. Thus the
question returns: Are these artists speaking of a harmony that can
truly be realized in everyday living or of only an imaginative ideal?

What is the relation between experience and art in expressionist thought? Are the two inherently different, or are they images for one and the same thing?

Here we might construct a hypothetical itinerary from one to the other. It is an itinerary that begins in consciousness of discordant historical experience and seeks unity within it. This "consciousness" is what the expressionists inherit as the cultural material of their time and with which they are forced to work: the dissonance of conflicting psychological, political, and ethical facts; of facts which may not even be facts but only values; of divergent "orientations" not unified by any coherent goal; of words opposed to things and of an "is" opposed to an "ought." The goal of these artists is to find unity in such sorely fragmented experience. In that respect, they work back from the surface contradictions of historical experience towards some unity (musical, pictorial, poetic, or philosophical) in which these contradictions might be bound. And this might make us suspect that, at this moment in history, the only true life-experience is polarity and that the coherence into which art might bring it is sheer rhetorical fancy.

But the suspicion would be insufficient. What art articulates is always, in some way, already experienced. The form of a work answers some call. Buber admits it himself: The "heightened meaning" of a poem can only stem "from moments of heightened existence, heightened humanity, heightened knowledge" (Buber 1913a: 67). Similarly, it is necessarily some "life-experience" that leads Michelstaedter, Trakl, and Campana to reinterpret this experience's material, rhetorical, or theoretical surfaces. Indeed, one can go further: An art of unified life-experience does not *imagine* such unity; such art arises from it. It is the form, or "expression," of a unity such is otherwise mute. It does not react to the disintegration of everyday forms in transcriptive, mimetic fashion; it responds to something beckoning within this disintegration, like a portraitist in front of a phenomenal figure. Such art is determined not merely by the confusions, dissonances, or conflicts of material history but also by a sense that, in a still inarticulate way, these differences are bound at the core. To put it more simply, if Trakl intuits a union of opposites, it is because that union is part of his life-experience. The same can be said of Kandinsky, Michelstaedter, and the others.

Their art moves to and fro—from the historical/rhetorical givenness of discord toward that "life-experience" in which the discord appears.

This life-experience does not name a transcendent harmonious unity over and beyond the fractured forms of conventional reality. It is not an abstract and metaphysical "oneness" at the bottom of all illusory forms. Indeed, when these artists seek a historical correlative of unity—especially an inner, autonomous, directing soul—they fail. In them, the I proves to lack any unitary intuitions or knowledge. It is never anything more than its life-experience: an experience of polarity, stream, and tension. The dissonance of being is a final condition.

The itinerary thus consists in three moments which depend on each other: (1) The consciousness of dissonance entails (2) a sense that some harmony within it is just outside the reach of one's available rhetoric. This sense, in turn, causes (3) a criticism and reorganization of those same deficiencies, oppositions, and contingencies that make up the dissonance (the interpretive labor of seeking the unity they mask). Insofar as no unity can be found at the bottom or outside any audible dissonance, but only *within it,* the movement from (1) to (2)—or the activity of (3)—is the only experience there is. This is the true nature of life-experience: the third of the three moments, not the first or the second. This is where unity resides, in the effort to articulate the relations of a dissonance emancipated from a rhetorical conception of unity. Dissonance already houses the unity that these expressionists seek, revealing all transcendence to be bound to immanence and all integrity to fragmentation. No experience can be reduced to unitary terms. This, too, is the experience that is heightened in art: the experience of a sign with multiple and indefinite meanings, of a "one" that is always two and three and four. It is the experience of constantly reading into and out of things from which one can reap no profit or of witnessing a surface whose depths cannot be plumbed.

The artistic process is the context and substance of persuasion, "realization," or unifying direction. It is there that persuasion occurs. The "moments of heightened existence," which are like the heightened meaning of a word in a poem, are also the moments "that fix speech, renew speech" (Buber 1913a: 67). Mere din, by contrast (the unharmonized dissonance of rhetorical, material commotion) only *passes on* the speech that it receives, not endowing it with anything further. The renewal of speech, and with it of life, is the very meaning of harmonization. "The creative hours, acting and beholding, forming and thinking," writes Buber, "are the unifying hours" (Buber 1913a: 72). These hours make up the "third moment" in the movement from dissonance to harmony—or the "content" of art, the *Bewegung* of the destiny it treats, the "necessity" it shapes. The life shaped by the movement is itself the movement.

Searching for unity in the dissonance of being, the artists of 1910 discover that unity is constituted in the dissonance itself. This is the endpoint of their journey (3). What remains to be seen in greater detail are the way stations (1) and (2). Potentially paralyzing encounters with the deficiency of being are the subject of (1), and of the following chapter. The unsuccessful quest for a transcendent principle of spiritual unity (2) is the topic of the chapter following that. Chapter four then circles back to examine how in (3), or in the conclusively inconclusive *Bewegung* of the world, appearance and essence, aesthetics and ethics, can no longer be separated.

CHAPTER TWO

The Deficiency of Being

Nowadays it is no longer possible to "compose" a funeral
march, for it already exists, once and for all.

—Ferruccio Busoni

THREE WOMEN

One of the most unusual romances that is recorded in 1910 takes
place between Scipio Slataper and his three Triestine friends remembered as Anna, Elody, and Gigetta.[1] The first friendship is erotic, the
second platonic, the third leads to marriage. However, before each relationship flowers into its own particular terms, Slataper is unable to
distinguish clearly between the three young women. We already sense
the complexities that will attend this ambiguous situation when the
twenty-one-year-old writer composes his first letter to all three women
in January 1910. Addressed to none in particular, it implicates them
all in the one identity that Slataper does name: his own. "Ah, you are
so close to me at moments," he tells them, "that I feel I am trembling
inside from joy, and then you are distant, lost in shadows that I cannot
solidify into bodies. . . . Sisters of my best soul, if I doubt you I doubt
myself. Who are you? At this moment I do not see you. But I write as
though in an effort to take hold of my soul that flees." He cannot see
these women, but writes to them in an effort to seize his fleeing soul.

---

1. One side of the romance is presented in the collection of letters by Scipio Slataper,
Alle tre amiche: Lettere (To His Three Women Friends; Slataper 1910–15). In his long
introduction to this collection, authorized by "Gigetta" and "Elody" sixteen years after
Slataper's death, the editor, Giani Stuparich, never feels the need to furnish the women's
surnames. (As it turns out Elody's maiden name is Oblath and her married name—
Stuparich! She is the editor's wife.) For additional information on Slataper's relationship
with the women, see Stuparich 1950. On Anna in particular see pp. 101–117. On Elody
Oblath-Stuparich, see Bertacchini 1980 and Maier 1981.

In Slataper's second letter, a few weeks later, the "sisters of his soul" have become individualized, for it is addressed "Anna. Elody. Gigetta." The letter begins by singling one out: "I am thinking of you, Anna. . . . It is very strange that we used to walk together, that once I even looked you in the eyes . . . and I did not see you, nor did you see me. No woman ever saw me." After lamenting his anonymous romantic failures to Anna, he turns to Elody, revealing that the preceding words have been intended for her as well: "And I have been alone for three years, perhaps even forever, Elody." Distant though he may be in space (he is in Florence, they in Trieste), Slataper assures the women that they have been fully absorbed into his own being. "You do not truly exist for me, in lives of your own, but are in me" (Slataper 1910–15: 32, 33–34). This tendency to incorporate the identities of others into his own "best soul" (which really means the *search* for his soul, and through writing rather than interpersonal relations) is common to the era.

In speaking of his encompassing but solitary being, Slataper is actually making a romantic overture: "I am alone. In my whole life there have been very few times when I have felt that someone, *outside me,* has helped me to victory. Maybe if I could truly rest for a few minutes on the soul of a woman, who could penetrate into me, I would experience a moment of companionship." The melancholic reflection is simultaneously an appeal. "Sometimes I think with immense joy that a woman (but who?) could give me that part which I lack in the world: human maternity: that is, the most profound thing, the only truth, of life." In making his confession, Scipio alerts each of the women, who registers the message in the privacy of her own consciousness, to just how much of a sacrifice he would be required to make for an intimate bond. To cede to the joy that he wants, he would have to stop being the person he thinks they respect: "I would not be a poet, I would not be a hero, I may not even be *alive*; and yet, I would rest in the fashion of a man. Do you know what it means never to be a simple man, who caresses without having a notion of a caress, who loves without knowing that he loves?" (Slataper 1910–15: 34–35).

The appeal proves irresistible. Anna becomes his lover (by the standards of the time, of course; it is unlikely that they exchanged much more than kisses). Elody becomes Scipio's traveling companion "and helps him in his work, recopying his manuscripts and correcting his proofs" (Slataper 1910–15: 19). Gigetta is wedded to him in 1913. The most interesting relationship, however, is the one with Anna, whom Slataper nicknames Gioietta (or "little joy")—not least because it comes to a violent and inexplicable end at the very height of its promise. Without warning, on May 2, 1910, Gioietta takes her own life, leaving Slataper to play out his grief and incomprehension in a series of letters addressed to the grave.

The suicide occurs after a botched tryst between the lovers in Florence. On a visit to Trieste in April 1910, Slataper had arranged for Gioietta to travel south to see him in Florence, where he was living. She arrives on April 27, but they fail to make contact. Scipio is not even sure whether she has actually arrived. The events leading up to the communicative mishaps are recorded in a brief note by the editor Giani Stuparich:

> Gioietta has indeed arrived. They are both in Florence, each expecting the other. They look for each other without success. Through a series of misunderstandings, Gioietta—who is not alone, and is thus unable to move about freely—awaits Scipio under the windows of her hotel. And Scipio awaits Gioietta in his room. Eventually, on the morning of the 28th, she decides to be driven to Scipio's residence; she sees him for an instant, the car is waiting downstairs, she barely has the time to grab the pages he has written for her and to repeat that he should meet her outside her hotel. But in his agitation and haste Scipio misunderstands; he thinks that she has promised to return and waits for her the whole afternoon of the same day to no avail. On the following day, the 29th, Gioietta returns with the same harried anxiety. Again they fail to reach a clear understanding. They see each other again on the morning of the 30th at the Exhibit of the Impressionists and Medardo Rosso, but in the company of many people. Gioietta lets Scipio know that she will be dining at the Trattoria Lapi. Even this invitation— only to see her, without being able to speak privately—confuses and mortifies Scipio, who lets his friends drag him elsewhere that night. So Gioietta departs from Florence, taking the steamboat from Venice to Trieste, and arrives at midnight of May 1st. On the morning of the 2nd she shoots herself with a revolver in front of the mirror.

Gioietta accompanies her final gesture with one last ambiguous message:

> *Scipio, I kiss you eternally.* This will be for your work. I will expect it. Do not despair, I am convinced that you love me and will feel how determined [*ferma*] I am. I give you my heart and all of me.
>
> Do not come to see me, for I do not want them to know you. Dear Scipio.
>
> I simply do not want them to speak to you, nor you with them. Please, please. Be always Scipio. Goodbye. I am joining you forever [*Vengo da te per sempre*]. (Slataper 1910–15: 503–504)

Scipio, too, finds it easier to express himself in writing—in five long letters to Gioietta and others about her to Elody and Gigetta. One letter responds to the suicide note directly: "Yes, Gioietta. Now I have read it, and truly feel peace, and am capable of believing that I will work. . . . Now I can really tell you: be still, Gioietta. I will write the work you expect and give it to you: to Gioietta" (Slataper 1910–15: 144). And so reads the dedication to the work to which Slataper is referring, the lyrical autobiography for which he is primarily remembered, begun before Anna's death and published in 1912 under the title *Il mio Carso*. But the guilt that fuels the writing cannot be erased. "I am capable of creating a work," he writes in September 1910, "but was incapable of making Gioietta live. I was the only one who could do so. And it is useless to try to escape. This is more than guilt" (Slataper 1910–15: 168–169).

Something more than guilt also accompanies the relationship between the two Hungarians Georg Lukács and Irma Seidler, one an essayist, the other a painter, and both in their twenties. Here, too, the consequences of the affair are as lethal as literary. "Does it not begin with her?" asks Lukács on the same day that Scipio and Gioietta failed to meet up in Florence. The "it" refers to his collection of essays called *Soul and Form*, published in Hungarian in 1910 under the title *A lélek és a formák*. "Does not even this journal perhaps begin with her?" (Lukács 1910–11b: 16, entry of April 27, 1910).

Lukács had met Irma Seidler nearly three years earlier, on December 18, 1907. After spending two guarded weeks together in Italy in May 1908, they correspond with each other in a series of tempestuous letters. For Lukács, however, the situation is a difficult one, especially theoretically. Among the intellectual influences that play strongly into his decisions at this moment is that of Søren Kierkegaard, the philosopher who fled from the marriage altar to pursue his unhappy existential analyses. Convinced that emotional fulfillment will obstruct the purposes of his writing, Lukács resists the temptation to join his destiny to Irma's. Instead, he writes an allegorical story of his relation to this "bella donna della mia mente" and publishes it as *Soul and Form*. The essay it contains on Novalis, he notes on May 20, 1910, expresses how he felt during their first encounter. Another essay hearkens back to their idyllic days in Florence and Ravenna. The essay on Theodor Storm reflects the letters he wrote Irma from Nagybánya, while the one on Sterne gives voice to the frivolous winter that followed their break in October 1908. Finally, the last essay on tragedy speaks of the engulfing reality to which it all led (Lukács 1910–11b: 16 and 23). Yet in 1910 Lukács still has no idea of how engulfing this reality would be.

On May 18, 1911, after a brief, unhappy marriage with the painter Károly Réthy and an affair with Lukács's close friend Béla Balázs, Irma leaps from a bridge in Budapest. According to his student Agnes Heller, Lukács suffers vertigo for the rest of his life. He knows that he could have saved her and in the process perhaps the better part of himself. His guilt has no bounds.

"I lay this book in your hands," he scribbles in a tentative dedication to the German edition of *Soul and Form* (on May 15, 1910). "For you have given me much more than it has been able to express: everything I have gained and become." Unsatisfied with this formulation, he commemorates the day they first met: "In memoriam 18 XII 1907." Memory, as Cacciari notes, is still the theme when he later singles out the place: "To the memory of my first Florentine days." Three months before she dies, he seeks Irma's permission to state merely, "Irma von Réthy-Seidler, in grateful memory." When the German translation of *Soul and Form* is finally published six months after her death, its epigraph reads also as her epitaph: "Dem Andenken Irma Seidlers."[2]

Two journal entries follow Irma's death in May. No others appear until Lukács's great friend, Leó Popper, the translator of *Soul and Form,* dies five months later. Lukács is now totally lost:

> Now I am thrown back on myself again. Night and vacancy is around me. . . . I have the feeling I am being punished for my pride, for believing in my work and the labor it has taken [*mein Vertrauen auf das Werk und die Arbeit daran*]. And this, too, will be taken away from me, along with life itself and the very possibility of life and everything that points to the future, in the absence of any definitive yes or no.

Negation and affirmation begin to exercise an equally powerful pull on Lukács's imagination. He finds himself in "an obscure and vacant place: nothing, no sign, no direction." Within three weeks he is on the point of taking his life, as though nonbeing were the only solution to this intolerable oscillation between negation and affirmation: "Whatever can be reached purely by means of the intellect," he remarks, "I have reached; it now turns out to consist in nothing. . . . And the more

---

2. These and additional drafts of the dedication to *Soul and Form* can be found in Lukács 1910–11b: 22, 23, 30, 38 (journal entries of May 15, May 18, June 9, and August 3, 1910) as well as in a letter to Irma of February 2, 1911 (Lukács 1982: 198). The dedication is missing from the English translation of *Soul and Form*. On the relationship between Lukács and Irma and how it affects his work, see Cacciari 1983, Congdon 1983, Heller 1983, Kadarkay 1991, and Schweikert 1982. As with Slataper, the *work* to which Lukács aspires is antithetical to the *Arbeit* of concrete, historical labor, including the labor that would have been entailed by a living relationship with Irma/Gioietta.

intensely I reflect on myself, the more clearly I see that death is the only decision" (1910–11b: 42, 47, 49; entries of October 22, November 17 and 23, 1911).

Romance, suicide, and writing are entangled in their own way in the relationship between Carlo Michelstaedter and a Russian divorcée he meets in the same dubious city that hosts Slataper/Pulitzer and Lukács/Seidler. A couple of years older than Michelstaedter, Nadia Baraden becomes his pupil in Florence for private lessons in Italian at the end of 1906. An affection grows between them, and Carlo makes advances. Nadia, however, wounded by past experience, preserves an appropriate distance. Some months later, at Easter, 1907, Carlo goes home to Gorizia for the holidays and sends postcards back to Florence—not to Nadia, but to a young woman he had met more recently called Iolanda De Blasi. There is no way of telling what responsibility Michelstaedter may have borne for what followed. This much, however, is sure. He instantly returns to Florence: Nadia has committed suicide. Whether he was philandering or not, the blow to the student can be felt in countless accents of guilt and ruminations on death that come gradually to pervade his work.[3] The blow is repeated in February of 1909 when news of a "cursed misfortune" (*maledetto accidente*) reaches Gorizia from New York concerning Carlo's elder brother Gino, who had emigrated to the United States in 1893 at sixteen years of age (Michelstaedter 1983: 352; letter to Gaetano Chiavacci of February 26, 1909). Michelstaedter's biographer Sergio Campailla, Daniela Bini, and the custodians of the Michelstaedter Foundation in Gorizia all believe that misfortune, cloaked by the family in silence, to have consisted in suicide.

Difficult as it is to assess the immediate effect of these deaths on Michelstaedter, they signal an intimacy with a condition he was increasingly to address in writing, indeed finally to make his own. As much as he tried to dispel the allure of this final solution, the thought of suicide revisited his mind on numerous occasions, perhaps already from the

---

3. Michelstaedter's guilt in the face of Nadia is most directly expressed in a fictitious dialogue in which she accuses him not only of betraying her, but also of being incapable of love. One of the final exchanges in the dialogue begins with Carlo: "Oh I would be able to love well a person who loved me—so much do I need it.—Poor Carlo! You will never know how to do it, for no one can love who loves only the love that he needs—for if he needs it, this means that he doesn't have it. You do not have anything and cannot give anything; ever more miserable, you will always request,—for you *are not* and cannot love, but ask for love in order to delude yourself into thinking that you *are* somebody. But no one can love who *is not*" (Michelstaedter 1988: 98). His incapacity to love Nadia is interpreted as an incapacity to love period—because Michelstaedter is nobody, with nothing to offer.

time when he was only eight and his cousin, Ada Coen Luzzatto, poisoned herself in 1895 (Altieri 1988: 38).

Many questions are raised by these suicidal relations—the motivations of the respective women, beyond all facile speculations on the "jilted lover"; the masculine rejection of the woman on behalf of the literary work; the role that may have been played by cultural models (Anna Karenina and Hedda Gabler for the women, Werther and Weininger for the men); the uneasy, reciprocal relations between the two elements in the pair (man and woman, work and life). The acts of the women precede but also replicate the spirit of the writings they help shape. They offer irrefutably dramatic, historical "proof" of the dilemmas the men go on to discuss in theory. At the same time these replications or anticipations also *vie* with the work they enable, preempting it of some of its validity. They embody the "reality" about which these writings only speculate. It is, after all, a certain type of life that is preserved by such voluntary deaths—or a certain idea of life—preserved from the deadliness of the word (the theories or the work) in which the three writers believe.[4] It is the freedom and "transcendence" of the word or work, rejecting the limitations of the life, that now appears to be a tightly sealed tomb, and the death of the women that is a life. Indeed, these deaths reaffirm a principle to which the young Lukács, Michelstaedter, and Slataper are absolutely attached: the autonomy of the single self, rejecting the effacements it risks in erotic fusion. Or is it the opposite? Could it be that the erotic (or at least practical) fusion would have preempted the deadliness of this self-assertion, more related to the principle of "work" than it seems? Whatever the case, the acts of the three women offer existential correlatives of principles conceptually explored by the men, and largely in response to such acts.

A DEADLY VOCATION

Numerous as these questions are, they arise in the context of an uncontestable fact: 1910 witnessed a profusion of suicide among the young, especially in that Habsburg empire to which Michelstaedter, Slataper, and Lukács belonged. The successor states to this empire, Austria,

4. Michelstaedter confirms Lukács's and Slataper's views on the opposition between work and life when he sketches the attic where he has secluded himself to write his thesis. He notes at the bottom, in Greek: "Here I live a life that cannot be lived [βιον αβιον], but it gives birth to a great work" (Michelstaedter 1992: 432). According to Michelstaedter's letters, the drawing is done on April 25, 1910, or two days before Gioietta arrives in Florence (Michelstaedter 1983: 438–439).

Hungary, and Czechoslovakia, have occupied top positions in world suicide rates throughout the twentieth century; more relevant, perhaps, is that suicide rose rapidly throughout the waning decades of the Austro-Hungarian empire to reach a staggering culmination in 1910.[5] Indeed, it was partially in response to this rise that on April 20, 1910, Freud's Vienna Psychoanalytical Society organized a symposium to address the phenomenon, particularly in its incidence among students.[6] Given the religious and social taboos that accompany suicide, and different methods of garnering and computing data, it is impossible to say whether the practice was more widespread in the first decade of our century than in the last (most indications point to the opposite). And yet it seems that then it was more ideological an act, more ethically respected a gesture, at least in intellectual circles; it was the mark of a passionate commitment to some principle without which life was not deemed worth living. On the heels of fin-de-siècle "decadent" culture, suicide was not only accepted among the options of those who insisted on ruling their lives; it was often viewed as the most laudable of acts.[7]

5. For documentation and interpretation of rising suicide rates in the Habsburg empire, see János Kristóf Nyíri, "Philosophy and Suicide-Statistics in Austria-Hungary," *East Central Europe* 5 (1978): 69–89. In tables published annually by the World Health Organization, Hungary often holds the highest national rate of suicide in the world, Austria third place, and Czechoslovakia fourth. On the ideological motivations of suicide in different groups of people see Shneidman 1979: 143–163.

6. Alfred Adler, chairman of the conference, traced suicide to uncompensated feelings of inferiority. Wilhelm Stekel speculated that "no one kills himself who has not wanted to kill another, or at least wished the death of another." Isidor Sadger saw it as a desire to expiate feelings of guilt. Freud, unsatisfied with these accounts, felt that no adequate explanation had been given for how the instinct for self-preservation can destroy itself. His own reflections on the issue did not appear until 1917, in his essay "Mourning and Melancholy," where he claims that in the process of depression the ego withdraws its libido from the environment and then identifies itself with all against which it has turned. On the symposium of April 20, 1910, see David Ernst Oppenheim, "Suicide in Childhood," *Minutes of the Vienna Psychoanalytical Society, vol. 2: 1908–1910,* ed. Herman Nunberg and Ernst Federn, trans. M. Nunberg (New York: International Universities Press, 1967): 479–497; *On Suicide, with Particular Reference to Suicide Among Young Students, 1910: With Contributions by Alfred Adler and Others,* ed. Paul Friedman (New York: International Universities Press, 1967); and Johnston 1972. The psychoanalytic discussion of suicide is subsequently renewed in thirteen articles in *Zeitschrift für psychoanalytische Pädagogik* 3 (1928–29): 333–442.

7. It was in precisely this fin-de-siècle spirit, notes Campailla, that the eighteen-year-old Michelstaedter responded to a questionnaire circulating in the drawing rooms of Gorizia in 1905. To the question "At what age would you like to die?" he answers, "Immediately!!" (To the question "What ideal would you like to see in your wife?" he answers "That she resemble my mother.") While Michelstaedter may have well been posturing, he makes a more telling statement much earlier in his life which could hardly have been feigned. His sister Paula records it in a memoir: "When he was three, I remember it well, and I was crying in horror over the death of a young girl who had drowned in the Isonzo—death being something I had not been exposed to at all at the

Five years after Irma's suicide Lukács speculates on the appeal of the act. Tellingly enough, he is not commenting on Irma, but on the fictitious scenario of *Anna Karenina*:

> At very rare, great moments—generally they are moments of death—a reality reveals itself to a person in which he suddenly glimpses and grasps the essence that rules over him and works within him, the meaning of his life. His whole previous life vanishes into nothingness in the face of this experience; all its conflict, all the sufferings, torments and confusions caused by them, appear petty and inessential. Meaning has made its appearance and the paths into living life are open to the soul. (Lukács 1916: 149)

Among the "crucial moments of bliss," Lukács repeats (149), belong "the great moments of dying."

One might wonder how Lukács *knows* this revelation is experienced by the dying (instead of merely imagined by the living). One might also wonder how well the concrete experience of the woman in question (Karenina/Irma) can accommodate the intellectual projections of the abstract, theoretical man. Be that as it may, the intellectual sect to which Lukács belonged *believed* in such moments of clarified experience, and frequently linked them to death. Here, too, the perception is more important than the fact. At recurring moments in history, Lukács notes before Irma dies, there arises "the ideology of the beautiful death." It stems from moments when culture recognizes its own decadence, and it becomes difficult "to assess values hedonistically," or to comfort one's mind with the thought that virtue receives compensation and sin can be explained as expiation. The ideology of the beautiful death occurs when "life, by the very fact that it has become problematic, ceases to be a prime value for the ethical person." When history contests "the fundamental values of humanity, one comes to bestow validity on the person who has been, or will be, condemned to death" (1911b: 56–57).

If this sounds impossibly romantic today, it is probably because we in our age are more bent on reaping the fruits of experience then were our great-grandfathers. We have lost the metaphysical unrest of intellectuals at the beginning of the century, including their insistence

---

time—he told me in all seriousness: 'But you know, even you and I, every one of us, must die some time.' And he said it with all the seriousness of a little philosopher. I was greatly moved." The seriousness of this three-year-old on the issue of death certainly grows in the next twenty years. Paula's recollections of her brother are in Winteler 1973. The questionnaire is published in Campailla 1981: 45–49. On ideologies of death and suicide in the Austro-Hungarian empire see Johnston 1972: 247–249 and 165–180.

on achievements more lasting than the pleasures of the day. On the threshold of the twenty-first century, after so much has been gained in the way of material benefits, it is difficult to understand those earlier creative thinkers who felt concrete possibilities of experience were inherently deficient, and who were inspired—in their very inability to discover an overall justification for life—to engage in martyric gestures. Most important perhaps, if we tend to assume today that the cause of every empirical act—including suicide—must also be empirical, we are nevertheless mistaken to project this assumption onto an age that did not share it, to project it onto others who did not share our respect for personal experience.

To take a case we know more about than the suicides of the three women, namely, the suicide of Michelstaedter, it elicits nothing but questions. Was it caused by a violent argument between himself and his mother the very same morning? Did the fact that it was her birthday play into Michelstaedter's decision, making his act a kind of retribution? A strange present indeed, transforming that day of celebration into one she would henceforth mourn. Was the suicide spurred by Michelstaedter's intolerable sense of guilt (ample evidence of which exists in his texts)—not only for what he perceived as his chronically unfilial conduct, but also for his inability to live up to his theoretical and moral demands? Or was his death really just a way to end a lethal ailment from which Michelstaedter knew he was suffering, manifested by pain in his feet, legs, and hip?[8]

Ninety years after the fact, it is difficult to understand why such a handsome, athletic, artistic, charismatic, and self-professed lover of life should have brought his life to such a fateful end. The truncation of a life as promising as his seems all but incomprehensible. If, as Giuseppe Papini wrote just two weeks after the suicide occurred, what really took place was a "metaphysical suicide"—or the consequence of a recognition of some unbearable truth or untruth of the world—then the distance between our time and theirs only grows greater.[9] Rarely do we grow so impatient as when we hear talk of "existentialism." And yet,

8. See his own references to a crippling condition in Michelstaedter 1983: 321, 361, 364, 379, 389–390, 393. See also Campailla's introduction to Michelstaedter 1988: 18, and Bini 1992: 277 n. 60, where she wonders whether the ailment may have been a bone disease.

9. Giovanni Papini, "Un suicidio metafisico," *Il Resto del Carlino,* November 5, 1910: 3; reprinted with the title "Carlo Michelstaedter" in *Tutte le opere di Giovanni Papini: Filosofia e letteratura* (Milan: Mondadori, 1961), 817–822.

what we often tend to forget in our postmodern content is the historical price this comfort has exacted—in the self-torment of hundreds of political leaders, in the intellectual intransigence of even more philosophers and artists, in the bloodletting of millions along our ostensible march to peace. We will never know what practical or psychological motivations Michelstaedter had for being so determined to end his life that (as one newspaper reports it) he fired not one but two shots from his revolver.[10] Perhaps the best we can do is to seek the causality of this suicide in his thinking—amply recorded in the dissertation he had just completed that morning, and addressing a world that he shared with others. Such a world is shaped not only by familial and psychological facts, by political and economic conditions, but by what gives them significance: cultural perceptions and beliefs, phobias and aspirations, forms of logic and illogic. Paradoxical as it may seem, suicide is never a personal act; it is the result of a series of tentacles in which the mind is caught, a reactive gesture or break in a system (a system, notes Shneidman [1979], that is necessarily ambivalent and dyadic, entailing not only a dialectic of self and other but also two parts of a single person). Before the Great War, suicide, pessimism, and despair were tied up with entirely different existential structures than those that surround us today, different ethical demands, different modes of significance and forms of conviction.

One of these forms of conviction held that life was not necessarily a self-legitimating process; it was not necessarily something to be preserved at all economic and cultural costs. In the prewar years thinkers tended to want to understand life "as a whole." They did not shy away from diagnosing local and universal deficiencies in conduct, often grounding their findings in physiology or metaphysics and proposing programs by which to achieve personal or social "authenticity." Death, at this moment in time, was viewed as more than an end to organic palpitation. Its negativity appeared to be inherent to life itself. What now seems to be the morbid thinking of the early twentieth century was largely the consequence of an unwillingness to acquiesce in the growing materialistic conviction that (a) all spiritual questions are foreclosed by the self-terminating flow of historical experience and (b) the human mind is accordingly well advised to limit its attention

10. "Tentato Suicidio," *Gazzettino Popolare*, October 18, 1910, reprinted in Antonella Gallarotti, *Il Fondo Michelstaedter della Biblioteca Civica* (Gorizia: Dispensa dell'Università della Terza Età, 1990), 12.

to the furtherance of its pleasures and chores. The "morbidity" is also the consequence of confronting what so many doctrines of happiness, rights, and empowerment tend to exclude from their moralizing pictures: the irrationality of physical and psychological suffering, the ineradicability of human pettiness and rivalry, the instability of destiny and the intellectual understanding of it.

Thinkers in 1910 were less interested in denying or eradicating pain than in comprehending it, in fathoming rather than erasing concrete signs of the demonic. A person of true faith, writes Buber, "would rather renounce salvation than exclude Satan's kingdom from it" (1913a: 138).[11] "People of our time who formulate new laws of morality," adds Schoenberg, "*cannot live with guilt!*" To hanker after the kitsch of moral comfort, in his view, is merely to deny or displace the fundamentality of guilt.

> The thinker, who keeps on searching, does the opposite. He shows that there are problems and that they are unsolved. As does Strindberg: "Life makes everything ugly." Or Maeterlinck: "Three quarters of our brothers [are] condemned to misery." Or Weininger and all others who have thought earnestly. (Schoenberg 1911a: 2)

If there is a sense of the deficiency of being at the beginning of the century, then, it grows out of an ethical and metaphysical unease that is much less common at the end of the century, or much more severely repressed (though not successfully enough to stop it from erupting in countless acts of violence which we call "isolated incidents," and which are more gruesome in nature than the suicidal violence of the earlier age). Accompanying the dozens of economic, psychological, and political reasons for the dark visions of 1910 is also a tendency to aspire to a more absolute ethic than we imagine to be within our reach today. "That there was dying in the world," says Buber's fictitious spokesman Daniel, "had become my sin, for which I had to do penance" (Buber 1913a: 133). Where our contemporary "optimistic" spirit continually risks being dismayed by all that it excludes from its vision, the earlier "pessimistic" one sought something more like what Trakl calls a "trans-

---

11. Two years earlier, in a text that appears to have left its mark on Buber, the young Lukács makes a similar point. Sin, he claims, "is no antithesis to goodness." It is rather that which "convulses our true reality," making an ethical approach to experience one that accepts the "unification of temptation and the tempted, of fate and soul, of the demonic and the divine in humans" (Lukács 1911c: 374, 378, and 382). But more on this in chapter four.

formation of evil"—an assimilation, rather than a negation, of destructive forces. What is "pathological" is hardly the feeling of life's deficiencies, it is rather the nosophobic refusal to acknowledge these deficiencies: the passive propagation of their morbid disguise.

IN THE BEGINNING WAS THE END

If death was still an exotic member of late nineteenth-century thinking, by 1910 it had received full citizen's rights. The turn is marked by a short essay called "The Metaphysics of Death" (1910) by the sociologist Georg Simmel. The essay rejects the most widespread European conceptions of death in order to portray it as a principle that structures all vital acts from within. Simmel's first target is the materialistic view of death as a mere cessation of breath. His second is the religious idea that death is a transitional event, a gateway to the One True Life. Both conceptions see death as different and separate from life—as an external intrusion, a truncation of action, a severing of the historical thread. Simmel instead describes death as "tied to life from within and from the very beginning."[12]

The actions and historical possibilities of an organism, argues Simmel, are circumscribed from the start by its end. Only within the borders of a mortal span of existence, and by virtue of the practical limitations on each possible experience, does a life acquire some identity and shape. In this sense, the moment to moment behavior of every creature is an implicit response to the fact that nothing it can do will last forever, to the impending fact that it too will die and must therefore accomplish its functions within a particular space and time. The considerations and acts of each moment, writes Simmel, "would be different if this were not our fate, which influences such a moment" (Simmel 1910a: 31). If we think that death is life's "opposite condition," marking only a limit to what we can do in life (as though this life would be exactly what it is, only longer, if death did not come to interfere with it), we simply ignore what we know before we start to think.

---

12. Congdon points out (1983: 36) that several of the central ideas of Simmel's essay can be found in a 1907 essay called "Death Aesthetics," dedicated to Simmel, and written by his student and Lukács's friend (and Irma Seidler's lover), Béla Balázs. Like Lukács, Balázs was studying with Simmel in Berlin in 1906–1907. For an excellent introduction to the many issues raised by the tragic philosophy of Simmel, see Alessandro Dal Lago, *Il politeismo moderno* (Milan: UNICOPLI, 1985).

Death rather shapes experience from the inside out, preselecting the nature of our strivings, desires, and decisions. Life has no trajectory at all except in and by means of its finitude.

Simmel's observations about the structure of organic behavior entail others about existential motivation. As he argues in his *Lebensanchauung* of 1918, we never act on behalf of life itself (as it is at any given moment), but always on behalf of "more life," and "more than life." We do everything we do in order to extend our possibilities beyond our actual and present conditions, to fight or flee those stand-ins for death which are obstacles, actualities, and diminutions. The greater the vitality of an organism, the greater its struggles against limitation. Even our repression of the sense of death is a surreptitious strategy to enhance our capacity to function. Thus, in general all of our

> gain and pleasure, work and peace, and all of our other modes of relation . . . are an instinctive or conscious flight from death. The life we employ to draw nearer to death we employ to flee it. We are like men on a ship who walk in a direction opposite to the one in which it is going: while they proceed to the south, the deck on which they do so is carried to the north with them on board. And this double direction of their motion [*Bewegtseins*] determines the position that they occupy at any moment in space. (Simmel 1910a: 32)

"With forehead bent forward, the demon of life sits at the rudder," notes Simmel's friend Buber, "and with head thrown back, the goddess of death sits in the prow" (Buber 1913a: 131).

The duplicity of the situation is more scathingly described by Michelstaedter. If he has one objection to life as it is commonly lived it is that, consciously or unconsciously, it involves precisely this flight from death, this delusory defense against the inevitable dissolution of all that we want to consider permanent. Such an ethic, if we may call it that, is just the response of an ostrich to the menace of time, a form of plastic surgery, a desperate ploy to deceive the truth. The values and meanings that we attribute to existence are in Michelstaedter's view almost invariably the fantasies of a desperate desire for stability:

> being *born* is nothing but wanting to continue: men live . . . in order *not to die*. Their persuasion is *fear of death*; being *born* is no more than *shrinking from death*. So that if death were ever made certain to them in a certain future—they *would show themselves to be already dead in the present*. Everything they do and say with firm persuasion, on behalf of a certain objective, with self-evident reasons—is nothing but fear of death. (Michelstaedter 1910: 69)

From the start, humans embark on a flight from the end—even though only this end helps us see the beginning.

We acknowledge such a beginning in Lukács's "great moments of dying." Why, he wonders, do we grieve at the death of a friend? Isn't it because this loss brings a larger set of issues to consciousness, the issue, for example, of impermanent companionship, or the impossibility of establishing absolute social bonds with our fellows? In the sudden and irrevocable termination of a friendship, claims Lukács, we face the "painful, forever fruitless question of the eternal distance, the unbridgeable void between one human being and another" (1910–11a: 107). Death is only the most dramatic instance of life's inherent disunity, the ultimate form of an alienation already embedded in its everyday processes. "The rupture caused by death, the great estrangement that falls between the dead friend and the living one, is perhaps the same as the thousand estrangements and pitfalls that may occur in any conversation between friends—only in more perceptible, more tangible form." In essence, the death of a friend is so painful because it is "a symbol of the survivor's aloneness [des Einsambleibens]" (Lukács 1910–11a: 108–109), an aloneness *predating* the death but not coming to the surface until moments like that. Death reveals the separation that has underlain and made possible the joining of lives. It unmasks the mortality that fuels the unions.

More metaphysical in his analyses than Simmel, Lukács goes as far as to characterize the entire fabric of such union as a tenuous and incoherent web:

> Life is an anarchy of light and dark: nothing is ever completely fulfilled in life, nothing ever quite ends; new and confusing voices always mingle with the chorus of those that have been heard before. Everything flows, everything merges into another thing, and the mixture is uncontrolled and impure; everything is destroyed, everything is smashed, nothing ever flowers into real life [zum wirklichen Leben]. To live: to be able to live something through to the end. *Life*: nothing is ever fully and completely lived through to the end. [DAS Leben: nie wird etwas ganz und vollkommen ausgelebt.]

The endpoint of Lukács's argument is thus extreme: Historical existence "is the most unreal and unliving of all conceivable modes of being; one can describe it only negatively—by saying that something always comes to disturb the flow [etwas kommt immer störend dazwischen]" (Lukács 1910–11a: 152–153). If "absolute life" can never take place in time, it is because change allows nothing to have an

essential and perduring identity. Temporal reality is ruled by a network
of accidental and meaningless necessities, with no other motivation
than that "of being empirically present, of being entangled by a thousand threads in a thousand accidental bonds and relationships" (Lukács
1910–11a: 157). Historical existence is not only a response to being-
unto-death; it is a literal enactment of it.

Persuasion and Rhetoric had reached a comparable conclusion in
its opening parable of the weight. Since the energy that moves things
is generated by a condition of privation—or by a desire for what "is
not"—all things, reasons Michelstaedter, are doubly nothing. Motivated by what they lack, things cannot even reconcile themselves to
the emptiness that they are. And this is why people lament their solitude: "*Being with themselves, they feel alone*: they feel they are *with
nobody*" (Michelstaedter 1910: 41). To engage in a "natural," everyday pursuit of historical fulfillment is to flee the nobody inside one
from whom none can escape. Michelstaedter is therefore the first to
agree with Lukács's belief that "real Life is always unreal, always impossible, in the midst of empirical life [*für die Empirie des Lebens*]"
(Lukács 1910–11a: 153). That Life in which "potency and act are one"
can only be an "*abios bios*," a Life without life (Michelstaedter 1910:
41). "Living life is beyond forms" (Lukács 1911c: 374).

What do Michelstaedter and Lukács mean by real Life? Don't they
characterize everyday existence as lifeless only because it does not incorporate what *they* believe that life should incorporate—namely, meaning and purpose, stability and order, permanent and unchanging identity? But these are only desires of the mind, intellectual wishes, to which
experience pays no heed. Life happily ignores them in its own quest
for power, security, or advancement. Is there not a "nihilism" at work
in this very attack on the nothingness of the world? In this condemnation of life for not living up to requirements that philosophical elucubrations feel it should meet? In this defense of "real Life" from all
"merging and smashing and flowing"? After his Marxist conversion in
1918 Lukács rereads his earlier work precisely in terms of such nihilism. And he links it to a more particular intellectual syndrome, namely,
the "idealism," "subjectivism," and "expressionism" of intellectuals in
an era unwilling to confront the true, material bases of their discon-
tent. By the thirties he has singled out a spokesman for this cultural
"flight from reality": the art historian Wilhelm Worringer (Lukács 1970:
33–34).

LIFE AS ABSTRACTION

In his major work called *Abstraction and Empathy*, printed as a dissertation in 1907 and published in book form in 1908, Worringer posits two different types of drives at work in artistic interpretations of life. Abstraction is one, empathy the other. Empathy is based on a "relationship of confidence between man and the phenomena of the external world," an "unproblematic sense of being at home in the world" (1908: 15). It views experience as patterned, secure, and meaningful. The artistic correlates of empathy are classicism, realism, naturalism, and other styles of representation that integrate spirit and matter. Abstraction does just the opposite. Taking root in "an awareness of temporality, contingency, and in a state of abject terror" (Waite 1981: 210), it is the "the outcome of a great inner unrest, inspired in humans by . . . an immense spiritual dread of space" (Worringer 1908: 15). Born from a "desperate psychological need for faith, repose, and stability," abstraction affords the "possibility of taking the individual thing of the external world out of its arbitrariness and seeming fortuitousness, of eternalising it by approximation to abstract forms and, in this manner, of finding a point of tranquility and a refuge from appearances" (Worringer 1908: 16).

Worringer does not locate this tendency towards abstraction in contemporary Europe until his 1911 article on modern painting. Its more obvious examples lie in Egyptian, Byzantine, and Romanesque art. While the urge to empathy finds gratification in the beauty of dynamic development, "the urge to abstraction finds its beauty in the life-denying inorganic, in the crystalline, or in general terms, in all abstract law and necessity" (Worringer 1908: 4). Abstraction offsets the horrors of realism. It endeavors

> to wrest the object of the external world out of its natural context, out of the unending flux of being, to purify it of all its dependence upon life, i.e., of everything about it that was arbitrary, to render it necessary and irrefragable, to approximate it to its *absolute* value. (Worringer 1908: 17)

In his great manifesto for abstract painting, Vasily Kandinsky gave no sign of knowing Worringer's work (although he probably did; *Abstraction and Empathy* had been published in Munich three years earlier by Piper, the same press that published his *On the Spiritual in Art*). Kandinsky's arguments in his manifesto and letters are similar to Worringer's. "Among us painters," he writes to Schoenberg on February 6,

1911, "it is the *res* which is forbidden."[13] *Res,* the word for thing in
Latin, is the external, material dimension of things, the dimension that
viewers had been accustomed to expect from painting for centuries,
assuming it to be one of the immovable laws of pictorial art that it im-
itates the forms of nature. On the deepest level, Kandinsky's statement
says that art can never convey an unmediated reality to its audience;
but if that is so, then art might also embrace the absolute consequences
of these expressive limitations, freeing itself from those outer forms of
things which are only carcasses of intentions, values, and "being" in a
more extensive sense. The historical, phenomenal *res,* writes Kandinsky, is the proper interest of "dull materialism," or of an art that "seeks
its own substance in *hard material*" only because it knows nothing no-
bler (1909–11: 135). Kandinsky, then, is less "reactionary" in his conception of abstraction than Worringer. He sees it not first and foremost
as a flight from the horrors of solid experience, but as a search for
something within or beyond such experience. (It is not certain, however,
whether this holds for his collaborator on *The Blue Rider,* Franz Marc,
who confesses, "I found people 'ugly' very early on; animals seemed to
me more beautiful, more pure; but even in animals I discovered much
that was unfeeling and ugly, so that my pictures instinctively . . . became increasingly more schematic, more abstract" [Marc 1985: 65;
letter to Maria Marc of April 12, 1915].)

With Kandinsky abstraction affects not only the manner in which
art mediates the real, without naturalistic or easily accessible content,
but also its position within political and historical processes. From those
processes it now asserts its independence. As in Schoenberg and Michelstaedter, art occupies a space radically different from life, and even
finds trouble reconnecting to it. Art speaks of an alternative order, a
militantly antihistorical one, where it almost makes no difference how
a composition "sounds" (or whether it caresses ears accustomed to the
ostensibly harmonic orders of everyday life), how easily it is understood, or how functional it may be in practical contexts. Art now tran-

---

13. Schoenberg and Kandinsky 1984: 27; letter of February 6, 1911. On the relations
between Kandinsky and Worringer see Waite 1981: 203; Long 1980: 10; and Weiss 1979:
7 n. 25. Franz Marc, the co-editor of the *Blue Rider,* mentions Worringer to Kandinsky
in a letter at the beginning of 1912 after *On the Spiritual in Art* is published: "I am reading Worringer's *Abstraktion und Einfühlung,* a good mind, whom we need very much.
Marvelously disciplined thinking, concise and cool, extremely cool" (Kandinsky and
Marc, eds., 1912: 30). The influence of Worringer's theories on modern art is treated in
Werner Hoffmann, *Grundlagen der modernen Kunst: Eine Einführung in ihre symbolis-
chen Formen* (Stuttgart: Kröner, 1966): 81–85, 109–110, and Weiss 1979: 158–159.

scribes a quest for an absolutely different type of understanding, a re-vision of the nature of vision, sound, and meaning.

Whether the Marxist Lukács is right or not in characterizing such abstraction as a "flight from reality," his analysis of at least one of its internal mechanisms is shared by other thinkers. The logical endpoint of all efforts to remake life in the image of abstract, metaphysical dreams, claim Nietzsche and Heidegger, is "completed nihilism": the sense that the solidities and structures by which we normally live are bridges over a gaping abyss, reassurances spurred by fear and need and spiritless survival. At the moment of completed nihilism, historical conduits of meaning grow clogged. One appears to lose access to any fundamental and substantial truth. Being, Michelstaedter confesses, re-mains "outside my consciousness and outside my life. I do not live the absolute, nor does my *nous* [intellect] know it—what I live and know with my *nous* is the nullity of everything that is visible and knowable" (Michelstaedter 1958: 803). "And thus the anguish," continues Gio-vanni Boine. The dilemma that follows such "knowledge," in ethical or behavioral terms, appears appropriately enough in a letter Boine writes on Christmas Day 1910, the anniversary of the birth of the su-preme martyr:

> Must I violate my moral conscience, must I restrict it and *do*? Or must I withdraw into the world of purity and *not do*? Action does not amplify you. It teaches you the low-lands and the *impossibilities* of the world, it re-inforces within you the bitter pessimism of the Christian tradition. Not God but sin circulates in each thing, and envelops and penetrates it:—The things of the world smack of sin just as sea water smacks of salt. (Boine 1983: xxxvi; letter to Casati)

If the forms of historical existence do not conform to theoretical ide-als, the argument runs, they are not fully real, at least not in the tradi-tional sense of reality as essential, sure, and lasting.

In the very years that this nihilistic idealism reaches its peak, phi-losophers like William James and John Dewey do everything they can to revise such a notion of reality, liberating it from ancient expecta-tions and redefining it as a function of purely pragmatic concerns. Yet the Americans enjoy great distance from the dispiriting history of Eu-rope, where reflections on the rift between the "is" and the "ought" are nourished by long moral, political, and philosophical practice. There are many reasons for the pessimism of Europeans in 1910, not just the assimilated clichés of nineteenth-century decadence (which weigh the negative and sickly dimensions of life more heavily than the positive and healthy ones) or the vitalistic creeds of Schopenhauer, Darwin, and Nietzsche (attributing all organic motivation to voracious, blind struggles of instinct). At work in the nihilism of Europe in 1910 is also a worry about the potential consequences of precisely the pragmatism that James and Dewey try to make philosophical: a culture, in Kandinsky's view, where people think only of "material well-being" and can judge nothing except by its outward results. In the practical, short-sighted, positivistic, and utilitarian age of which they were getting a glimpse, people who might have once turned into spiritual leaders, writes Kandinsky, are dismissed as "abnormal" and a technical product is hailed as "a great achievement" (1909–11: 135).

The abstract canvases of Kandinsky and Marc, the tone-color music of Schoenberg, the metaphysical reflections of Lukács and Michelstaedter crave alternatives to what they themselves perceive as abstract— what they see as lifeless, despiritualized action (even when it takes solace in impressionism or aestheticism). The abstract arts and thought of 1910 rebel against an abstraction *already at work* in pragmatic, positivistic, and materialistic reductions of historical practice to a set of predetermined goals, if not against the limitations of practice itself, especially where this practice allows no theory to be abstracted from it. To recover such a theory (or more properly speaking, to allow one to develop) thinkers and artists begin by exposing a whole series of unsubstantiated conceptions to which the practices of their time had led. This act of exposure entails more than metaphysical critique. Ultimately both Michelstaedter and the young Lukács are more interested in sociological fact than metaphysics. They accompany their visions of "real Life" with analyses of the configurations of actual, contemporary sociohistoric experience. In the final analysis, what they decry is not experience "in the abstract" so much as particular and "unnecessary" organizations of experience.[14] The ontological conditions that Lukács and Michelstaedter condemn are the ones particularly exacerbated by the culture in which they live, governed, as it seemed to them, by a collective reign of egotism, a failure of human solidarity, and the rationalization of social processes. If anything is abstract, these latter-day humanists would argue, it is life as it is institu-

14. See György Márkus's study of the organic relation between the young Lukács's metaphysical idealism and his later commitment to political practice (Márkus 1983). Another study examining similar issues in the broader context of Lukács's attempts to find more than an aesthetic or metaphysical solution to human isolation is that of Dennis Crow, "Form and the Unification of Aesthetics and Ethics in Lukács' *Soul and Forms*," *New German Critique* 15 (Fall 1979): 159–177.

tionally conceived and managed at the beginning of this century. There is a "kiss of death," writes Berman, already contained in the guiding structures of twentieth-century modernity, including the idea, shared by those who love it as much as by those who hate it, that "modernity is constituted by its machines, of which modern men and women are merely mechanical reproductions" (1982: 29).[15]

SOCIOLOGY OF DEATH

Long before Lukács attributes the demise of life to capitalist economy, he operates within the parameters of a cultural sociology related to that of Simmel and Max Weber. In his *History of the Development of Modern Drama* (1908–1911) he distinguishes between two types of society that he later comes to describe as (a) closed/organic and (b) open/mechanistic.[16] Open, mechanistic society, claims Lukács, is enabled by modern and bourgeois forms of association. It is "open" in multiplying the opportunities for individual decision, affording its members various choices of work and lifestyle. It is "mechanistic," however, in making this individualism possible only by means of a rationalization of the concrete relations between members of the society, and by recasting these relations in the form of financial bonds. The links between people in open, mechanistic bourgeois society are more abstract than they are in "organic" society, where the relations, performances, and roles of its participants grow out of a relatively closed tradition. Different as the persons composing an open society may be on the surface, each relies first and foremost on a hierarchical system of impersonal, mechanical, and "facilitating" networks: corporations, professional "friendships," post office clerks, credits and debits.

Conditions like these have a two-pronged effect. They produce a subjectification of the psyche—commonly called introversion—forcing citizens to seek their freedom and personal gratification in private, interiorized activity. They also subject these "subjects" to an unprecedented process of objectification, transforming them into functions and elements of complex, rational institutions. While adopting a sense of

15. The starkest articulation of this idea of life as mechanicity, published of course in 1910, is Mark Twain's dialogue *What is Man?* He takes a similar position in "The Turning Point of My Life," which also appeared in 1910, the year Twain himself died.
16. The distinction had already been drawn by Ferdinand Tönnies in *Gemeinschaft und Gesellschaft* (Community and Society) of 1887 and can be traced as far back as the *Monologues* of Friedrich Schleiermacher (1800).

abstract autonomy, a member of such a society exists "more and more only in relation to the things outside him, as the sum total of his relationships to them" (Lukács 1911a: 325).[17] Living people are mortified by the deadly complexity of socioeconomic ties.

In *The Philosophy of Money* (1900) Simmel had referred to the same process as spiritual objectification (*Vergegenständlichung*). Lukács calls it *Versachlichung* (thingification). Weber speaks of it as *Rationalisierung* (rationalization). What is named by each thinker is a commodified life in which most actions and thoughts are subsumed, a calculative, instrumentalizing life that evaluates experience on the model of quantifiable and manipulable things. Professions grow increasingly differentiated and detached from larger contexts of interest, visibly undermining the attitude of employees. As the relationships between them become opportunistic,

> an ever smaller part of the personality of the worker goes into the work and, consequently, even work requires less and less involvement of the personal capacities of the person carrying it out. Work takes on a specific and objective life of its own, over and against the individuality of the individual, so that the latter becomes forced to express himself elsewhere and not in what he does. (Lukács 1911a: 666)

Competition turns into the governing mode of human interaction, exacerbating the paradox by leading people to vie against each other in order to affirm the security and autonomy of their own identities. At the same time, however, competition makes self-assertion prey to a dialectic in which self-worth depends upon successfully opposing the will of others. In no way is it possible to affirm this new and contradictory type of personality "without suppressing the personality of others," writes Lukács in a passage describing the new way of envisioning one's colleague (especially a younger or more gifted one) as a threat, and making the others feel that they "can defend themselves only by destroying that individual" (Lukács 1911b: vol. 1, 161).

Without knowledge of Simmel, Tönnies, or other members of the German Society for Sociology (whose first meeting on October 19, 1910, took place two days too late), Michelstaedter has his own name for these reifying effects of modern society: rhetoric, the opposite of the condition in which one does what one believes to be right, even if this "right" should be based merely on an unquestioned, provincial or-

---

17. For a fuller account of this process in Lukács and Simmel, see Antonio De Simone, *Lukács e Simmel: Il disincanto della modernità e le antinomie della ragione dialettica* (Lecce: Milella, 1985).

ganic tradition. It names an *"inadequate affirmation of individuality"* (Michelstaedter 1910: 98). It is inadequate to the aim it pursues: self-expression, the achievement of power, the objective formation of "what one is." While Michelstaedter's terms are transposable to practically any social gathering in history, most of his examples are drawn from the society and the time in which he lived: the rhetoric of technology and progress, the rhetoric of civil rights, the rhetoric of property and work, the rhetoric of law and education. In 1910 "the rhetoric of the physical life is *sport*." The "religion of the *sportsman* is the 'record.'" The clichés about what is universally "enjoyable," coupled with the opportunities that society provides for its realization, are the "rhetoric of pleasure." Institutionally conveyed prejudice is the rhetoric of education (Michelstaedter 1910: 159, 107, 184). In modernist rhetoric, rituals "take on the name of sanctity, the manipulation of concepts the name of wisdom, imitative technique the name of art, and *all virtuosity the name of a virtue*." Society provides the means for its members to "find what they need in a preestablished form" and teaches them that they have learned proper conduct "when they have learned the norms of this form" (Michelstaedter 1910: 130, 174). Michelstaedter suggests that in his time, more than ever before, the possibility of honest human relations has been vitiated by calculation, reflection, and manipulation. If his analyses are frequently assimilated to Marxist frameworks, it is because they diagnose the deadly machinations of a commodified culture where work has become "violence against nature" and property "violence against humans." The result is an unavowed ethic of mutual slavery in which the self-assertion of one person means that "the other has a *truncated future* . . . he is material confronting the master; he is a *thing*" (Michelstaedter 1910: 146–477).[18]

In the year that Michelstaedter writes *Persuasion and Rhetoric*, the futurist F. T. Marinetti blasts the English for being so custom-bound, for their attachment to "masks and screens of every sort," for their "habitual and hypocritical formality" (Marinetti 1910: 68–69). Michelstaedter has even harsher invectives, even in his notebook sketches of

18. Marxist readings of Michelstaedter, based largely on his compelling "Discourse to the People" ("Discorso al popolo," 1909–1910, in Michelstaedter 1958: 669–671), can be sampled in Alberto Abruzzese, *Svevo, Slataper, Michelstaedter: Lo stile e il viaggio* (Venice: Marsilio, 1979); Cerruti 1967; Romano Luperini, "Carlo Michelstaedter, ovvero il coraggio della 'persuasione,'" *Il Novecento*, vol. 1 (Turin: Loescher, 1981): 217–223. Some limitations of these approaches are discussed by Bini 1992: 14–16.

pedants and society ladies, contrasted with other visions of noble, harmonious Florentine nudes. Towards the end of his life, his depictions grow increasingly dark, stiffening their critique of human duplicity into a meditation on grotesque and unbridgeable extremes. The gesture by which Marinetti provokes members of his audience to reflect on the difference between their inner interests and their outer, unreflective forms becomes, in Michelstaedter, a scathing denunciation of the difference itself, as though no world can be a world if it tolerates this opposition. The enemy becomes duplicity itself, the abstract, delusive shapes that distort all inner intention.

By the end of his life Michelstaedter's satiric caricatures share less with the avant-garde humorists of Milan and Paris than with the anxious expressionists of Mitteleuropa. He becomes incapable of addressing the social, political, or economic structures of everyday life without asking what principles they serve or betray. In this respect Michelstaedter's thinking follows the lines of the German *Lebensphilosophie* so popular in his time, which views sociohistoric phenomena as symptomatic of a greater, metaphysical complex in which they are gathered—one living or dying, constructive or destructive, true or rhetorical, cohesive or dividing. What other critics might characterize as purely local or contingent matters, perhaps only matters worthy of laughter, here assume ontological proportions. Vitalistic philosophy views them as constitutive issues, shaping the morality of the societies they mark. Here the critique of ideology, intuition, metaphysics, and sociological analysis are all interdependent. No surface remains a mere surface, no category a domain of its own. In this mixed climate it is no wonder that the richest depiction of historically reified selves in the first decade of the century occurs in a work that straddles the divide between France and Central Europe: *The Notebooks of Malte Laurids Brigge* (1910), a series of reflections on life in Paris of a man born in Prague.

DECREPITUDE IN BODY AND SOUL

"So, then people do come here in order to live," begin the *Notebooks,* the creation of Rainer Maria Rilke. "I would have sooner thought one died here." The speaker, Malte, is shocked by the fact that in the most vital city of the world life has been all but extinguished:

> I have been out. I saw: hospitals. I saw a man who swayed and sank to the ground. People gathered round him, so I was spared the rest. I saw a pregnant woman. She was pushing herself cumbrously along a high, warm wall,

groping for it now and again as if to convince herself it was still there. . . .
The street began to smell from all sides. A smell, so far as one could distinguish, of iodoform, of the grease of pommes frites, of fear. . . . And what
else? A child in a standing baby-carriage. It was fat, greenish, and had a
distinct eruption on its forehead. This was evidently peeling as it healed
and did not hurt. The child slept, its mouth was open, breathing iodoform,
pommes frites and fear. It was simply like that. The main thing was, being
alive. That was the main thing. (Rilke 1910: 13)

The last two statements clinch the distasteful irony of the situation,
or the deadly effects of the will to survival. Precisely in Paris, notes Rilke
in his personal letters, in the city where "the drive to live is stronger
than elsewhere," one senses the innumerable populations of the dead.
After Michelstaedter's and Lukács's remarks on the deadliness of the
unmediated will to live (or dissonant and insatiable self-interest) and
the deleterious effects of the rational, metropolitan forms into which
this will has been organized, is it any wonder that these armies of the
dying proliferate precisely where the forms and the will are mutually
corrupting? Is this "will to live" really life, asks Rilke? "No,—life is
something quiet, broad, simple. The drive to live is hurry and pursuit.
Drive to have life, at once, whole, in an hour. Of that Paris is so full
and therefore so near to death. It is an alien, alien city" (letter to his
wife, Clara, of August 31, 1902, in Rilke 1910: 219).

Where walls grow warm and babies turn green, the corrosive inver-
sions of human vitality are already foretold: "One arrives, one finds a
life, ready made, one has only to put it on" (Rilke 1910: 17). The in-
stitutionalized mortality of the metropolis suffuses itself throughout
the city's inhabitants, destroying them with its gangrenous effect.[19]

19. In 1910, and out of feelings similar to Malte's, Egon Schiele decides to move
away from Vienna, where "the city is black and all is formula," to the forest (Schiele
1921: 97, and Nebehay 1980: 71; letter to Anton Peschka, dated Spring, 1910). The
perspective is pervasive at the beginning of the century: "O the madness of the great
city," cries Trakl, "where stunted trees / Stiffen at evening along the black wall; / The
spirit of evil peers from a silver mask" (Trakl 1969: 124). "For the city," writes Martin
Buber, "for the crowd, for the wretched millions my heart swells and revolts. The unreal, the wretched. . . . The city, we say, but we do not, in fact, mean its houses and its
factories, it wares and its refuse; we mean, in fact, these millions of men . . . all these individual men, naked underneath their clothes, bleeding under their skin, all these whose
uncovered heartbeat united would drown out the united voice of their machines. These
men are wronged, . . . wronged in the right of rights, the gracious right of reality"
(Buber 1913a: 76 and 75).
  For depictions of the metropolis in this era see Burton Pike, *The Image of the City in
Modern Literature* (Princeton: Princeton University Press, 1981); Reinhold Heller, "'The
City is Dark': Conceptions of Urban Landscape and Life in Expressionist Painting and
Architecture," in Pickar and Webb 1979: 42–57; Cacciari 1993: 3–96; Simmel 1903.

Malte's notebooks reflect on this process as he wanders through
Paris and the rooms of his memory in an effort to exorcise his own fear
of death. He calls it the "Big Thing," the name he gave it when he first
experienced the terrors of childhood illness:

> Yes, that was what I had always called it, when they all stood around my
> bed and felt my pulse and asked me what had frightened me: the Big Thing.
> And when they got the doctor and he came and spoke to me, I begged him
> only to make the Big Thing go away, nothing else mattered. But he was like
> the rest. He could not take it away. . . . And now it was there again. (Rilke
> 1910: 58–59)

As Malte grew older, the phobia receded from his consciousness. But
in Paris it was suddenly returning, swelling up from within him.

> It grew out of me like a tumor, like a second head, and was a part of me. . . .
> It was there like a huge, dead beast, that had once, when it was still alive,
> been my hand or my arm. And my blood flowed both through me and
> through it, as if through one and the same body. (Rilke 1910: 59)

As the anxiety of this menace recurs, each of Malte's days becomes
like "a dial without hands." His most repressed fears become magnified by hallucination—the fear, for example,

> that this little button on my night-shirt may be bigger than my head, big
> and heavy . . . the fear that if I fell asleep I might swallow the piece of coal
> lying in front of the stove . . . the fear that I may betray myself and tell all
> that I dread; and the fear that I might not be able to say anything, because
> everything is beyond utterance. (Rilke 1910: 60–61)

Finally the Big Thing turns into dread pure and simple, a faceless
anxiety provoked not by anything in particular but by something
"unheard-of," something which can impinge on the soul whenever it

---

Good studies of Rilke's *Notebooks* or his general aesthetic include Claude David,
"Rilke et l'expressionisme," *Études Germaniques* 17, no. 2 (April–June 1962): 144–157;
Hartmut Engelhardt, ed., *Materialen zu Rainer Maria Rilkes "Die Aufzeichnungen des
Malte Laurids Brigge"* (Frankfurt am Main: Suhrkamp, 1984); Walter Falk, *Leid und
Verwandlung: Rilke, Kafka, Trakl und der Epochenstil des Impressionismus und Ex-
pressionismus* (Salzburg: O. Müller, 1961); Ulrich Fülleborn, "Form und Sinn der *Auf-
zeichnungen des Malte Laurids Brigge*," in *Deutsche Romantheorien*, ed. Reinhold Grimm
(Frankfurt am Main: Athenäum, 1968), 251–273; Erich Heller 1975, 1981; Ernst Fëdor
Hoffmann, "Zum dichterischen Verfahren in Rilkes 'Aufzeichnungen des Malte Laurids
Brigge,'" *in Deutsche Vierteljahrsschrift für Literaturwissenschaft und Geistesgeschichte*
42 (1968): 202–230; Wilhelm Loock, *Rainer Maria Rilke: "Die Aufzeichnungen des
Malte Laurids Brigge"* (Munich: Oldenbourg, 1971); Frances Mary Scholz, "Rilke, Rodin
and the Fragmented Man," in Baron 1982: 27–44; William Small, *Rilke: Kommentar
zu den "Aufzeichnungen des Malte Laurids Brigge"* (Chapel Hill: University of North
Carolina Press, 1983); Sokel 1980.

chooses (Rilke 1910: 62). It is that new twentieth-century emotion called angst—as ancient, no doubt, as existence itself, but collectively perceptible only in the new cultural conditions. It is the shadow of ni-hilism, the ailment of an age that feels stripped of the purposes in which it once was clothed, left to stare at the nudity of each of its acts. A sickness with "no particular characteristics," it "takes on those of the person it attacks [and] drags out of each his deepest danger . . . and sets it before him again, quite near, imminent" (Rilke 1910: 60).

It is a feeling or mood that arises when one grapples with that recurring problem of the *Notebooks* which are walls: severing one per-son from another, fragmenting both inner and outer experience, dis-connecting lives that are motivated neither from within nor from with-out. One of the most remarkable pages of the *Notebooks* dramatizes the conflict between such lives and the pressures attempting to efface them.[20] As Malte stops on a street to observe the remnants of houses that are partially demolished, he notes that their walls, their nails, and their floorings have been unable to shake off these lives, and now show them as fossils still alive in their death:

> But most unforgettable of all were the walls themselves. The stubborn life of these rooms had not let itself be trampled out. It was still there; it clung to the nails that had been left, it stood on the remaining handsbreadth of flooring, it crouched under the corner joints where there was still a little bit of interior. One could see that it was in the paint, which, year by year, it had slowly altered: blue into moldy green, green into grey, and yellow into an old, stale rotting white. But it was also in the spots that had kept fresher, behind mirrors, pictures, and wardrobes; for it had drawn and redrawn their contours, and had been with spiders and dust even in these hidden places that now lay bared. . . . And from these walls once blue and green and yellow . . . the breath of these lives stood out—the clammy, sluggish, musty breath which no wind had scattered. There stood the middays and the sicknesses and the exhaled breath and the smoke of years, and the sweat that breaks out under armpits and makes clothes heavy. . . . (Rilke 1910: 47–48)

---

20. Interestingly enough it is the same page of the *Notebooks* that so impressed Mar-tin Heidegger that he cited the passage in its entirety in *The Basic Problems of Phe-nomenology*, trans. Albert Hofstadter (Bloomington: Indiana University Press, 1982): 172–173. "What the exciting years between 1910 and 1914 meant for me," writes Heidegger, "cannot be adequately expressed; I can only indicate it by a selective enumer-ation: the second, significantly enlarged edition of Nietzsche's *The Will to Power*, the works of Kierkegaard and Dostoevsky in translation, the awakening of interest in Hegel and Schelling, Rilke's works and Trakl's poems, Dilthey's *Collected Writings*" (Heideg-ger 1957: 22).

And it is this life that artists like Rilke feel called on to salvage, precisely in these imaginative visions; it is the life that Michelstaedter was not able to salvage, at least not in his prose, overwhelmed as he was by the thought of its absence. His *Persuasion and Rhetoric* dramatizes the battle that life is losing more than the expanse of just what is lost.

"Is it possible," asks Malte, that "all realities are nothing" to the people who surround him in Paris? Is it possible that "their life is running down, unconnected with anything, like a clock in an empty room—?" "Yes," he answers, "it is possible." Is it possible that they still bandy about words like "community," "women," "children," and "boys," while it is so evident that "these words have long since had no plural, but only countless singulars? Yes, it is possible" (Rilke 1910: 29).

The animus of the contemporary metropolis destroys not only the *Gemeinschaft* of social relations, it also obliterates its symbols, its nourishment, and its places of dwelling. Museums, once intended as houses of tradition and communicated experience, are now structures where people go merely to "warm themselves." Malte tries to avoid these places, walking without aim: "I kept on the move incessantly. Heaven knows through how many towns, districts, cemeteries, bridges, and passage-ways" (Rilke 1910: 46). Rather than a center of habitation, the modern city is composed of cemeteries, bridges, and passage-ways: places of death and transition. The social abode has become the necropolis of what could have been. The place and the symbol with which Malte identifies the vitality of his childhood is his grandfather's house. When he tries to call it to mind he finds it "all broken up inside me . . . all dispersed within me." Even the spiral staircase, the very emblem of fluid continuity, in whose obscurity he used to move as effortlessly "as blood does in the veins," has not been spared (Rilke 1910: 30).

The syndrome is not changed by noting that Rilke's descriptions of the city are not accurate or "objective" assessments, but ghastly, distorted, and imaginative ones, saying more about Malte's frame of mind than about any truly external state of affairs. It changes nothing, for the distortion of the vision itself is already proof of the broken continuity of subjective and objective worlds. True, the subject of Malte's meditation on his grandfather's house is the disjunctiveness of subjective memory; but it is presented as the internal effect of a fragmented outer reality, the result of a contagion. The entire first part of the *Notebooks* is about this detachment of selves from a living, objective order. The "Big Thing" has assumed institutional power, running both cities and the organisms inhabiting them, producing a zombification that spreads from green, sick babies to speechless, clairvoyant phantoms, eternally on the lookout for characters who share their knowledge.

Malte encounters them periodically. At one moment he notices a tall, emaciated man in a dark overcoat who stumbles over something invisible. When Malte observes the situation more carefully, he sees that there is nothing there at all. This man was stumbling over nothing. "There was nothing there, absolutely nothing" (Rilke 1910: 63). And yet, this nothing has an undeniably palpable effect. The "horrible, bisyllabic hopping" with which the man walks climbs up from his legs to his neck. "From that moment," Malte thinks, "I was bound to him. I understood that this hopping impulse was wandering about his body, trying to break out here and there" (Rilke 1910: 65). It was an overwhelming, irrepressible anxiety, on the verge of taking his life.

Hard as it is to imagine grislier images of human degradation than these, they exist in great concentration at the very moment that Rilke is writing (in the visual art of Käthe Kollwitz, Alfred Kubin, the early Paul Klee, and Kokoschka). But the most striking examples may lie in the portraits of Egon Schiele, which do not belong on the cover of paperback editions of Robert Musil's *The Man Without Qualities* so much as on *The Notebooks of Malte Laurids Brigge*.

The progression in Schiele's own representations of death almost replicates his own biographical itinerary. First he shows death as creeping out of the body, later he allegorizes it as a powerful outside force. By 1918 he himself has died of the European epidemic of Spanish fever, at age twenty-eight. Early in his career, when Schiele is still under the spell of Gustave Klimt, his human figures are coextensive with an outside space, even if this space is projected by the figure rather than existing on its own. By 1910 he places the subjects of his portraits against the background of a stark and empty void. Dramatically organic and psychosomatic, human figures have been cut off from all contexts to suffer their intrinsic decay.

In portraits of this year—of Erwin von Graff, Karl Zakovsek, Max Oppenheimer, Arthur Roessler, Eduard Kosmack, and Herbert Rainer—one is struck above all by the portrayal of the hands, the members of the body through which the subject makes contact with the external world, fastening onto things solid, grasping and taking possession of

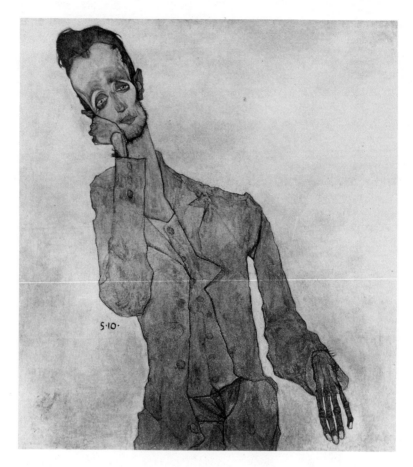

Fig. 9. Egon Schiele, *Portrait of the Painter Karl Zakovsek*, 1910, oil and charcoal. Courtesy Galerie St. Etienne, New York.

objects of desire. These hands are emaciated to the bone. The flesh that clings to them has withdrawn to the point of showing the skeleton. If there is any "will to live" in these clinging instruments it is a dying proposition. With their knuckles and nails protruding, long and thin, these hands of the living are the hands of death. They are attached, in turn, to unnaturally extended arms, protruding in paralytic gestures as though the sitters were subjected to arcane rituals of punishment. The left arm of Karl Zakovsek is extended in a crablike bend, resting upon nothing. One of his shoulders is three times as broad as the other, suggesting the pressure of an invisible weight. The remaining, peglike arm props up the head. More dramatic than the arms are the colors and shapes of the eyes and heads. These organs of vision are bulging, puffy, shut tight or transfixed—defiant, dejected, or forlorn. They glare at something distant, perhaps something even beyond the realm of the visible. They peer forth from bodies reclaimed by an "end" they have not yet reached, from faces cognizant of the oppression they cannot stop. The flesh is excessively pale or excessively dark, lacking blood in one case, life-moisture in another. Max Oppenheimer's face is green-yellow, like the children of Rilke's *Notebooks,* expanding in patches. Each of these subjects is an object, prey to an imponderably malicious, anonymous will.

In other portraits of this year, including many self-portraits, Schiele denudes the body altogether. Gesticulating, grimacing, writhing, or screaming, it seems to be acted upon by foreign and dehumanizing laws (fig. 24). Its veins and muscles burst the skin that contains them, in a manner first developed by Kokoschka. Later paintings personify the culprit, sometimes standing across or behind the main subject. In the self-portraits it tends to peer over Schiele's shoulder, claiming responsibility for the anxiety that haunts him (fig. 25). Elsewhere it embraces mothers and nuns. The children born from such unions have hollow and pallid features, with dark holes for eyes, like stillborns or puppets.

As with Rilke, Lukács, and Michelstaedter, it is difficult to sort out the difference between the psychological, metaphysical, and sociopolitical determinants of these depictions. Schiele focuses his art on the subjective experience of a psychosomatic deficiency abstracted from its surrounding objects and actions. As is clear, however, from his impulse to allegorize his subjects, something strangely universal is at work in this subjective experience, so universal that it cannot be separated from the objective conditions in which it is clothed. The body as it appears in Schiele is always an image of the historical *res,* if not of its incoherence, the image of a life riddled with forces it admits that it cannot control. Such an image is possible only after the spirit is reinscribed in the body, or subjects in objectivity, by modern philosophy, psychology, and anthropology. "Behind your thoughts and feelings, my brother, there stands a mighty ruler, an unknown sage—whose name is self. In your body he dwells; he is your body" (Nietzsche 1883–85: 146). By the beginning of the twentieth century, the spirit had been cast as libido, the instincts, or sheer will to power, bearing witness to a buried, impersonal, and autonomous self more sensitive to the creative and destructive forces of organic life than to rational purposes. By 1910 even the ostensible will to live was hardly to be separated from the body's own will to death. (The twenty-five-year-old Sabina Spielrein seems to have been the first to articulate the paradox in the context of professional psychology. Her findings, published under the title "Destruction as a Cause of Coming into Being" [1912], were presented to Freud in 1911 and shaped as early as 1910: "Secretly," she notes on October 19, 1910, "my new study, 'On the Death Instinct' is taking shape within me" [Spielrein 1909–12: 29].)[21]

The paintings of Schiele and other prewar expressionists reveal as much anxiety in the face of the deficiencies of physical reality as the writings of Michelstaedter, Simmel, Lukács, and Worringer. Schiele, too, makes occasional attempts to relate this deficiency to socioeconomics, as in the autobiographical poem "I, Eternal Child," which distinguishes the potential vitality of innermost subjectivity from the living death of commodified, institutional relations:

> Some say: money is bread. Others affirm: money is a commodity. Still others: money is life.—Who, however, dares say: Money, are you?—A product? . . . Oh, the lively living thing! (Schiele 1921: 49; Nebehay 1979: 163–164)[22]

Thus philosophical speculations on the deficiencies of everyday life in 1910 find support in pictorial depictions of the sufferings, confusions,

---

21. The theories of Spielrein might even help illuminate the suicides of the three women discussed at the beginning of this chapter. "A woman who abandons herself to passion," she claims "experiences all too soon its destructive aspect." There may be something in the way that women love that reveals this love to be inherently at odds with its surface interest. "One must imagine oneself as being somewhat outside bourgeois customs to understand the feeling of enormous insecurity which overtakes a person who entrusts himself or herself unconditionally to fate. To be fruitful means to destroy oneself" (Spielrein 1912: 466).

On Spielrein's anticipation of Freud's theory of the death instinct see Carotenuto 1982: 192, and Marthe Robert, *The Psychoanalytic Revolution,* trans. Kenneth Morgan (New York: Harcourt, Brace, and World, 1966): 330–331. On the reactions of Freud's Psychoanalytic Society to Spielrein's thesis, see *Minutes of the Vienna Psychoanalytical Society,* vol. 3: *1911–1918,* ed. Herman Nunberg and Ernst Federn, trans. M. Nunberg (New York: International Universities Press, 1967): 330 n. 4; Sigmund Freud, *Beyond the Pleasure Principle,* in *The Standard Edition of the Complete Psychological Works of Sigmund Freud,* trans. and ed. James Strachey (London: Hogarth Press and the Institute of Psycho-Analysis, 1953–1974), vol. 18: 55; and *The Freud/Jung Letters: The Correspondence Between Sigmund Freud and C. G. Jung,* ed. William McGuire, trans. Ralph Manheim and R. F. C. Hull. Bollingen Series XCIV (Princeton: Princeton University Press, 1974): 447.

22. This and other selections of Schiele in English (rendered differently) are included in Egon Schiele, *I, Eternal Child: Paintings and Poems,* trans. Anselm Hollo (New York: Grove Press, 1985): 6–8.

and anxieties of the body, the most obvious token for the historical determination of the spirit.

COSMIC GUILT

Nowhere does this anxiety take on a broader configuration than in the poetry of Trakl, the great genius of negativity, the "seer" of the epochal, spiritual death alluded to by his contemporaries when they reflect on mortality, decay, and decline. What concerns this poet of the night is not merely the horror or decrepitude of the body, not the rhetorical evasions of mortality or the rationalized death of industrialized citizens. It is a sickness built into the very order of being. Whatever the cause of this sickness, Trakl suggests, it can hardly be cured by knowledge, institutions, or social decisions. Politics and morality can do nothing to change it; it lies in the stars, in birth, in the predatory nature of life itself. Death is no more than its mask.

This sickness is known by its symptoms, recurring in the young man's verse: the green corruption of the flesh; blood and fever; icy winds and audible walls; lepers, cripples, and whores; people not yet born or deceased too soon; evening, night, and winter. Its motifs include estrangement, murder, silence, paralysis, fear, lament, holiness, transcendence, and rebirth. The titles that name it are "Winter Twilight," "All Souls Day," "The Wanderer," "De Profundis," "Decline," "Spiritual Twilight," "The Cursed," "Amen," "Rest and Silence," "To Those Grown Mute," "The Autumn of the Lonely One," "Human Sadness," "Dream and Derangement." Wherever we turn in this poetry we find the narrative of a fall from grace, a dissolution of soul into matter, a debasement of nature and childhood. In Trakl's mythology of cosmic malignance, the sublunary world is inhabited by evil angels. Love cannot be distinguished from hate. Madness, disease, and corruption are signs of a living conspiracy from which one can be redeemed only by expiation.

"Bitter is death," writes the poet, "the fare of the guilt-laden" (Trakl 1969: 150). Death is the "fare" (*Kost*), the means of sustenance, of those who are culpable. And who are these guilty ones? They are all who have existed and have yet to exist, including animals, for death spares none. Death itself is not the evil, but a manifestation of the evil, a symptom as it were of the crime. "Great is the guilt of the born" (Trakl 1969: 114, 1988: 64–65). In a poem of 1909 Trakl gives a name to this inbred existential guilt: "Blutschuld." Literally "blood-guilt," or "a crime of the blood," the title stands above lines that seem to refer so directly to Trakl's alleged incest with his sister that the editors of the first collection of his poems did not include the composition (Trakl 1969: 249). And yet it is a significance larger than "incest" in *Blutschuld* which resounds most strongly in Trakl's verse—the sense of *Blutschuld* as a criminality built into the blood from the start. Blood-guilt, Trakl's poetry reiterates, pervades the universe. This, if anything, explains the self-immolation and derangement of those few martyric figures who perceive it. Not just incest and murder, but sex and the very struggle for survival rehearse this violent depravity of organic existence.[23] Here Spielrein's "Destruction as a Cause of Coming into Being" is more explicit: "The reproductive instinct . . . is equally an instinct of birth and one of destruction" (Spielrein 1912: 503).

This sense of the violence and depravity of sex, stretching all the way up from the Christian theology of original sin to Schopenhauer's pessimistic metaphysics, reaches its culmination in Weininger's *Sex and Character.*[24] Weininger presents sex, or *Geschlecht*, as a fatality delimiting the very possibilities of spiritual achievement. In Trakl the word becomes as generic as every term he uses. Beyond the gender, sexuality, or copulative activity of creatures, it refers to their "creaturality," to their participation in the cycle of procreation. *Geschlecht* means the very principle at work in generation, including every "race of the begotten." Nearly everywhere the principle can be reduced to its opposite.

Trakl refers to *Geschlecht* five times in "Dream and Derangement," the poem equating death with the fare of the guilt-laden. The long prose poem opens with a boy, a figure for the poet, weighed down by "the curse of the degenerated race" [*der Fluch des entarteten Geschlechts*]. His hard father is now an old man and his mother has turned to stone. Twice the poet remarks on the curse of *Geschlecht*, both times in the context of a sexual scene: "O the accursed race. When, in defiled rooms, each such destiny is accomplished, death enters with mouldering steps into the house." The second mention is at the poem's end,

23. For an analysis of the poem "Blutshuld" see Sharp 1981: 59–62. On the associations between sin, guilt, and blood in Trakl's verse see Michel-François Demet, "Georg Trakl: Blood, the Mirror, the Sister," in Williams, ed., 1991: 167–190.
24. On Trakl's reading of Weininger, see Alfred Doppler, "Georg Trakl und Otto Weininger," *Peripherie und Zentrum: Studien zur österreichischen Literatur,* ed. Gerlinde Weiss and Klaus Zelewitz (Salzburg: Das Bergland-Buch, 1971): 43–54, and Sharp 1981: 53.

when, battered by "stony solitude," the boy is escorted by a dead man into the "dark house" of the father. Upon the arrival of the "sister," and the hint of an incestuous act, death and voluptuousness come together, revealing their bond:

> Purpurne Wolke umwölkte sein Haupt, daß er schweigend über sein eigenes Blut und Bildnis herfiel, ein mondenes Antlitz; steinern ins Leere hinsank, da in zerbrochenem Spiegel, ein sterbender Jüngling, die Schwester erschien; die Nacht das verfluchte Geschlecht verschlang.

> [A crimson cloud clouded his head so that he fell silently upon his own blood and likeness, a lunar face; stonily he sank down into emptiness, when in the broken mirror, a dying youth, the sister appeared; the night devoured the accursed race.] (Trakl 1969: 150; trans. Sharp 1981: 219)

Earlier in the poem Trakl had described this degenerative *Geschlecht* in terms reaching back to a primordial human family: "fruit and tools fell from the horrified race. A wolf tore the firstborn to pieces and the sisters fled into dark gardens to bony old men." The poet cannot suppress his cry: "O the voluptuousness of death. O you children of a dark race" (Trakl 1969: 149; Sharp 1981: 217).The generic language of the poem makes it impossible to associate the guilt of *Geschlecht* with only one family or only one group of acts. Rather, it refers to the transhistorical *origin* of the family, even to the voluptuous death of all spiritual concerns in rapacious, beastly behavior.

Is it any surprise, then, that Trakl chooses to cultivate the myth of unbornness? He recalls the ancient Greek saying of Menander, recommending the speediest of deaths, assuming one lacks the good fortune never to have been born at all. Figures so graced do exist in Trakl's poetry, especially Elis, the legendary boy buried in a mine, and Caspar Hauser, who was alleged to have spent the first seventeen years of his life chained to the wall of a dungeon-like room, only to be murdered by a stranger soon after seeing the light of day.[25] Shortly before his suicide, Trakl is reported to have said that he was only "half-born" and did not want to see his birth completed.[26] Did he mean that the blood-guilt of the generative-degenerate *Geschlecht* had not possessed him fully? Or that he was only half willing to accept the horror of aging in pursuit of lust and power? His other half would then have lived among those who refused to live by such rules, and whose refusal meant

---

25. The eighteenth-century mystery of Caspar Hauser was fictionalized by the Viennese novelist Jakob Wassermann in 1908.

26. Hans Limbach, "Begegnung mit Georg Trakl," *Erinnerung an Georg Trakl: Zeugnisse und Briefe* (Salzburg: Otto Müller, 1966), 121–122.

death. Michelstaedter entertained a similar notion, frequently returning in his writings to the ancient Greek wisdom that the truly blessed
of the gods are those who die young.

Never so much as at the beginning of the twentieth century, states
Trakl's poetry, have the degenerate effects of *Geschlecht* been felt so
starkly. It is now—and not in every possible historical world—that one
hears the lament of the "solitary grandchild," the spokesman for countless generations. It is now, in the forlorn present, that the gods have
been ravaged, that faces appear speechless and stones fall silent. It is in
Trakl's own time that "the spirit of evil peers out of white masks" and
the "self-spilt blood gushes forth from the heart" (Trakl 1969: 68, 29,
97; Sharp 1981: 212). As a "muter mankind bleeds silently," whores
give birth to dead infants (Trakl 1969: 124, 1988: 81). The term *Geschlecht* weds Trakl's vision of ontological destitution to an indict-
ment of that cultural history which the early twentieth century called
the *Abendland,* the West, the land of the declining sun, playing out its
twilight.

Indeed, twilight pervades the only language a poet of this era can
speak. Like the boy in "Dream and Derangement," he is the voluntary
victim of the epoch in which he lives. "Silvery shimmer the evil blossoms of blood on his temple, the cold moon in his shattered eyes." Thus
Trakl, the child of a dark race, cannot but be a "deranged seer," announcing the "unspeakable guilt" of his own "cool grave" (Trakl 1969:
148–149; Sharp 1981: 216–217). The vision of degeneration and decline increases steadily from the idyllic struggles of Trakl's early poems
to the terror and regret of the final ones. His entire poetic corpus is a
"Song of the Departed One," as the title reads to the penultimate section of the last collection he composed, *Sebastian im Traum* (1915).
The poet of *Blutschuld* can find no redemption except in voicing his
resistance to existence.

If such an individual isolates himself in modern society, Trakl writes
to a friend, it is "because he prefers to be dissolute rather than inau-
thentic. I anticipate world catastrophes, I take no part, I am not a revolutionary. I am the departed one, in my epoch I have no choice but
that of pain" (Letter to Johannes Klein, cited by Magris 1983: vii). The
present is a "bitter hour of decline, / when in black waters we gaze at
a stony face" (Trakl 1969: 119). If "we" are here cast in the role of
Narcissus, then the self-knowledge we obtain from our surroundings
(in the image reflected by the waters) is that these surroundings have
acted as Medusa, turning us to stone. Our spokesman, the poet, folds

in on himself and his participatory guilt, acquiescing in the derangement of his final *Umnachtung*. Nothing positive can be uttered in a
night without revelation. Like Ludwig Meidner, with his *Apocalyptic
Landscapes* of 1912–13, Trakl imagines himself to be the representative of a world at its end. His silence can speak only in the vocative
mood, appealing to the consciousness of need.

IMPOTENCE

Instead of offering the metaphoric shelters of the benighted poet,
Michelstaedter speaks discursively—in syllogisms and axioms, philo-
sophically explaining the pain, sterility, and impotence expressed by
Trakl. The most dauntless theoretician of the deficiency of being also
reaps guilt from this deficiency, projecting it onto the cosmos. Death,
for him, is not merely Simmel's prerequisite for the conduct of life. It is
not Lukács's feature of actual, contemporary existence when measured
by a utopian ideal, or Trakl's metaphor for spiritual corruption. It is
these and more. As well as the only positive truth of life.

We have seen Michelstaedter argue that the flight from death governs the most banal, everyday decisions. He characterizes everything
mortals do as a conscious repression of their itinerary toward non-
being. By fastening their will on the "life" they lack at any particular
moment, they transform their present into absence and perpetual death.
This is the *"continuous deficiency . . . which everything that lives is
persuaded is life"* (Michelstaedter 1910: 43). Vitalism, desire, or *philopsychia,* the love of life, becomes for Michelstaedter the very source
of death. The constitutive deficiency of experience is never filled by
the satisfactions and achievements to which we direct our attention.
These apparent accomplishments only mask the universal and ubiquitous pain, the "dull and continuous grief [*dolore*]" that "seethes beneath all things" and "unites all things that live" (Michelstaedter 1910:
55, 57, 59). The truth is experienced when the thread of one's illusory
pleasures suddenly snaps:

> As when, in the dimming of the light of one's room, the image of one's inti-
> mate things . . . becomes more tenuous, and the invisible grows more visi-
> ble, just so, when the woof [*trama*] of illusion becomes more thin, unrav-
> eled, or torn, humans, *made impotent,* feel themselves in the throes of what
> *lies beyond their power, of what they do not know: they fear without know-
> ing what they fear.* (Michelstaedter 1910: 56)

Michelstaedter's *dolore,* like that of Malte, is an objectless anxiety: One fears without knowing what one fears. When the fabric of one's pleasures is rent (but *trama* also means plot, the false continuity of a life story) one cannot single out a particular thing to redress. The invisible *grows* more visible: Not an absence of visibility, but the absence itself comes into sight.

The pain consists in recognizing that one is prey to "what lies beyond one's power." What is it that Michelstaedter imagines to be beyond one's power? The adversity and contingency of fate? A demonic principle? Or is it the permanent possibility of impotence itself, the risk of not achieving the power one covets, as though this were the real obscurity that made all pleasure flicker? Impotence is a more primordial condition than any that occurs in historical experience. While power is necessarily limited, impotence is potentially infinite (Michelstaedter 1910: 61). Obscurity, impotence, and pain are more "positive" than any of the forces they contest, a positive negativity underlying whatever we might construct. Is this a specious argument or does Michelstaedter just take a truism to an extreme that few thinkers would be willing to accept? In essence his position radicalizes Schopenhauer's idea that we never really feel the overall health of our body (the positive), but only the spot where the shoe pinches (the negative). Suffering, not joy, is the prime mover of action. If this is so, then the only practical question is how large this negativity can loom if we fail to contain it.

Michelstaedter allows it free rein. He speaks, for example, of what happens to children when they are subject to boredom and their attention is not firmly held by outside things (the condition of *noia*). They eventually "find themselves *looking at the darkness* with their little minds." And the darkness becomes peopled with menacing, humanoid figures, with eyes and ears, with arms that clasp at the small creatures "with a thousand hands," making them "flee madmen in terror, and shriek in order to deaden their senses" (Michelstaedter 1910: 57). Given the imaginative force of this description, it will come as no surprise that Michelstaedter himself was terrified of the darkness as a child. "It was I," writes his sister Paula, "who made him overcome his instinctive fear of the darkness by closing him in a dark room, and made him overcome his fear of storms by dragging him onto the terrace during lightning and thunder" (Winteler 1973: 149). As an adult Carlo still remarks on the "threatening darkness" outside his window, explaining in a poem to his sister on her birthday, two months before his suicide,

in an airtight place dissolves when exposed to the open" (Michelstaedter 1910: 58–59).

This final "improvisation" overturns common sense in the most unabashed of ways. It likens open-air, daylight activity to existence in an airtight coffin. What appears to be a living, historical person—the one of waking hours—is only a mummy. The *real* open air—from which we try to conserve our lives—is darkness, non-being, nothingness. This is the reality that threatens the corpse. Everyday zombies are thus doubly unfortunate: their empirical lives are walking deaths, while the true life they encounter in vacancy, obscurity, and dread does them in for good. The same reversals of life and death recur in Michelstaedter's poetry.

It is difficult not to read this fear of impotence of which Michelstaedter speaks in terms of fear of historical others, if not of all things outside the self-contained subject. We can recall another "improvisation," this time a parable. Hydrogen and chlorine, when they come into the proximity of each other, show an innate compulsion to join (Michelstaedter anthropomorphizes the valences of these elements, as he does the gravitation of the weight). But what happens when these elements achieve the union for which they pine? They lose their separate, independent natures, forming the noxious new compound, hydrochloric acid. The "love" by which they are moved is "a lethal embrace," a murder and suicide for the sake of a debilitating union. Just as these elements live for "death," comments Michelstaedter, "so their love is hate" (Michelstaedter 1910: 47).

The main purpose of this simile is to convey the deadly implications of a life that cannot stand on its own two feet. But why does Michelstaedter use an erotic metaphor to describe the union of chemicals? What light does this rhetoric shed on his own persuasion? The "lethal pleasure of the embrace" recurs throughout *Persuasion and Rhetoric,* as though Michelstaedter, like Weininger, Schiele, Freud, and Kokoschka, was unable to steer clear of the sexual unease of his age. One remembers, for example, that he personifies rhetoric as a demon of pleasure: the god of *philopsychia,* pandering illusory pleasures that only distance ourselves from ourselves. The cadaver that rots in the air of insecurity is the demonic result of the pleasure principle.

The identification of impotence and insecurity with the pursuit of pleasure is common to Michelstaedter's time. Just a year after the Italian's suicide, the psychoanalyst Alfred Adler breaks with Freudian doctrine on similar grounds. He rereads the "will to pleasure" not as a primary interest, but a secondary one, a response to universal and congenital insecurity. We seek pleasure or power to compensate for conditions of incompleteness and privation from which we can never be free. And yet, for Adler as for Nietzsche before him, there is nothing intrinsically unhealthy in this primordial deficiency of being. Unhealthy are the elaborate ploys to which we resort in order to *deny* this privative state, whether by fleeing from the risks run in satisfying it or by cultivating illusions of self-sufficiency. In the light of Adler, one is compelled to ask whether Michelstaedter, too, wants to flee from the insecurity that he spies in the everyday operations of life. The love of life, in him, is insecurity itself, and his first reaction is to battle this love. His equation of eros and impotence becomes a strategy to repress his own desire, an admission that he does not know how to establish a system of reciprocities that would enable him to overcome his alienation. The "impotence" is not the *effect* of the outside world; it is the effect of having no means—no language, no mode of behavior—*by which to affect* that outside world. The desire for bonds goes unappeased.

Both Campailla and Bini have noted that Michelstaedter's Florentine studies in the nude avoid representing the genitals. We also find sexual transpositions in his paintings, as in the watercolor of his father ascending to heaven in a feminine pose and dress (fig. 10). To illustrate the effects of *philopsychia* Michelstaedter calls on sexual metaphors. The word *amplesso* ("embrace," a euphemism for copulation) appears not only in his description of the union of hydrogen and chlorine but also in his account of the symbiosis of bee and flower: "In the bee the flower sees the propagation of its pollen, in the flower the bee sees sweet food for its larvae. In the two organisms' embrace each sees in the other's disposition 'its own self as in a mirror'" (Michelstaedter 1910: 63). What Michelstaedter finds grotesque in this "reciprocal love" is that it is merely a mask of self-interest. The situation is further complicated by the fact that this self-interest is actually an illusory one: the seeming egocentricity by which the flower or the bee says "yes" to its lover only in order to affirm itself turns out to be "ego-eccentric," for each loves the other out of desire for an offspring outside the two. And this is a rhetorical form of self-affirmation, a shirking of solitude. The "selfish" interest in propagating the species is just a knee-jerk reaction to death.

Such eros is *anteros,* transforming subjects into objects and ends into means (Michelstaedter 1910: 63). A participant in the erotic relation never asks whether its self-affirmation enables the self-affirmation

Fig. 10. Carlo Michelstaedter, *Assumption II*, no date, watercolor and pencil. Courtesy Gorizia Civic Library, Gorizia.

of the other, "or whether, instead, it does not take away [the other's] future—whether it kills it. Each only knows that this [act] is good for itself, and makes use of the other as a means toward its own ends, as material for its own life, while at the same time it too is a material means to the life of the other." And so out of "reciprocal need" the affirmation of illusory individuality "takes on the appearance of love." Instead of eros "it is a travesty of *neichos*"—contention, strife, or battle (Michelstaedter 1910: 63).

By 1910 the association between sexuality and death had already been 2,000 years in the making. It was beginning to call for resolution. The matrix of the problem had been articulated in Schopenhauer's supplement to the Fourth Book of *The World as Will and Representation,* "The Metaphysics of the Loves of the Sexes" (1844), arguing that erotic attraction was the expression of a blind metaphysical compulsion towards procreation which no higher or rational force can hope to withstand. Moreover, there was no individualism in either the act of sex or the choices it made; it was merely the "genius of the species"—not of individuals—that was voicing its will in *Geschlecht.* But Schopenhauer himself was already elaborating on Kant, who had viewed sexual interaction as nothing more than "the reciprocal use made by one person of the sexual organs and faculties of another." Marriage is the institutionalization of this reciprocal use, a "union of two people of different sexes with a view to the mutual possession of each other's sexual attributes for the duration of their lives."[28] More recently, Michelstaedter's generation had Nietzsche's philosophy on which to base their sense of the *anteros* involved in eros: "Has my definition of love been heard? It is the only one worthy of a philosopher. Love—in its means, war; at bottom, the deadly hatred of the sexes" (Nietzsche 1908: 723).[29] And this notion, in turn, was linked to Richard Wagner's *Liebestod* and to the battle of the sexes in Bizet's *Carmen,* and received further elaboration in the Pre-Raphaelites, Gabriele D'An-

28. Immanuel Kant, *Metaphysik der Sitten* (1797), ed. Karl Vorländer (Hamburg: Felix Meiner, 1966), 91.

29. The most dramatic expression of the erotic antagonism occurs in Kokoschka's short play *Murderer, the Hope of Women,* where, upon sight, a man and a woman attack each other in a battle to the death. See Kokoschka 1907 and Bettina Knapp, "Oskar Kokoschka's *Murderer, Hope of Womankind*: An Apocalyptic Experience," *Theatre Journal* 35 (May 1983): 179–194. On the intricacies of the masculine struggle with the feminine in turn-of-the-century Europe see Bram Dijkstra, *Idols of Perversity: Fantasies of Feminine Evil in Fin-de-Siècle Culture* (Oxford: Oxford University Press, 1986).

nunzio, August Strindberg, Franz Wedekind, and Jugendstil art of the early twentieth century.

In the years following Jugendstil, however, this clever idea of sexual strife becomes truly tormented. In Michelstaedter, Schoenberg, Kokoschka, Trakl, and Schiele sexuality faces up to the barrage of obstacles to its expression that had been accumulated over the course of two thousand years of Christian culture. And the confrontation proved cathartic, as we know from the "roaring twenties." But the situation was hardly as easy for those who enabled the catharsis. Before sexual energy could enjoy its freedom, homosexuality, misogyny, monogamy, propriety, guilt, and repression—in short, the question of what exactly was at stake in the sexual act—first had to be understood. The first phase of such understanding saw the questions being marshaled in consciousness. The second and more difficult phase—represented by Weininger, Trakl, Schiele, Michelstaedter, and Freud—sees the ranks of the wounded. Before sexuality can doff its connotations of victimization, depravity, and abuse, its martyrs will have been even more numerous.

One of the emblems of the prewar identification of love and hate is a hand-colored lithograph of Edvard Munch. *Loving Woman* depicts a contemporary image of *philopsychia*: a voluptuous, naked, demonic female with thick wild hair, in a gesture of sensual abandon. Frenzied sperm cells climb up and down the margins of the illustration. The fruit of the sexual union, however, is not life, but an incarnation of death, a stillborn fetus in the lower left corner, doomed from the very moment of conception. Extreme desire and revulsion are mixed in this vision, bespeaking the fear of losing one's life in eros. And that fear is exorcised by means of deathly equations. Sexual catharsis will not be complete until it has exorcised such demons, haunting the freedom for which it strives.

Egon Schiele has his own images of *philopsychia*, some reached for directly by the hand of death (*Female Nude*). But whose hand is this that reaches for the naked woman, her nose suggestive of a syphilitic infection? Is it the hand of death or is it Schiele's—which kills its object? Or is it just an image of the risks of reaching out, of the fears of doing so? "Our extremities, including our hands," writes Schoenberg, "serve to carry out our wishes, to express, to make manifest, that which does not have to remain inside. A fortunate hand operates externally, far outside our well-protected self—the farther it reaches, the farther it is from us" (Schoenberg 1988: 35; "A Lecture About *Die Glückliche*

Fig. 11. Edvard Munch, *Loving Woman (Madonna)*, 1895–1902, lithograph. Courtesy Munch Museum, Oslo.

Hand," 1928). The problem that is treated in Schiele's painting as in
Michelstaedter's compulsively erotic rhetoric is that of bridging the
gap between self and other, of *possessing* the nakedness of another. In
most of Schiele's paintings, if not this one, the nudity is of a shocking variety, directly countering the effort to aestheticize the object of
desire, frequently contrasting the overall beauty of the body with the

Fig. 12. Egon Schiele, *Female Nude*, 1910, watercolor and charcoal.
Courtesy Graphische Sammlung Albertina, Vienna.

Fig. 13. Egon Schiele, *Embrace (Lovers II)*, 1917, oil. Courtesy Öster-
reichische Galerie, Vienna.

coarse exposure of the pudenda. While Schiele's libidinal instincts are
admittedly stronger than Michelstaedter's, their expression is stifled,
nearly choked by the crudity of the pornographic. Both males and
females are brutalized, their gestures and poses aggressive. When a
woman does hold a man in Schiele, as in *The Embrace,* her deep and
lyrical allegiance is contrasted by the effort of her knees and elbows to
keep her lover at bay. The parts of the body one expects to see closest
are the ones at furthest remove. The woman's fingers are positioned as
scissors. This embrace is the desperate clasp of two suffering solitudes,
each terrified of being left alone.

The couplings in Schiele are failures. *Coitus* (1913) shows a female
posing for the viewer while her man, passive and awkward, gazes off
into a distant space, unable to rise to the occasion. Vibrant as sexuality may be in Schiele, it seems rarely to know its aim, much less the
steps to achieve it. In a self-portrait Schiele directly reproaches his
organ for not measuring up to the dimensions of his forearm, held
forward from an impossibly low joint. The axis of Schiele's neck par-
allels this subjugating ideal, bowed down as though for the guillo-
tine, in a confession of impotence. The portrait is appropriately called
the *Preacher* (1913): the spokesman for guilt. Schiele's most dramatic
scenes of sexuality are accordingly onanistic, as in *Seated Couple,* where
the woman laments the misguidance of the man whose affection she
seeks. With swollen red eyes she clasps him from behind, an unwilling

Fig. 14. Egon Schiele, *Seated Couple (Egon and Edith Schiele)*, 1915, gouache and pencil. Courtesy Graphische Sammlung Albertina, Vienna.

accessory to a stubborn exhibitionist who is bent on offending public decorum. Thus the ultimate result of the libinal urge is self-absorption, the energy folded back on itself (*Self-Portrait Masturbating*, 1911).

Self-absorption, on a more spiritual level, is also the result of the antierotic polemic in Michelstaedter. His solution to the impossible union of blossom and bee, or man and woman, is a life of free and autonomous individuality, of pure and unadulterated self-reliance. Persons who seek themselves instead of a means to themselves require an uncorrelative existence: Persuasion *"does not live in him who does not live on himself alone"* (Michelstaedter 1910: 42). Does it come as a surprise that Michelstaedter rejects actual, concrete love on the very same ground? The object of desire is Argia Cassini, in whom Carlo had invested much feeling in 1910. On one of the final days of his life, he addresses her in the most intransigent of metaphysical love poems. Its purpose: to explain why there is no reason whatsoever for him to bring his love to fruition:

> Parlarti? e pria che tolta per la vita
> mi sii, del tutto prenderti?—che giova?
> che giova, se del tutto io t'ho perduta
> quando mia tu non fosti il giorno stesso
> che c'incontrammo? . . .
>
> [Speak to you? and before you are taken from me
> for life, seize you completely?—for what reason?
> for what reason, if I lost you completely
> when, the day we first met,
> you were not mine?]
> (Michelstaedter 1987: 95)

The fact that Argia was not already his on the day that they met—that she was irremediably "other"—means that she was lost to him forever (for "life": for another, not living life). At best, to seize her completely would have been an injustice, at worst, an illusion. Even if he succeeded in winning her completely, Michelstaedter continues— "by means of your will," he adds, reaffirming his phobia of hetero-determination—Argia would never be fused with his being. If "I do not know / how to create your life from within my own," the poem concludes, the enterprise is doomed to fail (Michelstaedter 1987: 95–96).[30]

The words of Rilke in *The Notebooks of Malte Laurids Brigge* help illuminate the syndrome of Michelstaedter: an "unspeakable fear for the liberty of the other" made him yearn "to remove from [his] love all that was transitive" (Rilke 1910: 212, 208). If love is motivated by a self-interested desire for possession, neither subject nor object of love can do themselves justice. Indeed, this motivation cannot even abolish

---

30. Another poem to Argia proposes a more absolute, perhaps even literal, death over and beyond the "bitter" historical one of coupling (which provides illusory rest to those who are "dead by birth"): "the young death that smiles / to those who do not fear / death that does not separate / but unites man and woman / and does not press them with dark sorrow— / but receives them both in her womb, / as a harbor of peace receives him / who was able to sail / in the stormy sea, in the deserted sea, / and did not turn to land for comfort" (Michelstaedter 1987: 88–89; trans. Bini 1992: 168).

that difference between self and other at which it aims. For eros to be eros it must resist the suicide and murder of possession. The question then becomes the one that Lukács poses in *Soul and Form*: "Whom can I love in such a way that the object of my love will not stand in the way of my love?" (Lukács 1910–11a: 34). This is the question that causes his separation from Irma and nourishes the "work." Slataper too accepts an irremediable distance between self and other as the prerequisite for the expression of his subjective potential. "I cannot yet rest," he states ten months after Gioietta's death, "because I have not created a book." Whatever one might achieve short of this "is not work but the restlessness of impotence" (quoted by Stuparich 1950: 115). Love not sublimated into work—"transitive" love, fastened on an object—is self-dispossessing, a desperate disguise of deficiency.

Michelslaedter, Lukács, and Slataper eventually find a way to reinvest this love with such intransitive value that no single object can exhaust its attention. In the meantime, however, like Schiele, Kokoschka, and Schoenberg, they express misgivings about its everyday forms.[31] Attachment to another, and probably even *resistance* to such attachment (no longer "fear for the liberty of another," but fear for the liberty of oneself), is fear of impotence. And this is no avenue to self-possession—without which a person is no more than "a son and a father, and a slave and a master, of what surrounds him" (Michelstaedter 1910: 42). We do not need Hegel's pages on the master and slave dialectic to seize Michelstaedter's meaning. In the context of his argument about treating the other as a means rather than an end, his more immediate reference is probably Weininger. When a person "can only think of things as possessions," writes Janik, paraphrasing arguments in Weininger's posthumous *Ueber die letzten Dinge* (On Ultimate Things, 1904), "he relates to persons as master or servant, never as comrade" (Janik 1985: 72). And this is a sure way to lose the very autonomy one thinks one has, for where "there is no Thou there is certainly no I" (Weininger 1903: 180). Unless one acknowledges the separate independence of another, one cannot even begin to affirm one's own. In the context of Michelstaedter's work, however, one can also

---

31. The theme of love in a condition of solitude, of love in and despite mortality, pervades Schoenberg's work, especially *Erwartung* and *Transfigured Night*. Kokoschka's prototypical vision of distance in togetherness, which was probably the inspiration for Schiele's *Embrace*, is *The Tempest* (1914). Its real title, conceived by Trakl when, dressed in black and mourning the near death of his sister-lover, he silently watched Kokoschka complete it, is more revealing: *Bride of the Wind*. The phrase finds its way into Trakl's poem "The Night" (Trakl 1969: 160, 1988: 115).

turn Weininger's statement around, saying there can be no I where there *is* a Thou, for it is precisely this Thou that threatens the I.

LOSS OF SELF

The recurring antagonist in these philosophical, literary, and pictorial texts is oppression, repression, limitation, and decay. Figured in various prisons of the body, historical constraint, and social convention, objectification is the final opponent, threatening that bundle of intention, feeling, and thought that we call the self. In 1910 these forces seem all to explicitly conspire against the independence of subjectivity. In early twentieth-century culture "humans have been distanced, so to speak, from themselves," writes Simmel. "Between themselves and their most authentic, essential part there has been erected an insuperable barrier of instruments, technical conquests, capacities, and commodities" (Simmel 1907: 484). The casualty of this rhetorical network is the possibility of coinciding with one's inward nature. Even that metaphysics of "vitalism" which posits an unconscious and organic becoming beneath the rhetorical rigidifications of commodified culture has an analogous effect, leaving no point of reference upon which to construct a life one can call one's own. "Impressions do not take hold in my soul," writes Michelstaedter in 1905, aware of the risks of living a pure flux of becoming. "Every instant I feel as though I were another; I have lost the sense of the continuity of my I" (Michelstaedter 1958: 418–419). No identity can be properly affirmed in empirical change, says Lukács. In Trakl the pronoun I becomes impossible to pronounce. He must scratch it out of his poems and replace it with words like the "stranger" and "the departed one." If one can speak at all of something like the soul, one must say that it is *etwas Fremdes auf Erde*, "something strange on earth" (Trakl 1969: 141).

As the face of the Austrian poet turns stony, that of others suffers corrosion. At the corner of Notre-Dame-des-Champs, Malte observes a woman whom an external force has made to collapse into herself. Her face remains in her hands:

> I could see it lying in them, its hollow form. It cost me indescribable effort to stay with those hands and not to look at what had torn itself out of them. I shuddered to see a face from the inside, but still I was much more afraid of the naked flayed head without a face. (Rilke 1910: 16)

The objectified life of these metropolitan denizens does not merely render them faceless; it gives them faces that are not theirs, masks that are ridden with holes, withering and peeling away. And in time, "little by little, the under layer, the no-face, comes through." The alien life implodes. Even one's death is assigned by outside forces: "Voilà votre mort, monsieur." This completion of a life, which should have grown out of it in the manner of its innermost conclusion, is now an abstract event, belonging "to the diseases and not to the people." One dies in hospitals, and from one of the deaths "attached to the institution" (Rilke 1910: 15–18).

In the pestilent atmosphere of the *Notebooks* as well as *Persuasion and Rhetoric* "one has nothing and nobody." Malte drifts through the streets like "a sheet of blank paper." The deficiency of being robs all things that are not fully objective (physical, testable, or practically useful) of language, killing the very spirit that presumably gives them life. "I sit here and am nothing," Malte remarks. And yet in his recognition of nothingness Malte "begins to think" (Rilke 1910: 24, 66, 28). This seemingly casual step—by which a nothing begins to think—is of utmost importance. It almost suggests that the inner activity one *can* control begins only now, that thinking is *originated* by this experience of lifeless negativity, by this negative life, by this perception that the structures of historical being eclipse the very consciousness they were presumably designed to serve.

And what does this nothing think? It thinks, "I have an inner self of which I was ignorant. Everything goes thither now," to that inner, but unknown realm (Rilke 1910: 14–15). If thinking has a task in the face of the deficiency of being, it consists in constructing a means of revealing this unknown self, including an idea of humanity itself, its languages and truths, its nature and measures of knowledge. Thinking, in 1910, does not come to an end with a meditation on negativity; it is there that it begins, as a search for persuasion. It seeks form for what now seems to be the only alternative to lifeless being: "something strange on earth," lacking its own manner of expression.

The moment is reached when a confrontation with this voiceless subjectivity becomes the only promising project of life, the moment when, as Michelstaedter writes beneath his final self-portrait, "man lights a light for himself in the night" (Michelstaedter 1992: 444). The investment of hope in the innerness of the human being is the logical development of the dualistic thinking of 1910, where the scientific, industrial, and technological furtherance of "life" seems to have obliterated the real "thing-in-itself" and produced only phenomenal appearances. If value cannot be located in any solid objective facts then it would seem to reside in their opposite, or in that which this objectivity lacks: the motivations of soul, the inward interests of human beings—who rebel against their reification and strive to reestablish their autonomy, as though that were the only means of asserting a thing-in-itself. The deficiency of being reveals the need for another mode of *experiencing* being, and it appears to lie in self-experience. At the moment when nihilism reaches its culmination, something unprecedented happens on the plane of expression. An inner vacuum speaks out. "Let me go, Paula, into the night, to create a light for myself" (Michelstaedter 1987: 72).

The "death" haunting the characters of 1910 is thus double, beginning with the decrepit, intransigent rule of the physical and cultural body and then stifling the spirit. It is this spirit, or soul, that is done in by the zombification of rhetorical and material history. It is the soul that is trapped and silenced, recast as a function of its everyday practices. And the loss is a considerable one, for in the more than two thousand years of Western history that follow from Anaxagoras, Parmenides, and Protagoras, some principle of spirit, subjectivity, or consciousness had always been posited at the heart of being, as either its formal or final cause. Redefined at crucial periods like the Renaissance, the Enlightenment, and the age of Romanticism, this basis for Western humanism is the ultimate casualty of the ontology of death. Before it can be abandoned or reconceived, however, a concerted effort must be made to see what life, if any, it might still harbor.

CHAPTER THREE

The Hole Called
the Soul

I am the dark side of the moon; you know of my existence,
but what you establish concerning the bright side is not valid
for me. I am the remainder in the equation which does not
come out even.

—Martin Buber

One aspect of the privation of existence that Michelstaedter did not appreciate as much as Rilke or Kandinsky is its complicity with everything that we conceive of as positive in life. It is Adriano Tilgher who first makes this point in his 1922 review of *Persuasion and Rhetoric*. Michelstaedter never understood, or never had the time to understand, in Tilgher's reading, that "what seems to be the deficiency, condemnation, and misery of man is also proof of his incorruptible and celestial essence." The sense that something necessary is conspicuously missing from life is itself evidence that this something "informs one's true being." It is an image of what "one has mysteriously fallen away from and to which one must return," or more simply put, an image of an intuited condition of totality and wholeness

> outside of which everything else is only appearance and dream—[an intuition of wholeness] which instills in [a person's] soul the fecund disquietudes and healthy torments in which his nobility lies, and which saves him from the atomic and molecular dispersion of a life lived minute by minute, instant by instant, and which binds the unique instants of his life to one another, transforming them into moments in the development of a single energy. (Tilgher 1932: 295–304)

In 1916 the philosopher Giovanni Gentile remarks much the same thing about evil, negativity, and pain: "The spirit's non-being," as he calls it, is undoubtedly the most painful aspect of human experience; but it is also what "spurs us on from task to task, and what has always been recognized as the inner spring by which the mind progresses and lives" (Gentile 1916: 244).

By the time Tilgher wrote his review of Michelstaedter he had carefully studied Simmel's "The Metaphysics of Death." In essence he is applying the same perception as the German, to the effect that only the implicit recognition of death, deficiency, or negativity allows humans to posit values at all. Precisely *because* everyday life is "casual and fleeting," observes Simmel, we characterize some of its contents as universal, absolute, and lasting. We consider that not *all* dimensions of life have to share "the destiny of life's process; in this way alone the meaning of certain contents is stipulated as valid beyond life and death, independently of all flux and end" (Simmel 1910a: 34). The awareness of mortality compels us to abstract values from the senseless process.

The production of meaning in the face of fragile experience also gives rise to the idea of a basic and lasting self, irreducible to its historical experience. Among the values detached from physical and practical fluctuations of life is the concept of a unique, fundamental subject, affirming its own identity in the face of its scattered surroundings.

Similarly, Lukács associates the recognition of death with an "awakening of the soul to consciousness or self-consciousness." We experience something we call the soul, he notes in "The Metaphysics of Tragedy," in and through its historical limitations—and "only because and in so far as it is limited." The opposition between life and death from which Michelstaedter suffered, then, is the very thing that "extracts the soul's essential nature" and "gives to this essential nature the existence of an inner and only necessity" (Lukács 1910–11a: 161–162).[1] Where the difference between life and death appears to be absolute, interiority and exteriority oppose each other as "the real and the unreal, the necessarily thought and the unthinkable and absurd." The experience of deficiency has its positive dimension after all. It is of a piece with the "longing of man for selfhood, the longing to transform the narrow peak of his

---

1. On uses of the term soul in Lukács see Márkus 1983 and Elio Matassi, *Il giovane Lukács: Saggio e sistema* (Napoli: Guida, 1979), 44–45. A dialectical conception of negativity was already present in Lukács's *The History and Development of Modern Drama,* spurred by a reflection on the theories of Theodor Lipps. Tragic pain, writes Lipps, allows for "the flowering of a certain positive value of the personality. . . . In our feeling of compassion or sadness . . . is mixed a higher awareness of value, a higher enjoyment, rendered deeper by pain itself." Lukács comments: "We feel the value of something with greater intensity precisely in the moment of its decadence . . . a life acquires its own expression as it declines, in its ruin. . . . Tragedy renders the vital processes self-conscious" (Lukács 1911b: 64–65). This thought is intimately tied to Lukács's valorization of the "beautiful death."

existence into a wide plain with the path of his life winding across it [*den Gipfel seines Daseins in eine Ebene des Lebenswege*], and his meaning into a daily reality" (Lukács 1910–11a: 161–162).

For Michelstaedter, the goal of such longing is self-certainty. In Simmel it is "pure self-determination," or the "being-itself-of-the-soul" (Simmel 1910a: 36). And yet there is a difference in the ways in which the two thinkers assess the goal. Where Simmel sees self-determination as an ideal that can only be realized in an imaginary or otherworldly realm, the young Lukács and Michelstaedter view it as a program to be accomplished on earth.[2] The idea is born that persons must be fully self-determining here and now, translating their innermost being into action. They must actualize their souls in the contingent world, shaping their life in practice as much as in theory. It is a challenge that accompanies that dissonant and antithetical world in which "naked souls conduct a dialogue with naked destinies" (Lukács 1910–11a: 155). The investing of all hope in human subjectivity is not just a logical response to the deficiency of being: to many it is the only response.

AUTOSCOPY

"When religion, science and morality are shaken [and] the external supports threaten to collapse," writes Vasily Kandinsky, "then man's gaze turns away from the external *toward himself*." It turns to "materials and surroundings that give a free hand to the nonmaterial strivings and searchings of the thirsty soul" (Kandinsky 1909–11: 145 and 146). The soul becomes the only true seat of the real and must look at itself (autoscopy).

These materials and surroundings that give a free hand to the soul assume various shapes in 1910. They are the subjective excavations

2. Although noting the relationship between Michelstaedter's "persuasion" and Simmel's "pure self-determination," Piero Pieri (1984: 110–111) overlooks Simmel's implication that this pure self-determination is not possible except in a life that is free from death; and that, of course, is not the view of Michelstaedter, who wishes persuasion to be actualized in concrete, historical practice. Ranke (1961) notes another apparent agreement between Michelstaedter and Simmel (though Ranke's explicit comparison is between the Italian and Heidegger): the fleeting admission in Michelstaedter (1958: 824–825) that all values are founded upon a recognition of death. But Ranke, too, fails to acknowledge that Michelstaedter's own values—being, identity, eternity, etc.—are thoroughly antihistorical, incapable of assuming concrete form. With Michelstaedter it is difficult to make the case that applies to Simmel and Heidegger and even Gentile (the latter being the subject of comparison in Arangio-Ruiz's study of 1954): that the deficiency of being serves a productive function in the everyday conduct of life. Like Weininger before him, Michelstaedter is led by the thought of negativity to dream of an absolutely opposite form of being, all plenitude, and categorically opposed to everyday practice.

of psychology, phenomenology, theosophy, and philosophical idealism. They are daring experiments in atonal music and pictorial abstraction, both seeking to convey spiritual possibility in perceptible form. The moment of this "turning" of which Kandinsky speaks is one where the political and technological world appears to reflect a distorted image of the inner life, in which works like *The Notebooks of Malte Laurids Brigge* try to formulate new methods of seeing and understanding, new strategies for gathering more in consciousness than passive impressions of lifeless things. As the canvases of paintings become vehicles for feeling and intuition, portraits and self-portraits try to convey something internal to objective appearance. Schiele paints himself nude. Michelstaedter seeks a language for voiceless persuasion. Kandinsky and Kokoschka "paint pictures the objective theme of which is hardly more than an excuse . . . to express themselves as only the musician expressed himself until now." Schoenberg, the author of this statement, hopes that the freedom enjoyed by music can finally be shared by the visual arts—and that "those who demand a text, a subject matter, will soon stop demanding" (Schoenberg 1912a: 144–145). And yet there is still a text in this new expressionist art, and it is the self, more solitary and naked than ever in history.

In Kandinsky the words "spirit" and "soul" mean more than the respective natures of individual, historical beings. They refer to the "inner necessity" of an age, which comes to expression in art. But even in Kandinsky this necessity cannot discover its form unless it travels the route of human interiority. There is only one step between the theories of *On the Spiritual in Art* and the memorable distinction that Paul Kornfeld draws between expressionist and non-expressionist art: the first concerns itself with "souled man," the second with "psychological man."[3] Psychological man, comments Walter Sokel, "is man *seen* from the outside, as an object of portrayal and scientific analysis. 'Souled man' is man *felt* from inside, in his ineffable uniqueness" (Sokel 1959: 52). In the analogous terms of Giovanni Gentile, the souled person is "the subject truly conceived as subject," not "reduced to one of the many finite objects contained in experience" (Gentile 1916: 5). The psychological person is the self-viewed-as-object, the souled person is the self-experienced-as-subject.

Alessandra Comini draws a similar distinction in her study of Schiele.

---

3. Paul Kornfeld, "Der beseelte und der psychologische Mensch" (Souled and Psychological Man), *Das junge Deutschland* 1 (1918): 1–13.

The portraits of the young Austrian, she claims, are not interested in the external "façade" of a person but in the interior psyche, not in the "political, religious or economic man" of earlier art but in the "inner self." And in exploring such a subject, Schiele mirrors the collective quest of his time. The new hero of the expressionist generation—presented for the first time on stage in Oskar Kokoschka's *Murderer, Hope of Women*— is "Man-the-Self, transparent and painfully autobiographical" (Comini 1974: 1–2 and 5). The wish to penetrate essences "as though by X-ray" is shared by a host of Schiele's contemporaries, even if they do not agree on how to achieve this penetration.

An entire philosophical spectrum separates Kandinsky's abstract ramifications of the spirit from Schiele's graphic psychobiography. At one end lies the idea of a collective and perhaps even cosmic soul with which a sentient person might come into contact through art or thought. At the other lies the sense of a thoroughly historical and finite I, whether ego or id, libido or morality, male or female, or some such combination. Conceptions at the first end of the spectrum—theosophy, anthroposophy, occultism, even Jungian psychology—tend to emphasize the unity and continuity between living beings. Those at the other extreme stress the disjunctions. In 1910, however, the gradations along the spectrum are not that easy to distinguish. No theory entirely excludes another. The colors bleed into each other, offsetting categorical distinctions. Indeed, this uncertainty about the very modalities of spirit—this ontological "confusion," as it were—is immanent to the autoscopical turn, to a workshop of subjectivity simultaneously fueled by different elements, energies, and interests.

The object of the turn in Kandinsky is that "living spirit" of human experience which he believes to be the true content of art (Kandinsky 1912a: 250). In fact, only this content distinguishes the "necessary" new arts of his time from contemporaneous developments in the sciences and "unnecessary" arts.[4] For Kandinsky the latter are rhetorical and formalistic in manner, offering a mere symbolism of the real. Their content, assuming they have one, is dictated in advance by the forms and the methods of articulation. For Kandinsky, by contrast, no form has relevance except insofar as it is *the external expression of inner content.* The true artist has no formal concern but one: the question "which form should I employ . . . to achieve the necessary expression of my inner

---

4. On Kandinsky's ambivalence toward "formalist," avant-garde painting in Paris see his 1909–11: 151–152, 207–209.

experience" (Kandinsky 1912a: 237, 248). This is the new sense of "ne-cessity" that is born in 1910, the new meaning that is given to a quality that philosophers had traditionally attributed to the realm of hard, ob-jective fact. "To neither the joinings of human need between birth and the grave," writes Buber in 1913,

> nor to the fate of all life that is scattered abroad in the world, nor to all the counterplay of the elements, nor even to the movement of the stars them-selves, not to all these investigated and registered things may I grant the name of necessity, but only to the directed soul. (Buber 1913a: 57)

In this argument, everything outside the soul's direction, even what can-not be changed, has no necessary reason for having the form that it has. History and politics themselves are but the cluttered externals of an "unknown Inward which is the most living thing of all" (Buber 1909: 1). A similar distinction underlies Lukács's difference between the real and the unreal. The real is the "inner and only necessity of the soul," playing itself out in its "experience of itself" (Lukács 1916: 147). In an unreal epoch—where "no things, no houses, no exterior" still harbor any meaning, as Rilke notes in his study of Rodin—innerness comes into its own. And this innerness "is formless, inconceivable: it floats" (Rilke 1902–07: 240). The distinction of the art of his time is that it seeks "equivalents among the visible for the inwardly seen" (Rilke 1910: 76). The "inwardly seen" is more than what lies in the eye of the artist; it is what lies in the innerness of things themselves, and can never be illumi-nated by mere scientific descriptions. Schoenberg says much the same thing about his own paintings: "I never saw faces, but because I looked into people's eyes, only their 'gazes'. . . . A painter . . . grasps with one look the whole person—I, only his soul" (Schoenberg 1938: 237). But this soul is more than the whole person.

Franz Marc addresses the same issue from the position of the viewer. What struck him like a lightning bolt when he saw the NKVM exhibit in late 1910 was that the works of Kandinsky's group put art to a radi-cally new purpose. The originality of their works lay in their "utterly spiritualized and dematerialized inwardness of feeling"—a feeling which "our fathers, the artists of the nineteenth century, never even attempted to achieve in a 'picture'" (Marc 1910b: 126). Within a month Marc is corresponding with fellow painter August Macke on the subject of color theory. In it both seek a means "to express oneself naively with art" (Macke and Marc 1964: 25; letter from Macke of early December, 1910). And to express oneself naively means to escape the rhetorical traps of the European artistic tradition, above all the notion that painting must mimic historical appearances. "We must feed our ideas and ideals," exclaims Marc, "with locusts and wild honey, and not with history" (Macke and Marc 1964: 40; letter of January 14, 1911). Instead of adhering to the picture of nature, artists should "annihilate" it, seeking "the powerful laws that rule beneath a beautiful appearance" (Marc, quoted by Vogt 1980: 81). Following their research in 1910–11, Marc and Macke come to agree that no form can be anything more than a cipher of these other, more powerful laws: "Man expresses his life in forms," writes Macke. "Each form of art is an expression of his inner life. The exterior of the form of art is its interior" (Macke 1912: 85).

The strongest apology for this new, autoscopical art still lies with Schoenberg and Kandinsky, who learned even more from each other in this period than Marc and Macke. At its highest level, claims Schoenberg, art "is exclusively concerned with the representation of inner nature." It is "born of 'I must,' not 'I can.'" This is as true of music as of painting: "Every chord I put down corresponds to a necessity, to a necessity of my urge to expression" (Schoenberg 1911a: 18, 1911b: 365, 1911a: 417). "One must express oneself!" he exclaims to Kandinsky on January 24, 1911. "Express oneself *directly*! Not one's taste, or one's upbringing, or one's intelligence, knowledge or skill. Not all these *acquired* characteristics, but that which is *inborn, instinctive*." Two days later Kandinsky replies in agreement: "I am very pleased that you speak of self-perception. That is the root of the 'new' art"; there "the 'inner voice' alone should speak" (Schoenberg and Kandinsky 1984: 23 and 25).

Strong as this inward turn is in Germany and Austria, it is just as evident in Italy, where Boine, Slataper, and other members of *La Voce* cultivate a new aesthetics of the lyrical, autobiographical fragment. "So far," writes Giovanni Papini in 1911,

> art has nearly always expressed the most common and most universal feelings and facts of men . . . descriptions of external things, on the basis of ordinary studies of consciousness. Now, as I see it, art should refer more to the *interior*, should interiorize itself more than it has done so far; it should start *with the I* and not with things, expressing spiritual realities more than material appearances. (Papini 1911: 107–108)

Was it not for the same reason that Virginia Woolf announced that human character changed "in or about December, 1910"?

> All human relations have shifted—those between masters and servants, husbands and wives, parents and children. And when human relations change there is at the same time a change in religion, conduct, politics, and literature.

> Let us agree to place one of these changes [i.e., the change from the Edwardian novel to the Georgian writings of James Joyce, T. S. Eliot, and D. H. Lawrence] about the year 1910. (Woolf 1924: 320–321)

By 1910, her essay argues, human nature had suffered an alienation from its sociopolitical conditions, requiring a tortured new language to find its voice. And if, when we move from Woolf's England to France, we do not see the inward turn quite so clearly, it may be because a magnetic gathering of bold and innovative artists in Paris kept aesthetic issues firmly focused on the new promises of formal invention. But even in France there were the André Gides and the Henri Bergsons, the Paul Claudels and the moralists of the *Nouvelle Revue Française*. A new sense of the primacy of the subject had pervaded Europe. Among the many reasons for these new arts of subjectivity there are three in the realm of ideas: the sociopolitical thinking of the eighteenth and nineteenth centuries, and the joint rise of philosophical egoism and idealism.

QUALITATIVE INDIVIDUALISM

In 1908 Georg Simmel attempts to account for the new subjectivism of the century by reference to two inherited styles and concepts: the "quantitative" individualism of the eighteenth century and the "qualitative" individualism of the nineteenth (Simmel 1908: 527–545, 552–565, 568–570 and Simmel 1971: 268–274). Beneath the Enlightenment effort to liberate humans from the servitude of traditional political institutions, argues Simmel, lies the supposition that individuals are at bottom essentially the same. Different as they may seem to be on the surface, citizens of a state are all instances of a general rule. In the light of this rule varieties in lifestyle and interest are merely contingent, trivial, atomic reflections of a universal human order. This is why Simmel calls the individualism of this period "quantitative," saying that it essentially envisages the singleness rather than uniqueness of persons (*Einzelheit*, not *Einzigkeit*).

In the following century things change. The belief that persons are monadic instantiations of a general essence gives way to an emphasis on their uniqueness. In German romanticism the individual is no longer primarily a political animal or an exemplum of universal humanity. The social rule is now a context against which persons stand out as irreducibly singular. Individuality comes to mean uniqueness, irreplaceability, "qualitative" incomparability with every other being, including one's most intimate friends and social groupings.

If the Enlightenment subordinates the individual to the universal principles of natural right and equality, the nineteenth century strives to accommodate society to individual deviations. No longer is it self-evident that the social domain can be justly and homogeneously organized, enabling the emergence of equal and comparable human beings. It appears rather to be fueled by differences, legitimated through competition and the division of labor. The principles at work in this qualitative individualism are not reason and necessity but freedom and will, not the actualities of history but the potentialities of subjective creativity.

The twentieth century inherits both species of individualism, complicating their implications in unforeseen ways. Qualitative, romantic individualism becomes even more radical, nurturing differences among human beings as never before. Simultaneously, however, the social and economic structures that appeared to *serve* the qualitative individualism come to appear as clandestine methods for *quantifying* individuals once again, reducing them to functions of abstract, objective rules. By the late nineteenth century a whole series of opponents of bourgeois culture—bohemians and dandies, advocates of the genius, the saint, and the criminal—strengthen their position; the pursuit of uniqueness rebels against the social structures in which it once hoped to achieve its actualization. Subjectivity becomes increasingly worried by the gap between theory and practice, between inner and outer worlds of human comportment. If this process begins in nineteenth-century disillusionment with the French Revolution, it comes to fruition in the early twentieth century, in what Lukács comes to call romantic anticapitalism: the association of individualism with internal, subjective freedom rather than with a concrete reorganization of socioeconomic activity. And this is when artists and philosophers take to bemoaning the deficiency of being, when political faith breaks down, and when individuality seems achievable only in conceptual and imaginative self-discipline.

Whether properly diagnosed or not, this development is exacerbated by another event: the growth of a metaphysics of egoism. Most of it can be traced to the influence of Schopenhauer, Darwin, and Nietzsche, who locate a lust for survival or power beneath the orderly progression of rational, scientific, and political logic, pitting every organism against its constraining external conditions. Whether it is called will to survival or will to power, self-assertion motivates all individuals and groups. People appear even more unequal than the romantics thought. Qualitative differences in resourcefulness and strength involve a type of constitutive alienation between every ego and the things outside it, whether they be homeostatic material conditions or enabling social structures. Individualism appears to be the result of an agonistic process of individualization, the product of a contention with and within historical becoming. This is one dimension of the philosophical heritage underlying the theoretical developments of the turn of the century, including Freud's libidinal psychology and the fluctuant metaphysics of the *Lebensphilosophen*. It is also why Schoenberg can say, with all apparent ease, that an objective assessment of any historical condition "reveals the living personality poised for the struggle, in vigorous conflict with its environment" (Schoenberg 1911a: 412). Six years later William Butler Yeats elevates the struggle into a categorical opposition between Creative Will and the Body of Fate into which that will is thrown.[5] In Michelstaedter the struggle takes the shape of a hankering for life—and more-than-life—which keeps creatures eternally distant from each present moment.

If ever there was a culmination of this qualitative individualism it lies in *Persuasion and Rhetoric,* the most eloquent account for why expressionism becomes so necessary in the early twentieth century. Impelled by its own inner desire, writes Michelstaedter, each creature "moves differently from things different from itself, different even itself from itself" (Michelstaedter 1910: 41). As long as a person is alive, the condition continues unabated: "he is here and the world there: two and not one. And as long as he is conscious of it, the world does not consist all in one point, but always in one thing and another, in a now and an after, in a more and a less . . . *ta polla* instead of the one."[6] Individualism is not merely a goal, but a destiny. In this scenario no attempt to transcend one's difference can ward off failure:

> if I jump into the sea, if I feel the wave on my body—where I am the sea is not; if I wish to go where the water is and to have it—the waves cleave before the man who swims; if I drink the seafoam, if I exult like a dolphin—if I drown—still I do not possess the sea: I am *alone and different* in the midst of the sea. (Michelstaedter 1910: 40–41)

The situation is even more fruitless in the company of one's fellows: "Neither kisses, nor embraces, nor any of the many demonstrations that love devises will ever succeed in making one person interpenetrate the

---

5. W. B. Yeats, *A Vision* (New York: Macmillan, 1978), 261. The work, writes Yeats, was conceived before the first volume of Spengler's *Decline of the West* was published (before 1918).

6. Carlo Michelstaedter, "Critical Appendices" to *Persuasion and Rhetoric* (Appendix II, "Decadence") in Michelstaedter 1958: 192.

other; rather, they will remain eternally two, and each alone and different in front of the other" (Michelstaedter 1910: 41). These differences
reach even into the innermost recesses of an individual self. And that,
once again, is why people lament their solitude: "*being with themselves
they feel alone*: they feel they are *with nobody*" (Michelstaedter 1910:
41). The inward turn is thus intimately tied to the perceived difference
between an I and the company it keeps, between even its internal and
external nature.

The condition in which a living personality is eternally poised for the
struggle calls for unique new forms of expression. If art becomes more
audacious than ever before it is because it appears to be the proper realm
of activity for unique individuals—if not the activity by which individuals *become* unique. "He who really has principles," writes Schoenberg,
"lives according to his own inclinations." It is no surprise that he defies
all universal and quantitative "laws" (the law of four-part harmony, for
instance) in deference to qualitative and individual ones. The artist is ir-
resistibly drawn to precisely "what is *not common usage*" (Schoenberg
1911a: 413, 11). In a similar declaration of independence, Schiele contends that those people who are most "themselves" are necessarily at
odds with industrious, law-abiding humanity. "To be oneself!—Oneself! . . . Oh, the lively living thing! . . . Oh—the perennial wearers of
uniforms! . . . The living person is unique [*Der Lebende ist einzig*]"
(Nebehay 1979: 163–164). To say that the living are unique is also to
say that *only* the unique are living—only those, like Schiele, who inhabit
the fringes of conventional society. Normalcy, once again, is a mask of
death. "The absolute duty of the new artist," he writes in 1909, is to find
"in himself the ground on which to construct, without relying in any
way on the past or tradition" (Nebehay 1979: 112). Agreeing with
Schiele, Schoenberg, and Michelstaedter is also the young Lukács: "Only
the individual," he writes in *Aesthetic Culture,* "only individuality pushed
to its furthest limits, really exists" (Lukács 1913: 29; cited by Márkus
1983: 9).

SUBJECTIVE TRANSCENDENCE

This association of individuality with a higher degree of reality would
not be possible without a third development that accompanies the notions of qualitative individualism and the vision of the world as a battle-
ground of egos. We might call it the transcendentalization of the I.
Not only is the I separate and different from all things around it; it also

underlies whatever we can say about them—everything we can perceive and value. The qualification of the I is now complete. Here the sense of a radical difference between ego and world joins a belief that the forms of historical life are contingent on how we see them—representations, in Schopenhauer's terms, of subjective will. Widely diffused in Europe by 1910, this essentially Kantian doctrine does not mean that empirical phenomena have no existence outside the ego; it just stresses that the features, the value, and ultimately the truth of these phenomena are consciously or unconsciously determined by the subject. They are functions of consciousness, feeling, desire, and interest.

Again it is Michelstaedter who exemplifies the position most radically. "If I am hungry, reality for me is no more than a set of more or less eatable things; if I am thirsty, reality is more or less liquid, and more or less drinkable." If I am neither hungry nor thirsty, nor in need of anything in particular, he adds, then all I can say is that "the world is a great set of grey things whose nature I do not know, though I certainly know that they have not been created to cheer me up" (Michelstaedter 1922: 85–86). No disinterested, universal, or objective knowledge can ever be achieved. Either things serve some practical interest or they have no meaning. The I determines the nature of all things. And art will inevitably mirror this situation, beginning with impressionism and building up to the subjective distortions and abstractions of expressionism.

Michelstaedter's position has many variants in the prewar years, especially those of Hans Vaihinger, Otto Weininger, the German neo-Kantians, and the British and Italian idealists. But the most sophisticated argument for the transcendence of the subject occurs in the phenomenology of Edmund Husserl. In a work he had already begun in 1910 (*Ideas: General Introduction to Pure Phenomenology*, 1913) Husserl traces all phenomena and meanings in history to their source in the intentional nature of the mind. This mind, or consciousness, is not "a human Ego *in* the universal, existentially posited world, but exclusively a subject *for* which this world has being." In fact one could go so far as to say that "the transcendental Ego exists [*ist*] absolutely in and for itself prior to all cosmic being (which first wins, in and through it, existential validity)" (Husserl 1913: 8). No aspect of existence is more real for Husserl than this invisible, theoretical recess of world-constituting subjectivity. All other things are of a "second order" of reality, a function of the structures in which they appear.

One also finds a transcendental theory of subjectivity in the work of Ludwig Wittgenstein. Like Michelstaedter, Wittgenstein takes Schopenhauer's notion of the representational nature of the world—or the "propositional" nature of the world, as Wittgenstein calls it in the *Tractatus Logico-Philosophicus* (1922)—as the starting point for his reflections on the nature of intelligence and subjectivity. The subject, he writes in 1916, "is not a part of the world but a presupposition of its existence." Beneath the physical apparatus of the self lies an unspeakable I that feels, judges, and wills. This I, writes Wittgenstein, is "not the human being, not the human body or the human soul with psychological properties, but the metaphysical subject, the boundary (not a part) of the world." The human body, by contrast, is just "a part of the world among others, among beasts, plants, stones, etc." (Wittgenstein 1914–16: 79–80; notes of August 2, and September 2, 1916). Six years later, in his *Tractatus*, the second note becomes: "The philosophical I is not the man . . . but the metaphysical subject, the limit—not a part of the world" (Wittgenstein 1922: #5.641).

Such a conception of subjectivity entails considerable distance from the practical, political, historical world. "What has history to do with me?" exclaims Wittgenstein. "Mine is the first and only world!" Even the physical, empirical ego "makes its appearance in philosophy through the world's being *my* world." That the world is my world originates even the inventions of culture: "Only from the consciousness of the *uniqueness of my life* arises religion—science—and art. And this consciousness is life itself" (Wittgenstein 1914–16: 82, 80, and 79; notes of September 2, August 12, and August 1–2, 1916).[7]

In Wittgenstein the transcendence of the subject means that all metaphysical and ethical questions—for example, the ultimate nature and value of reality, how one should behave within it, and so on—lie outside the realm of the knowable. They are the *basis* for knowledge, not its object. For another thinker of the time, however, the transcendence of the subject means that even the nature of action must be reassessed. Giovanni Gentile first introduced the principles of *The Theory of Mind as Pure Act* (1916) in a paper of 1912 called "The Act of Thinking as a Pure Act." Difficult as it is to condense Gentile's complex argument, its main steps are these: All historical reality "resolves" itself into the

---

7. But both the style and the substance of these notes is indebted to *Ueber die letzen Dinge* by Weininger: "Culture is *transcendental*. . . . It is *transcendentality* that first *furnishes* culture [Erst die *Transzendentalität schafft* Kultur]" (Weininger 1904: 155). On the relations between Weininger and Wittgenstein see Janik 1985. On Weininger's impact on Italian thinking see Alberto Cavaglion, *Otto Weininger in Italia* (Roma: Carucci, 1982). On Weininger in general see Le Rider 1982 and 1993, who in the 1993 volume also has a useful exegesis of Simmel's qualitative and quantitative individualism.

subjectivity in which it is thought; it processes itself as subjectivity. As
with Kandinsky, the two apparent components of experience—historical materialism and spirituality—stand in tense opposition. According
to Gentile, "the spirit is the negation of Being" in the measure to which
"it is precisely the non-being of Being." That is to say, spirituality battles the inertia of developed, material reality (Being) in an effort to actualize its latent potential (or non-being). The paradox of spiritual reality is that it "is in not being: it fulfills its real nature in so far as this
is not already realized and is in process of realization" (Gentile 1916:
244). While spirit, in the ordinary conception of the word, is everything
that matter is not, this "not" supplies the impetus for change, development, and progress. One actualizes spirit by negating particular aspects
of the practice which that spirit itself has produced, by negating the
"history" and the "nature" which appear to be the basis of the spirit but
are really no more than its products. In the philosophy of pure act, historical becoming is the outcome of a spiritual battle against objectivity
and "naturalism," or against that Being which is in truth the non-being
of a spirit eternally becoming.

Gentile's idea of subjectivity is not solipsistic. Spirit does develop into
objective reality; it lives in the effort to produce what is not in the present, but will be in the future—in the form of practical, concrete history.
In this sense, Gentile's philosophy of the *atto puro* is analogous to
Kandinsky's conception of spirituality as the motor drive of history, a
movement "forwards and upwards." Moreover, it is in the interests of
"pure objectivity" that Gentile's spiritual action militates against the
sclerotic, contemporary forms of thought and act into which subjectivity is periodically reduced. "Man is man," he writes, "by denying, loath-
ing to be what he is, and by turning his eyes to the ideal that he must realize. And were he to confuse this ideal with what he is already, he
would acquiesce so perfectly in his condition that he would fall into the
deep sleep of a stone." Against all present appeasement and acquiescence, then, Gentile advances a demeanor of "perpetual spiritual vigil."
The inherent impulse of a person is "to go out from himself . . . 'to dissolve' and absorb himself into the ideal which is the object" (Gentile
1920: 106).

Can these notions of a transcendental ego and of a constitutive, ontological subject be reconciled with the bodily, psychological ego of paintings like Schiele's? With Kandinsky's sense of an inner necessity? How
do they stand with Lukács's form-making "soul" or the Freudian psyche? Different though the conceptions are, they all belong to a single

chapter of thought. They all inherit and explore that Cartesian legacy of Western philosophy which mandates a turn away from an objective tradition (history, science, or fact) to subjectivity as the foundation of truth. Consolidated in particular ways by the quantitative and qualitative individualisms of the eighteenth and nineteenth centuries, this Cartesian turn does not achieve its ultimate implications until human subjectivity is explicitly declared to be the sole hinge of action, morals, and understanding. And that is the conclusion of 1910. Even where no arguments are made about the spiritual transcendence of subjectivity, the I at this moment is still posited as the center of things. And in one way or another it is elevated to the status of a universal. Its uniqueness and unspeakability are the basis for everything that *is* divulged by speech.

Why, for example, does Schoenberg maintain that the artist's only significant activity is introspection and "absorption with his own nature"? Because this autoscopical activity is ultimately the means "to express: the nature of mankind" (Schoenberg 1911a: 412). The "souled," expressionist artist is not only a person but an instance of cosmic truth. What is really at work in introspection and self-absorption, for Schoenberg, is a demolition of the rhetorical acquisitions of finite, historical selves in order to restore the essence they share. Thus Schoenberg, too, ends up reconnecting subjective uniqueness with everything from which he had appeared to distinguish it: intractable materiality, other subjectivities, and historical destiny, for it contains their blueprint. In the words of Lukács, "the way of the soul is to strip away everything that is not truly part of oneself; to make the soul truly individual; yet what results transcends the purely individual" (Lukács 1913: 28).

By the beginning of the twentieth century, the philosophical *principium individuationis* becomes an avenue to quite the opposite—the overcoming of individuation, difference, and separation through a transpersonal unification of experience.[8] "The entire world is nothing but my 'I' and my 'I' is nothing but the world," writes Julius Hart, one of the founders of Berlin's mystical circle of the *Neue Gemeinschaft*. "He who appreciates that he is the thing-in-itself has overcome time and space, and has become the universe; indeed eternity. His I has become the great axis about which infinity spins" (Hart 1901b: 40 and 1901a: 24). In 1909 Martin Buber describes the same seemingly egocentric condition

---

8. On this paradoxical overcoming of the principle of individuation see Le Rider 1993 and Mendes-Flohr 1989. The same paradox is discussed by Sokel 1980 in reference to Rilke's *Notebooks*. For a thorough account of the flourishing of philosophies of subjectivity in German culture see Ascheim 1994: 51–84.

as all-unifying ecstasy. It is the "Inward" experiencing itself, achieving "the unity of the I, and in this unity the unity of I and world; no longer a 'content,' but what is infinitely more than any content" (Buber 1909: 2). In his remarks during the first conference of the German Society for Sociology a year later, Buber elaborates further: "In the intense exaltation of the self one establishes a relationship to the content of his soul, which he perceives as God" (Buber 1910a: 206).

This recuperation of the exterior in the interior, of the cosmos in the I, and of identity in difference traverses the entire spectrum of subjectivist thinking in 1910, whether it upholds the psychosomatic degradation of finite, historical persons or a world spirit which such complexes of mind and body might discover within themselves. In life philosophy, even the most fragmented acts of a purely physical person unfold as aspects of an overall process of vital development. In every case the subjectivist move of the prewar years appears to follow the same three steps: from the rejection of external, repressive, or "conventional" history to an interest in the innermost nature of the individual self, to a relocation of everything that matters in this nature. At the moment when the interior self appears to be the excluded topic of historical experience, it also comes to offer the transcendental "content" of that same experience, its only real basis and truth. Kandinsky's gaze in on oneself becomes the first act in a search for this self's proper language, a language that can be translated into history, articulating that self-presence of consciousness on which good actions and decisions are seen to rely.

SELF-POSSESSION

Michelstaedter describes the deplorable condition in which everything "moves differently from things different from itself" only to draw some conclusions: What a person really wants from all objects of desire, he claims, is

> what is missing in himself: *the possession of himself*. . . . What he wants is given in himself, and wanting life he distances himself from himself: he *does not know what he wants*. His aim is not his aim, he does not know why he does what he does: his action is a *form of passivity*. (Michelstaedter 1910: 41)

On the surface the argument is structured as follows: (1) One desires only what one lacks; (2) since desire means reaching beyond oneself, what one lacks most in desire (or suppresses, or fails to appease) is oneself; hence (3) what one desires in desire is self-completion, the wholeness and independence of a self-sufficient I. Whatever unavowed considerations may also be embedded in this argument, by claiming that in things we desire ourselves Michelstaedter addresses the primary concern that ensues upon the nihilistic recognition of the deficiency of being: how to recapture that which one has lost in the process of living—or perhaps never had: that soul which is "a stranger on earth," the "nothing" that eventually begins to think, and thinks: "I have an inner self of which I was ignorant." Once the mind no longer discovers identity, permanence, or value in outside things, it searches for the only identity that may have survived: the *source* of all values, the desiring I, the key to all other identities. If the experience of all historical things is at bottom just an experience of self, then possessing oneself means possessing the all.

Michelstaedter's sketches and paintings are almost all portraits. Rarely does a setting interfere with his anthropocentric focus. Similarly, his philosophy and poetry have no use for the historical attributes or contingencies that typically inform the experience of an I. For the I to be itself, everything must be necessary and nothing accidental. The absolute self "affirms itself absolutely in absolute value," not as a function of "more or less, before or after, if or maybe, in the throes of need" (Michelstaedter 1910: 94). Self-possession is the only true interest of this artist. And if the self is the real center of being, it must live accordingly. Empty as it may appear in its ordinary experience, it still has the task of transforming this negativity into positive terms. This "missing" or transcendent foundation of the universe must act out its own transcendence. Recognizing the ontological deficiency of life outside it, the self must *make itself into* that absolute, unshakable point of the world that it already is. It must recognize and embrace its solitude:

> Whoever is for himself (μένει) needs nothing else to be for him (μένοι αὐτόν) in the future, but possesses everything in himself. "It will not take place, has been, or was / But simply is, in the present, today and now / And is simply eternity gathered and whole" (Petrarch). . . . *Persuasion does not live in whoever does not live on himself alone.* . . . Persuaded is he who has his life in himself: the naked soul in the Isles of the Blessed. (Michelstaedter 1910: 41–42)

The Isles of the Blessed are those of the Orphic myth discussed by Plato. According to the myth, before being able to pass true judgment on the souls of the dead, Zeus must first strip them of everything they have acquired in the course of their mortal existence: their clothes, their

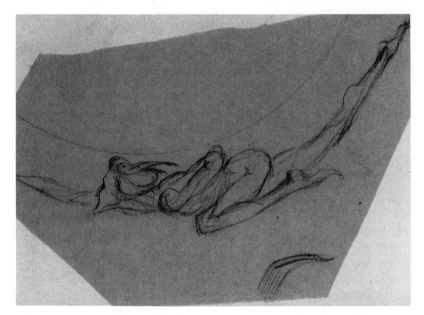

Fig. 15. Carlo Michelstaedter, *Flying Figure*, no date, pencil. Courtesy Gorizia Civic Library, Gorizia.

body, and so on. He must see them exactly as what they are.[9] Michelstaedter calls for this denuding operation in life itself, where the self will finally be exactly what it inherently is. The persuaded person lives as *"the first and the last,* and finds nothing that was done before him, nor does it avail him to believe that anything will be done after him . . . he must create himself and the world, which does not exist before him: he must be master and not slave in his house." The best example of such persuasion is Jesus Christ, one of those few who "saved himself by the fact that out of his mortal life he knew how to create the god: the individual" (Michelstaedter 1910: 73, 103–104). This is what it means to become oneself: in the nakedness of persuasive self-affirmation, to become the god-individual that one already is. Indeed, Michelstaedter could have borrowed the title of another work of 1910 to capture the theme of *Persuasion and Rhetoric,* Jules Romains's *Manual of Deification.* "The first way to become concentric to a god," writes Romains,

9. Michelstaedter alludes to the same passage in Plato's *Gorgias* when stating, in a letter to his friend Enrico Mreule, that absolute judgments of value can be pronounced only if and when "the naked contemplates the naked." "Only the naked soul is free," he claims a few lines earlier. Both phrases are in Greek (Michelstaedter 1983: 362).

"is to stop up your eyes and ears, to suppress the universe. For the universe means your insistence on being who you are," or who you have so far believed you are (Romains 1910: 63–64).[10]

Indeed, Michelstaedter suppresses the universe more unsparingly than the most violent expressionists. To the persuaded person "the world must be a man who ever says 'no' to each of his acts, to each of his words, until he has filled the desert and illuminated the darkness on his own." One cannot discover what one is except by *"making one's life always richer in negations"* (Michelstaedter 1910: 84), to the point of recognizing that

> the needs, the necessities, of life are not necessities . . . one cannot affirm oneself by affirming [the needs] that are given to him . . . by a contingency that is outside and prior to him: one cannot move differently from things that *are* because he *needs* them. (Michelstaedter 1910: 70)

To stand on his own, a person must first "make his own legs for walking—and make a path where there is no road" (Michelstaedter 1910: 73). While scholars are right to distinguish Michelstaedter from the most extreme philosopher of individualism, Max Stirner, few lines are more reminiscent than Stirner's "I am the creative nothing, the nothing out of which I myself as creator create everything" (Stirner 1845: 41).[11]

Thus does objective nullity provide the foundation for plenitude. And subjective plenitude, in turn, restores the value of objective, historical being. While the search for oneself in things constantly transforms each empty moment into another, persuasive self-possession "makes time stand still." Every instant in a life of this sort "is a century in the life of

---

10. Several other positions taken by this book strike chords in Michelstaedter: "La vérité? Elle est si près de vos yeux qu'ils ne la voient pas. Fermez vos yeux. Vous la sentirez avec vos paupières. / La vérité? Je vous assure qu'elle est chez vous, dans votre maison. / Ne sortez pas ce soir avant de l'avoir découverte [7–8]. . . . Vous dormirez entre des murs qui ne contiendront que vous. Le sommeil est à l'individu [12]. . . . Quand les dieux seront pleinement réels, les hommes n'auront plus de devoirs [58]. . . . Nous ne créons pas de dieux pour qu'il y ait une morale; nous voulons une morale pour qu'il y ait des dieux [59]. . . . Mais la naissance du moindre des dieux suffirait à la gloire de la terre [66]." Six years before Michelstaedter, Weininger had reached the same paradoxical conclusion: "Das realisierte Ich wäre Gott" (Weininger 1904: 104).

11. Max Stirner, *The Ego and His Own* (1845), ed. John Carroll (New York: Harper & Row, 1971), 41. Once again the intermediary between Michelstaedter and Stirner is Weininger: "Man is alone in the world, in tremendous eternal isolation. He has no object outside himself; lives for nothing else; he is far removed from being the slave of his wishes, of his abilities, of his necessities; he stands far above social ethics; he is alone. Thus he becomes one and all; he has the law in him, and so he himself is the law, and no mere changing caprice. . . . Nothing is superior to him, to the isolated absolute unity" (Weininger 1903: 162). On the subject of Michelstaedter and Stirner see Pieri 1989: 33–36 and 272–273; Bini 1992: 13, 15.

others—until one *turns oneself into a flame* and succeeds in consisting in the ultimate present." In this ultimate self-presence the individual "is everything," having, "in the possession of the world, the possession of himself—*being one, himself and the world*" (Michelstaedter 1910: 89, 82).

What is clear, however, from the very extremity of this rhetoric, clearer here than in any previous philosophy of subjectivity, is the obstacle that awaits this solution to the deficiency of being: This "actualization" of the pure, unadulterated subject abolishes that same subject from the confines of history, at least if we understand history as an interactive, temporal process. When the idea of the subject as the *fundamentum inconcussum* of all reality is taken to Michelstaedter's extreme, the I becomes detached from everything that can be experienced, understood, and spoken. In possessing itself, Michelstaedter's subject possesses none of the things with which history identifies it: its physical and social characteristics, its beliefs and actions, its finite perspectives and contexts. It is only the missing essence of its "accidents," too naked to step into the world. By insisting on being what it is "in itself," the I becomes the same nothing that it shunned in outside experience, not made into something, but abandoned to the greatest possible deficiency of being. "*I know that I want and* [*that*] *I do not have what I want*," says the opening sentence of *Persuasion and Rhetoric* (Michelstaedter 1910: 39). Trakl, by the same logic, is forced to abandon the *Erlebnislyrik,* or the confessional lyric, by 1912. All that remains is negative knowledge. "What must I do?" Michelstaedter asks Nadia in a dialogue. "You know. —I do not know. —But you know that you are not doing it" (Michelstaedter 1988: 97).

Thus does the subjectivist tradition of Western philosophy come to its end. The Greek "Know thyself!" was based on a disparagement of objective self-evidence: The outer world was a deceptive and corrupting one; truth could only be discovered by turning inward and admitting to oneself what the world did not know. But when this project is taken to its extreme—or when the faith in outside knowledge is so broken that nothing appears to be real but the self—then one discovers that even this "self in itself" is nothing. It is nothing whatsoever outside of its objective relations. It is speechless and can attain no self-knowledge. Even if the I seems to achieve a type of mystical self-transformation at the height of persuasion, affirming the unspeakable reality of each of its historical experiences, it still loses its features. It dissolves into the arena of pure objectivity, where all "essences" are momentary and fleeting appearances, and no subjects can be distinguished from objects. Here, too, the metaphysics of the subject is overcome (Harrison 1991; Cacciari 1992a; Perniola 1989).

Michelstaedter needs no critics to point out the impossibility of his ideal of persuasion. On the very page where he advocates knowing oneself he also admits that self-knowledge is a chimera, a "seeking with negative data." We lack the tools for the job. We only know—or would like to know—that the essence of such a self *should not be related to the irrationality of need*" (Michelstaedter 1910: 85). Where knowledge is inevitably mediated by rhetoric and action by form, one can neither know nor become oneself. In his battle against *philopsychia* Michelstaedter despairs of the sense that the true being of all subjects and objects "cannot be defined in another way than by negating all the attributes of the will. . . . And even if my individuality points toward the absolute, I am always the negation of the absolute 'insofar as I want it.'" Thus *ousia*, or primal being, "remains outside of my consciousness and outside of my life" (Michelstaedter 1958: 803). In *Persuasion and Rhetoric* he acknowledged the impossibility of bridging the I and the All even more decisively than in this note: "I have never known the absolute; rather, I know it as one suffering from insomnia knows sleep, as one peering at the darkness knows light" (Michelstaedter 1910: 96). If persuasion means self-possession, the self is now impossible to characterize in positive terms. It is not equivalent to its needs, it is not what the mind says that it is, it is not the sum of its achievements or satisfactions. It is a mere dream of itself.

As Gentile recognized in the twenties, Michelstaedter's thinking undoes itself (Gentile 1922). It suffers the contradiction of the terms in which it operates (Cacciari 1992a; Bianco 1993). An effort to achieve form beyond form, its wedding of soul and experience joins an empty self to an empty present, both dissolved into a play of rhetorical appearance. The synthesis of I and world is an imaginary alternative to this only historical reality, this ubiquitous and omnipotent rhetoric, its pendant or mirror-image. Self-actualization is self-dissolution.

The marks of this dissolution are borne on every page of *Persuasion and Rhetoric*, beginning with its opening sentence: "I know that I am speaking because I am speaking, but that I will persuade no one; and this is dishonesty—but rhetoric ἀναγχάζει με ταῦτα δρᾶν βία [compels me to do it]" (Michelstaedter 1910: 35). The "rhetoric" that forces

Michelstaedter to speak dishonestly is not only the academic jargon that professors require of dissertations like his. It is also the conceptual vocabulary on which Michelstaedter himself relies, which makes him believe in an *alternative* to rhetoric, in the abolition of masks, deception, contingency, and appearance. It is rhetoric, and rhetoric alone, that makes Michelstaedter believe that his Parmenidean concepts of being, identity, and permanence have possible correlates in the historical world. It is rhetoric that seduces him into believing in persuasion. How lucid Michelstaedter might be about this paradox is hard to say. But it is clear to most of his readers that in his withering critique of rhetoric even the concept of persuasion is destroyed. Once one has understood that identity is an empty concept, or an illusion produced by historical and linguistic form, then the being and the self that one tries to distinguish from illusions also fall.

The breakdown of the I and its means of expression is just as apparent in Michelstaedter's dialogues and drawings, in his lyrical poems and paintings. Most of the drawings are caricatures, blending sympathy with aggression (Campailla 1980b; Bini 1992). These are not celebrations of an I. Rather, they bring as stern a judgment to bear on their subjects as do the critiques of *Persuasion and Rhetoric*. Just as the critiques push their arguments to the margins of self-parody, so the drawings turn satirical. However much Michelstaedter wanted to believe in self-determination, what he offers in his drawings are pictures of unaccomplished and rhetorical selves, trapped in conditions they cannot control. True, a handful of works do depict self-knowing, ecstatic, or seemingly self-possessed individuals (fig. 17). But what they convey most strongly is the preternatural strain of the effort, offering images of selves imbued with pain, wrinkled and frowning from the pressures of their voiceless suffering. The forces they battle are the same ones that Michelstaedter's dissertation and caricatures deride: the social, biological, and moral laws of rhetoric from which none can escape.

Michelstaedter's pictures of solitary human beings bear witness to an insuperable contest between unspeakable essence and clichéd appearance. His typical modes of articulation—including caricature, satire, and parody—are perversions of form, distortions of form's *own* distortion. They are critical rather than constructive procedures, strategies for speaking when speech is imperiled. They expose rather than reveal a subject, presenting it as divided and contradictory. It is the stage of a drama where, in Buber's words, "understanding and misunderstanding

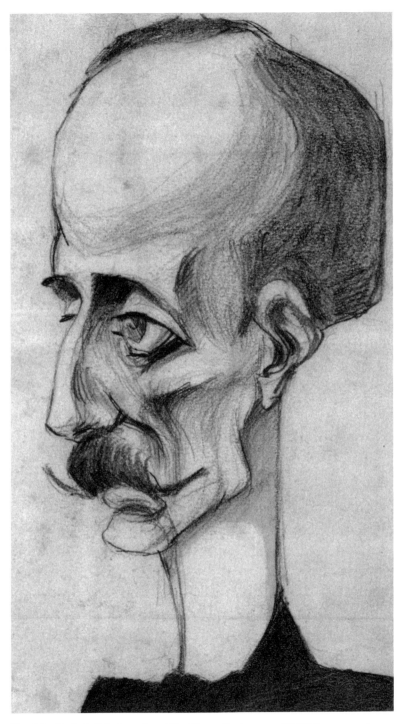

Fig. 16. Carlo Michelstaedter, *The Great Caricature*, 1908(?), watercolor and pencil. Courtesy Gorizia Civic Library, Gorizia.

Fig. 17. Carlo Michelstaedter, *Revelation*, 1906, oil. Courtesy Gorizia Civic Library, Gorizia.

are interwoven" (1925: 63). The duplicity informs each of Michel-staedter's art forms. His lyrical poems are extraordinarily cerebral, too conceptual in nature to stand as pure records of feeling. The axiomatic arguments of his thesis are filtered through emotions that frequently border on hallucination. Even his last and surest refuge—the I of his

Fig. 18. Carlo Michelstaedter, *Self-Portrait of 1908,* watercolor and pencil. Courtesy Gorizia Civic Library, Gorizia.

own self-portraits—comes to suffer dissolution, as the final depictions
transform even their maker into "another person, a stranger, he too a
member of the petty community of evil" (Campailla 1980b: 144).

   Michelstaedter, the heroic nihilist, performs the last concerted effort
in the West to ground all experience and value in a place where they cannot grow. A similar itinerary is followed by others in his time, who are
bent on the same end but who discover in the process that the project
cannot succeed. Kandinsky, Kokoschka, and Schiele wish to uncover
some hidden and essential dimension of subjectivity; they critique the
arbitrary traits in which it is materially or historically cloaked. But even
they end up affirming not the autonomy of self, but the autonomy of the
materials out of which it is built.

PICTURES OF SOUL

The inward gaze has its pictorial awakening in the work of Vincent van Gogh and Edward Munch. Not that artists had never taken a hard look at the self before, but few had attempted to penetrate its invisible, unspeakable uniqueness, despoiling it of connections to the external, operative world. What assumes form in van Gogh and Munch is the spiritual "aura," as it were, of the individual, qualitatively different self, its voiceless fears and aspirations, its struggle against forces bearing down upon it. The same thing occurs in the *Urschrei,* or primordial scream, of later expressionist poets: the first impetus for their labor is an encounter with anxiety. And its most celebrated example is Munch's *The Scream.*

The face of Munch's howling man on a bridge is almost bereft of features. His eyes and mouths are holes, as though nature had made these organs of perception and articulation dysfunctional out of malice. The man cups the ears of his hairless head with his hands, trying to block out the piercing sounds of the swirling, circumambient universe. Wandering away from dark, retreating figures impervious to this clash of abstract forces, he is witness to a nightmare outside himself. Internal though it be, his anguish is caused by cosmic pressure. If there is anything about this depiction that can be tied to debates about the "rights of the fetus," as some claimed when the painting was stolen during the winter Olympics in Norway, it is the suggestion that the *actual life* of this man is an abortion, and that he would have willingly refused such an indignity had he known, in the womb, what awaited him. The man is screaming about the monstrosity of the so-called right to life.

Munch's later *Self-Portrait with a Cigarette* (1895) shows a rigid man isolated from his background, facing a bright light illuminating his dazed and unseeing face. He has been caught by surprise; his startled and silent eyes show the passivity of an objectified subject. The smoke rising from his cigarette blends into the obscure and hazy background, while his torso fades away at the bottom of the frame; both reinforce the insubstantial, apparitional nature of the life in question. Something previously unseen comes into view in this apparitional life: an unfamiliar and impenetrable spirit that never developed out of it, now exposed to a light to whose warmth the subject is unaccustomed, like a creature of the shadows that he casts. His attempt to appear dignified in evening wear only makes the illuminated stress more clear.

In 1908 Munch suffers nervous collapse. During his treatment he paints a portrait of his doctor Daniel Jacobson (fig. 20). Everything in

Fig. 19. Edvard Munch, *The Scream*, 1895, woodcut. Courtesy Munch Museum, Oslo.

this portrait conspires to convey an impression of the internal energy of the doctor: the towering, full-length view; the bursts of orange, green, red, and brown; the ethereal, dynamic movements of the space that he occupies with his arms akimbo. Whether these distortions of nature emanate from the doctor or are projected by the suffering patient's vision, the drama is an internal one. The resources of Munch's art are all geared

Fig. 20. Edvard Munch, *Portrait of Dr. Daniel Jacobsen,* 1909, oil. Courtesy Munch Museum, Oslo.

toward uncovering what does not appear on the natural, objective surface of things, or what appears despite this surface.

The bridge between Munch and expressionist portraiture of 1910 is built by the artists who went by that name: Erich Heckel, Ernst Ludwig Kirchner, Karl Schmidt-Rottluff, and Fritz Bleyl, who announce the formation of the *Brücke* (Bridge) on June 7, 1905. Nourished on readings of Nietzsche and the vitalist philosophers, these young Germans make the pictorialization of the *élan vital* a programmatic objective. They associate much of this vitality with creative, libidinal energy, with sexuality, dance, and human communion. To express these spontaneous forces they emulate the "primitive," "elemental," and "instinctive" techniques of tribal art. By 1912 the exuberance of human subjectivity finds form not only in nudes but also in paintings of circus performers, artists at work, and music hall revelers. At the same time, the artists of the *Brücke* produce dramatic woodcuts of solitary faces, of figures set against metropolitan or natural contexts, many of them heroes and saints. In their view the "new human being" to whom they wished to provide a bridge would henceforth rely on the most intense, direct, and immediate forms of expression. "We claim as our own," writes Kirchner in a program of 1906, "everyone who reproduces directly and without falsification whatever it is that drives him to create" (Dube 1990: 21). Here the gaze in on oneself is intimately tied to ethical and aesthetic liberation. As the years go by, however, this liberation proves increasingly agonizing, leading to religious self-questioning on the part of the artists and, in the case of Kirchner, to suicide.

The generation of the *Brücke* was influenced not only by Munch and van Gogh but by the French Fauvists and Jugendstil, whose most interesting pictorial results lay in the work of Gustave Klimt. With their stunning blend of atomism, eroticism, and symbolism, Klimt's portraits always show links between figures and something that transcends them, whether it be mortality, languishing sexuality, an intricate, unreal surrounding, or the unwritten rules of social decorum. In the context of the towering influence of Klimt, it is ironic that the beginnings of Austrian, rather than German, expressionism are announced by an artist who refused to let his paintings be hung in the same room as the works of the master: Richard Gerstl.

Gerstl was a brilliant young artist who might have been more acclaimed had he not burned so many paintings before taking his life at the age of twenty-five. It all occurred at the end of 1908, after Gerstl had eloped with Schoenberg's wife, Mathilde. When Anton Webern convinced Mathilde to return to her husband, Gerstl positioned himself in front of his atelier mirror, tightened a noose around his neck, and plunged a butcher knife into his chest. The importance of Gerstl lies largely with the emotional range and intensity of his portraits. One of them, notes Whitford (1981: 51), may be the first nude self-portrait since the sketch by Albrecht Dürer of 1503. Another shows the painter laughing at the spectator in demonic defiance. Both paintings glorify the subject as a shameless rebel. Whether their interest lies in self-analysis, however, or in parodying an image others might have of this self is hard to say. In either case the self-consciousness is ill at ease, inviting the audience to reflect on the mystery of a secret it is not disclosing. The true object of Gerstl's ironic laugh may be the futility of the hope of getting to the bottom of the self in question; for most of his portraits are of people who seem, like wraiths, "to be attempting to re-materialize in a world they have long since left" (Whitford 1981: 55). Indeed, in the *Group Portrait* of the Schoenberg family, Gerstl's brushstrokes and colors on the faces are so thick that "the identities of the subjects are all but obliterated" (Kallir 1984: 51). The members of this family lack the distinctive features by which we recognize persons. The self is Gerstl's subject, but it has become a conundrum.[12]

The two painters who do the most with the lead of Gerstl are Schiele and Oskar Kokoscha. Here, what is only implicit in van Gogh and Munch—though overexplicit in postwar expressionist painting—becomes a whole story: the dramatic efforts of a subject to come to expression. The drama is as clear in their portraits as in their self-portraits. In fact, at a cer-tain point one cannot even distinguish between the two types of self in question. By his own confession, Kokoschka took to painting portraits in order to overcome "self-alienation" (Kokoschka 1974: 36–37). What he sought in ostensible representations of others was actually self-knowledge. The explanation for how the distinction between I and other is blurred by his art is addressed by his 1912 lecture on an issue that he calls *das Bewusstsein der Gesichte*: the consciousness of visions, or the imaginative apprehension of a face, where seer and seen are both subsumed in an act of seeing. The vision, countenance, or face (for *Gesicht* is simultaneously all three) is not simply a depiction of some "consciousness" or knowledge; it is an appearance that *motivates* consciousness. It is neither an objective image nor an artist's subjective im-

---

12. On Gerstl's art, life, and relation to Schoenberg see Breicha 1991 and 1993; Kallir 1992; Schröder 1993.

pression, but a "stream" of understanding in which subjects and objects first receive their forms.[13] Consciousness of vision, claims Kokoschka's elusive essay, reproduces the functions of an oil lamp: the artist is a wick sucking up the oil provided by the aspects of others and then bursting into a flame of imagination. Consciousness of vision is not the form of an appearance, but *consciousness of* the form, or of appearance itself, a type of self-perception of that "nature, *Gesicht,* life" without which things have no form at all (Kokoschka 1912: 12). Vision-consciousness is Kokoschka's counterpart to the art of inner necessity in Kandinsky and the art of persuasion in Michelstaedter.[14] The "self" of which it speaks is one that has always already transcended itself.

Two works from 1909–1910 offer results of this consciousness of vision. One is a portrait of the architect Adolph Loos, the other of Herwarth Walden. Both faces are highlighted in a manner reminiscent of Munch's self-portrait of 1895, composed of jagged, almost animated layers of matter. The left eyes are surrounded by large rings of darker flesh, suggesting either an external bruise or the emanation of some energy deep inside the body. As frequently occurs in Kokoschka, the eyes speak of great spiritual distance from this body, a vision-consciousness transcending the medium through which it works. The distorted features of these two subjects—abstracted from every natural setting—not only suggest the oppression of consciousness by physical forces; they also suggest its rebellion against its palpable shapes (pictorially speaking: volume, line, color, gesture, and expression). What Schoenberg called the inborn and instinctive dimensions of the I, which have never

13. If "two selves" are fused in Kokoschka's portraits one must also recognize a third—that of the person observing the painting, especially where its subject stares straight into his or her eyes, as occurs so often in expressionist portraits. These paintings interpolate the subjectivities of not only their sitters but also their viewers, as though asking, "Who are you to be shocked by the countenance you see? And what of your own case? Have you ever questioned your own self-vision?"

14. In a defensive statement twenty years after the fact, Schoenberg upholds the "complete independence" of his paintings from those of Kokoschka, Gerstl, and Kandinsky (Schoenberg 1938). In the process he also sheds light on the distinctions within their conceptual vocabularies. Schoenberg recalls that he named his own paintings of 1910 "gazes" (*Blicke*); Kandinsky later called them "visions" (*Visionen*); Kokoschka spoke of his own paintings in terms of *Gesicht* (a word central also to Trakl; see Williams 1991: 153). Kokoschka's image of the artist as an oil lamp, fueled by a "superabundance of life," finds another link in Michelstaedter. On the title page of *Persuasion and Rhetoric* (which frequently describes persuasion as a process of transfiguring things into flames) Michelstaedter draws a lamp overflowing with oil. Next to a similar drawing in the margins of one of his books, he comments: "The lamp goes out because of lack of oil / I extinguished myself out of overflowing superbundance" (Michelstaedter 1975: 140–141). On Kokoschka's consciousness of vision, see Schorske 1981: 339–344. On Schoenberg's "gazes" see the essays in Schoenberg 1991b.

Fig. 21. Oskar Kokoschka, *Portrait of the Architect Adolf Loos,* 1909, oil.
Courtesy Bildarchiv Preussischer Kulturbesitz, Berlin.

found adequate expression in history, can only lacerate the appearances they physically inherit. This laceration is even more severe in Kokoschka's self-portraits, particularly the poster for *Der Sturm* of 1910
(fig. 23). If the aim of Kokoschka's art is to overcome self-alienation,
the cure lies in taking the disease to its extreme. The autoscopical self
confesses to its own mutilation, its victimization, its inability to discover
a true source of persuasion. At the same time this self has also left its
body. In consciousness of vision, its eyes are outside; it exists in subjective transcendence. None of the "three selves" involved in the process of vision—the artist, the sitter, the viewer—is constituted except
through this transcendent activity of seeing. No ontology of the I can be
represented.

Schiele's portraits reveal a comparable search for an identity that cannot be portrayed. If people who commissioned their portraits from the
young Austrian were frequently offended by the results (Otto Wagner
was one), it had to do with the fact that they did not recognize themselves in the forms they were given. Like Kokoschka, Schiele exagger-
ated their features, making them look older or more pained than they

Fig. 22. Oskar Kokoschka, *Portrait of Herwarth Walden,* 1910, oil. Courtesy Staatsgalerie Stuttgart.

were. In 1910 and 1911 he isolates his subjects from natural and imaginative settings. The atmospheric backgrounds of Gerstl, Kokoschka, and Max Oppenheim disappear, leaving only an emptiness from which the subject stands sharply out, sometimes isolated by the shielding margin of a halo. The "expressive solid inserted into a void" (Comini 1974:

Fig. 23. Oskar Kokoschka, *Self-Portrait* (Poster for *Der Sturm*), 1910, lithograph poster. Courtesy Robert Gore Rifkind Collection, Beverly Hills.

77) becomes an icon of pure subjectivity, a subjectivity as independent in Schiele as it is in Michelstaedter. Moreover, as with Kokoschka, such encounters between "naked souls and naked destiny" are just strategies for Schiele to make his own self-encounter.

In 1910 he adds two other kinds of compositions to the subjective analyses of others: female nudes and self-portraits. Beginning with secret paintings of his younger sister Gerti, Schiele's nudes eventually include a whole repertoire of females, many prepubescent. Concurrent to the nudes, Schiele turns increasingly to depicting himself—scowling, screaming, gesticulating, naked, masturbating, and finally inviting or fending off death. While Schiele sometimes attaches allegorical depth to these self-representations, calling them *The Lyric Poet, The Prophet,* and so on, this is an attempt to ennoble or universalize the findings of what is primarily an exercise in self-perception. Whatever their names, all subjects are Schiele.

In these examinations of the only true topic of human experience—the nature of the solitary, subjective, desiring I—Schiele attains the peak of his art. The nakedness of his own body in his self-portraits suggests that the "erotic" female nudes are not an entirely separate issue: The effort to strip the other of clothes and the willingness to expose oneself are aspects of a single quest for the naked self. By penetrating the defenses of another, one attempts to penetrate one's own. The reflection on eros leads inevitably to a reflection on the I that is its source. In Schiele everything comes back to the desiring subject, to the narcissistic, onanistic seat of all shimmering interests of self. "I am for myself," he writes in his "Self-Portrait" of 1910, "and for those to whom my thirsty, drunken craving to be free gives everything, and also for all, for I love —I also love all. I am the noblest of the noble" (Schiele 1921: 19; Nebehay 1979: 142). In his self-portraits, the noblest of the noble gives all that he knows of himself to the world.

The most sensational of these offerings is the writhing, paralytic, agonized figure of the *Nude Self-Portrait, Grimacing*. On the surface the most striking thing about this self-portrait is its absolute refusal to let anything stand in the way of complete and pure self-perception. The self has decided that it must see how it looks naked, with no added distractions in front of the mirror. Like Zeus and his souls in the Isles of the Blessed, it has stripped off its "acquired characteristics" and confronted the reality that remains: a desperately feeling and thinking body, a self-confined self exposed to the world. Autoscopy could hardly prove more

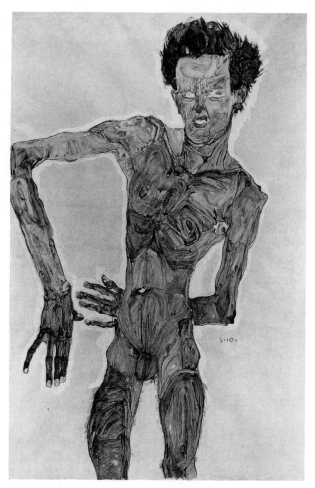

Fig. 24. Egon Schiele, *Nude Self-Portrait, Grimacing*,
1910, pencil, watercolor, and gouache. Courtesy Graphische Sammlung Albertina, Vienna.

troubling than it is in the portrait. Here the literally and painfully naked
self is the only frame of reference for human experience, tortured
against the void of a bad and empty infinity. The umbilicum, its original
source of nourishment, is a hole. We, the ostensibly dispensable audience, are made privy to the delirium of he who looks too hard at himself, finding no selfsame person but only the actor of his role.

As though to reinforce the intent of these self-portraits, Schiele embarks in the same year on a series of "self-seer" compositions in which

Fig. 25. Egon Schiele, *The Self-Seers I*, 1910, oil. Courtesy Galerie
St. Etienne, New York.

the topic is explicitly the self that looks at itself. More specifically, there
are two selves in the paintings, each looking at the other in a mirror
and yielding the plural *Self-Seers* of the title. The self has broken apart.
In *Self-Seers I* we have two identical and easily recognizable Schieles,
both naked, one kneeling behind the other and leaning out his head to
observe the reflection of the other—or of himself in the company of his
intimate other—in the mirror. The faces, bodies, and postures of each
are nearly identical. One is the perceiving self, the other the self perceived. And the self perceived—the image contemplated in the mirror
and committed to canvas, the I that is seen and known—is gripped by
theatrical tension and subjective defiance. The implicit role of the mirror in this double portrait makes the existential connotations of such

self-reflection clear: The subject is caught in a narcissistic circle of interest that has no other outside it. The I communes with the I, a puppet-like entity that it seeks to prop up and bring into obeyance.

If self-knowledge or self-possession is the objective of this type of autoscopy, it fails as much here as in Michelstaedter. The seemingly closed circle of the self is broken even before it is drawn—broken *in order* to be drawn. *Si duo idem faciunt non est idem,* Michelstaedter writes: "if two make one, it is not one" (Michelstaedter 1983: 423). The effort to know oneself is hindered by the self-splitting by which it is enabled. Self-knowledge, like self-expression, is a double mediation of appearance, a double rhetoric of form, a seeing that is twice removed, a seeing of seeing. And this is, of course, an impossible dialectic. There is also the presence of the audience, for whom this self-view is performed. Positioned as the reflecting mirror, the audience is the mediating element that validates the "other" which the autoscopy seeks to exclude.

That self-mastery does not succeed in Schiele is suggested not only by the brutalization of the two aspects of the self in the subsequent self-seer portraits, but also by Schiele's permanent failure to represent a fully dignified, self-possessed subjectivity in his portraits. As the years progress (and there are only eight before Schiele dies of the Spanish fever in 1918), he moves beyond the self to depict landscapes and human relations. But never does the historical, empirical self come under the domination of an ideal, transcendent one. Instead, it remains hounded by the same impersonal forces it hoped to put to its purposes: artifice, libido, mortality, dumb feeling. The effort to discover self-rule ends in the way it began—in a scream, not addressed to the world, as in Munch, so much as to the self this world has abandoned.

Do Schoenberg and Kandinsky follow similar patterns? While advocating adventures in self-absorption which lead one to express "the nature of mankind," Schoenberg gives us the *Red Gaze*: a vision of subjectivity as sheer fright. He gives us encounters with that hypothetical situation in which the individual "*is alone in the desert* and must create everything by himself." He gives us the self-portrait of the Blue Rider Exhibition in 1912: the backside view of a slight, bald man walking wearily away from the frame. Above all he gives us the harmonies of dissonance—correlates, in Adorno's view, of a "lonely subjectivity which withdraws into itself," where voyaging home means entering "a vitreous no-man's-land in whose crystalline-lifeless air the seemingly transcendent subject . . . finds himself again on an imaginary plane" (Adorno 1985: 142). Coupled with his ontology of individual solitude, the fragmentations and contractions of free atonal music entail a reduction of the self into virtual silence (a silence which literally follows this phase of Schoenberg's music, not broken until he formulates the principles of serial composition nearly ten years later). That which is "inborn, instinctive," and literally unconscious cannot be conceived or grasped in a common, universal language. Schoenberg's ostensibly subjectivist art thus issues into an impersonal aesthetic. "Think what self-denial it takes to express oneself with such brevity," says Schoenberg of Webern's breathlessly short *Six Bagatelles for String Quartet*:

> Every glance can be expanded into a poem, every sigh into a novel. But to express a novel with a single gesture, or a (person's) happiness with a single deep breath: such concentration is only to be found where there is a corresponding lack of self-pity. (Schoenberg 1992)

If this is an art of self-expression (and in Schoenberg's view it does intend to be), it is one that arises out of a virtual bereavement of language, aesthetics, and rhetoric. While Schoenberg views each of his compositions as "a self-portrait which should be presumed to bear a close resemblance to its creator" (Fleisher 1989: 22), the art to which this endeavor leads leaves no self behind. It issues into the very opposite of self-expression, a situation where

> no Ego oversees and directs the operations of transformation and organization—no Subject who . . . might comprehend and dominate the [musical] material. . . . Where there is no Thing there cannot even be a Subject. (Cacciari 1982: 156)

The inevitable consequence of the quest for self-expression is the dissolution of subjectivity into pure composition, into a "necessary" form of rhetoric with neither everyday nor metaphysical cogency.

A similar process can be traced in the artist who most explicitly defends the value of the inward turn. After dividing experience into the two antithetical categories of spirit and matter, content and form, intention and expression, Kandinsky recommends that art devote itself to the first set of terms (of which form, material, and so on, are only the instruments). But this conception of art already transcends an aesthetics of the subject, at least if subjectivity is associated with the emotional or historical constitution of a living human being. Kandinsky has no use for psychological or physiological approaches to the self. This, indeed, is the basis for his criticism of the paintings of Kokoschka, Schoenberg, and the *Brücke,* which in his view used art for predominantly confessional purposes. The true content of art, Kandinsky writes, is "the emotion in the soul of the artist" (Kandinsky 1910b: 87). And yet, this emotion is not the feeling of a person in a particular situation. Rather, it is a transpersonal "mood" in which all people can participate (Kandinsky 1914b: 403). "The birth of a work of art," he claims elsewhere, "is of cosmic character. The originator of the work is thus [not a particular artist but] the spirit. Thus, the work exists *in abstracto* prior to that embodiment which makes it accessible to the human senses" (Kandinsky 1914a: 394). If a work exists prior to its embodiment in form, its content transcends any given form of nature or historical experience. "As long as the soul remains joined to the body, it can as a rule only receive vibrations via the medium of the senses" (Kandinsky 1910b: 87); but in Kandinsky this soul is precisely *what is not represented* by the body— or by material and existential facts, by objective logic and philosophy, by historical and rhetorical form. The "true subject" is as transcendent here as the I in Husserl and Wittgenstein. It is not "in" the world; it is something that marks its borders, not a constituted form but an act of formal constitution, an "intention" exceeding expression.

The final nature of the I dissolves into something beyond the reach of all language and form. Its only form is one that it creates, and until it does so, this I or spirit can only be described in negative terms. "I do not want to paint states of mind. I do not want to paint coloristically or uncoloristically. . . . I do not want to show the future its path" (Kandinsky 1914a: 400). The absolute I is nothing that can be named before its forms have been invented. What lies beyond form can only be expressed by a form that is purified of empirical content: by shapes that are not representative, by unique new signs, by aesthetic surfaces not endowed with preestablished meanings. If the inner content of human experience is expressed by a form that is not recognizable (not "picturing" an entity or experience we can already conceive), the content is fully etherealized—no longer self but soul.

It is hard enough to experience spirit in everyday life, much less in the forms most proper to it: "The spirit is often concealed within matter to such an extent that few people are generally capable of perceiving it. Indeed, there are many people who are incapable of seeing the spirit even when incorporated in a spiritual form" (Kandinsky 1912a: 235). It is the second sentence that is crucial, for it suggests that there is such a spiritual form, an art of pure composition, of autonomous rhetoric without any criterion of evaluation. In practical terms, it takes an already cultivated audience to distinguish the "content" of a Kandinsky from the mere "formal exercises" of other types of painting. How can the viewer *tell* whether a work embodies spiritual content or not? "Only its author can fully assess the caliber of a work of art" (Kandinsky 1910b: 87). An artistic procedure "is only and exclusively *good*, properly speaking, if it has come of its own accord" (Kandinsky 1914a: 394). But no such judgment can be confidently made by someone outside the creative process. Indeed, as many conservative critics of art have charged throughout our century, objective criteria for the "aesthetically good" are in a very real sense made obsolete by the work of Kandinsky and Schoenberg. Such criteria can only be re-created by each work anew, each on its own individual terms. No work can be properly read until and unless its hidden, internal mechanisms are discovered.

After Schoenberg and Kandinsky, the aesthetic validity of a work no longer lies in any self-evident subject—for here such a subject is no longer self-evident, and does not even exist *before* the work—but only in the communicative lines that it establishes with its audience, in the relationship that it instills between audience and artist. And this changes the very notion of a work's "inner necessity." Now this necessity is present only where "the vibration in the soul of the artist [finds] a material form, a means of expression, which is capable of being picked up by the receiver" (Kandinsky 1910b: 87). The choice of colors, forms, and subject matter in painting *"can only be based on the principle of purposefully touching the human soul*. This basic tenet we shall call the *principle of internal necessity"* (Kandinsky 1909–11: 160; cf. 165 and 169). The innerness or content of art thus lies outside it, in the activity it engenders in human beings, in the manner of Buber's moments of "heightened experience," where no subject confronts an object, but rather a significant occurrence absorbs them both in its flow. By pursuing a spirituality that can withstand the deficiency of being, Kandinsky abolishes the subject standing over and against the object in at least three ways: He makes it fully abstract (i.e., not reducible to a concrete, historical self); he dissolves its content into form; and he notes that even this form cannot be understood as a "sign" for a content, but only as the medium of a hermeneutical activity in which that content *occurs*. Less than anyone else can the artist say "I."

Thus Schoenberg and Kandinsky duplicate the path of Schiele, Kokoschka, and Michelstaedter. The soul, not the self, is their true subject of interest and knowledge. Yet this most "intrinsic" of realities, this "noumenon" contrasted with all phenomena, is no longer intrinsic or self-contained. The gaze inward yields nothing but the process of gazing, not focused on any fixed subject or object.

After these prewar attempts to give form to soul, the very notion of the soul is lost. It naturally and inevitably erases itself, living on, at best, as a name for its absence, as an announcement of the definitive impossibility of possessing a language for what is most real.[15] Innerness, subjectivity, persuasion, individualism, and the self—by dint of the effort to discover their nature (or to accomplish the goal of Western humanism)—lose their meaning. After the expressionists, artists no longer even believe in self-constituting realms of subjectivity. Futurism, imagism, dadaism, and surrealism—not to mention the emotional outcries of postwar expressionism and irrational new arts of the id—wittingly or unwittingly espouse the end of the I as "the measure of all things." All this replicates the catastrophe of collective and historical self-determination in the Great War of 1914. Believing that their action was self-determining, the warring powers discovered instead that the selves and the passions they were serving were almost totally at the mercy of outside forces. Bent on controlling its own destiny, each national or ethnic group was forced to recognize that such destiny was a thoroughly contextual matter. The world of victors and vanquished alike was one in which Michelstaedter's principles of dependent, rhetorical, and correlative existence were more real and intractable than all self-governing dreams.

The great pathos of prewar expressionist art thus lies in its pursuing a Western ideal to the point where it collapses in exhaustion. As Kandinsky puts it, "the seeds of the struggle toward . . . *inner nature* . . . obey the words of Socrates: 'Know thyself!'" (Kandinsky 1909–11: 153). The ideal of self-expression appears predicated upon the possibility of self-knowledge, but this, in turn, relies on a belief in the self. One can

15. The most eloquent postwar descriptions of this unliving "center" of subjective experience are achieved (in negative terms) by Robert Musil's *The Man Without Qualities*. Having established that every person has at least nine selves or characters (national, sexual, unconscious, etc.), the narrator of the novel concludes that "every inhabitant of the earth also has a tenth character that is nothing else than the passive fantasy of spaces yet unfilled." The true essence of a person, or the only innerness that is not contingent, now appears to be this empty space (or better, this *illusion* of an empty space). "Whether one is at rest or in motion, what matters is not what lies ahead, what one sees, hears, wants, takes, masters. . . . Something is not quite in balance, and a person presses forward, like a tightrope walker, in order not to sway and fall. And as he presses on through life and leaves lived life behind, the life ahead and the life already lived form a wall, and his path in the end resembles the path of a woodworm: no matter how it corkscrews forward or even backward, it always leaves an empty space behind it. And this horrible feeling of a blind, cutoff space behind the fullness of everything, this half that is always missing even when everything is a whole, this is what eventually makes one perceive what one calls the soul" (Musil 1930–40: vol. 1, chaps. 8 and 45).

express oneself only if one (a) possesses such a self, (b) is properly attuned to it, and (c) gives it a convincing form. In the period separating Socrates from twentieth-century vitalism these principles encounter no absolutely insuperable obstacles. The problems arise when everything appears to hinge on these principles and them alone. At the height of its cultural appeal, self-expression begins to look like an ideal but unreal plan. There no longer exists any measure for the "measure of all things." Subjectivity, the only true content of objective experience, proves to be the ultimate bastion of otherness, the absolutely self-alienated object. The ideal of self-expression leads directly to suicide.

But in this death begin ethics and aesthetics.

CHAPTER FOUR

An Ethics of Misunderstanding

If a man could write a book on ethics which really was
a book on Ethics . . . this book would, with an explosion,
destroy all other books in the world.
                                        —*Ludwig Wittgenstein*

As György Márkus notes in a classic essay on the young Lukács, the
antinomy of life and the soul makes it impossible to mold experience
into a personal destiny. Empirical life cannot be turned into a coherent
totality that is governed by the ethical will. Yet this is precisely what
Michelstaedter and the young Lukács seek most ardently to do: to make
rhetoric submit to persuasion, to reconcile the necessity and the contingency of human experience. In 1910 neither succeeds in offering more
than an image of their nonreconciliation, whether in such figures as
Kierkegaard, Socrates, and Christ or in such works as Giovanni Bat-
tista Pergolesi's *Stabat Mater.* On the one hand, both thinkers consider
artistic expression to offer a means by which to transcend the relativity of arbitrary, fluctuant, historical life. Articulating the "true essence
of life," artistic form offers proof that faith in subjective transcendence
"is justified, for it is its living realization, more truly alive than all of
life" (Lukács 1910b: 28). On the other hand both thinkers admit that
the abstractness of artistic expression sets it apart from the concrete
experience that gave it birth. Although it mediates between the soul
and everyday life, artistic form "can never finally resolve the antagonism, the dualism, between them." While persuasive form springs from
life, it also "breaks away from it, and breaks away sharply, simply because it is totally self-enclosed. . . . It is a new life which . . . has (and
can have) no point of contact with anything beyond itself from the moment it comes into being" (Márkus 1983: 11, 12). As Martin Buber
expresses it, artistic experience

transposes us into the midst of a world which we are incapable of entering. Living so enclosed by it that it appears that nothing could separate us from it, penetrated and confirmed by it, we still recognize it as the forever remote distance. This world is reality, unified and certain as no natural world can be; it alone is finished reality. We abandon ourselves to it and breathe in its sphere. Yet it is also image: its essence is withdrawn from and inaccessible to us. (Buber 1913b: 67)

Hence, even if art provides evidence that "the alienation of 'ordinary' life can be overcome," it still does not eradicate this alienation from historical practice. Nor does it ensure the communication or communion of souls which it was designed to serve. In truth, the persuasive forms of art only carry the inadequacy of everyday processes of communication to a higher level (Márkus 1983: 11, 12). The possibility of "misunderstanding, which in empirical reality was only a *verité de fait*," writes Lukács, becomes in art "*a vérité éternelle*" (Lukács 1912–14: 56). This truth—that no truth can be free from misunderstanding and no language can unify life and the soul—"is not abolished by art; it is merely eternalized. It is changed from an empirical to a constitutive category" (Márkus 1983: 13).

Upon this realization arises the tragedy of artists: "All the perfection they give to works, all the depths of experience they pour into them," writes Lukács, "are in vain. They remain more silent, less able to express themselves, than people in ordinary life, who are all locked up into themselves" (Lukács 1912–14: 80). These other people have at least the unifying bonds of gossip and chatter. Artists, by contrast, place all their bets on the possibility of a transcendent, universal communiqué. But this still leaves the contingent historical experiences of which they speak without a voice of their own, still formless and mute.

Neither Lukács nor Michelstaedter has a solution to this tragedy. On the contrary, they suggest that the creative process can only be played out in its space, in the distance that separates persuasive and timeless forms from the historical labor of rhetorical hours. It is precisely this distance which nourishes and sustains all ethical and aesthetic achievements. Ethics concerns the question of how to live; aesthetics involves the procedures for addressing the question. Ethics evaluates the situations and conditions of historical experience; aesthetics is the *instrument* of evaluation, the set of interpretive strategies for making such evaluations, including the feelings or desires we make them serve. Taken together, the two categories name the conscious motivations of human beings, inevitably unfolding between an ideal and an actual realm, between persuasive goals and the philopsychic interests to which they cater or with which they vie. In essence, the rift between theory and practice which characterizes the human condition is the soil from which ethics and aesthetics spring. It is also the soil to which these seeds fall back, submitting their ideals to the judgments of the historical world. In this perspective, ethical and aesthetical activity does not articulate "goodness" or "beauty," affirming an imaginary value over and against a historical one. It does not abstract a vision or an idea from experience and give it a form. It enacts an irresolvable *battle* between idea and experience.

To submit to this battle is not to throw up one's hands in a gesture of spiritual defeat. It is to adopt a more complicated understanding of spiritual activity, including a more dynamic conception of the nature of human motivation, expression, and will. Where harmonic ideals are contested by the dissonance within and against which they strive, aesthetic or ethical responsibility is not relinquished; it is embraced for the very first time.

ETHICAL AND AESTHETIC TRANSCENDENCE

Ethics and aesthetics involve consciousness and language. But language, as Buber claims, "is adequate to everything, only not to the ground of experience" (1909: 7). The ground of experience, which consciousness would like to seize and fix in form, can only be obscured by the "commotion" of things linguistic, whether they serve logic or just personal desire (that desire which originates language, in Augustine's and Michelstaedter's view, making us point to the things we want and then gives them names). "Language is knowledge," Buber continues, "and knowledge is the work of the commotion" (1909: 6).

Language is not only the realm of signs rather than things. It is also "a function of community, and it can say nothing except what is held in common." To voice a truly individual experience one would have to transcend such language and speak in a way no one could understand. By transcending language one would also transcend one's bonds with one's fellows, experiencing a condition in which "one no longer has others *outside* oneself, no longer has any communion with them or anything in common with them." Indeed, that true realization of experience which the young Buber calls ecstasy "stands beyond the common experience. It is unity, solitude, uniqueness: that which cannot be transferred" (Buber 1909: 6).

Ironically, the philosopher who did the most to defend the validity of that realm of linguistic "commotion" agreed with his fellow Austrian about all that its communal, rhetorical knowledge excludes from its reach. A few years after Michelstaedter's death, Ludwig Wittgenstein began to jot down the notes that found their way into the only work he signed in his lifetime, the *Tractatus Logico-Philosophicus*.[1] A systematic treatise on everything that can be properly said, the *Tractatus* opens with the proposition, "The world is all that is the case." All that is the case is all that comes to pass as well as to pass away. It is that, and only that, which can be described as historically occurring. Historically means in a contingent rather than necessary way, for, as Wittgenstein sees it, "all happening and being-so is accidental." One cannot explain *why* whatever happens *has* to happen, or why events occur in any particular way. While contingent, historical events cannot be explained, however, they can still be described, and in a rhetoric on whose rules we can communally agree. This rhetoric for the young Wittgenstein (or commotion for Buber) amounts to a system of objective reference, where words name things, and the relations between them can be organized in a propositional grammar. Proper use of the system supplies us with the certainty we associate with science.

The self-professed mission of the *Tractatus*, then, is to prescribe the proper usage of language—the limits within which things can be legitimately described. And as for everything else, the conclusion of the work is clear: "Whereof one cannot speak, thereof one must be silent" (Wittgenstein 1922: #1, 6.41, 7).

In another reading, however, the *Tractatus* appears even more interested in carving out a space for what *cannot* be said in propositional language, as though to preserve it from violation. This unspeakable space is the space of everything that colors the facts—the space of ethics and aesthetics, which make use of "what is the case," subordinating it to intentions and goals. Ethics and aesthetics are stipulations of value: the right and the wrong, the good and the bad, the beautiful and the ugly, what is or is not desirable, what should or should not be done in a given situation. In the mildest reading, the stricture of silence that the *Tractatus* passes on these types of issues, by eliminating them

1. The *Tractatus Logico-Philosophicus* was first published in German in 1921 as *Logisch-philosophische Abhandlung* and a year later in a definitive edition, with facing English translations and an introduction by Bertrand Russell. Citations from the *Tractatus* will henceforth be identified by the number of the propositions rather than the pages on which they appear. The English translations have sometimes been revised.

from the realm of what can be meaningfully said, only cautions that a rhetoric of denotation cannot posit the value of anything. The true interest of ethics and aesthetics—the ultimate "sense" or value of what is the case—transcends the perceptible world of observable facts:

> 6.41 The sense of the world must lie outside the world. In the world everything is as it is and happens as it happens. . . .
> If there is a value which is of value, then it must lie outside all happening and being-so. For all happening and being-so is accidental. . . .
> 6.42 Hence also there can be no ethical propositions.
> Propositions cannot express anything higher.
> 6.421 It is clear that ethics cannot be expressed. Ethics are transcendental. (Ethics and aesthetics are one.)

A third unspeakable subject, beyond ethics and aesthetics, is metaphysics: the study of why some aspect of totality of world events is *not* accidental. "What makes it non-accidental cannot lie *in* the world, for otherwise this would again be accidental" (Wittgenstein 1922: #6.41). To argue the necessity of a certain state of affairs one would also have to explain why this argument *itself* is necessary, and so on ad infinitum.

In the describable world "all propositions are of equal value (*gleichwertig*). . . . In the world everything is as it is and happens as it happens. *In* it there is no value—and if there were, it would be of no value" (Wittgenstein 1922: #6.4–6.41). All meaningful propositions, or statements of fact, are value-free. Every occurrence in history (which the soul would like to mold into a meaningful destiny) is equi-valent, in Cacciari's phrase—meaningful and valid to the same degree, "just" in the degree to which it actually occurs and therefore requires no justification (Cacciari 1980: 41–49, 135–140).

Hence by separating speakable facts from the concerns of ethics/aesthetics, Wittgenstein divides consciousness into two different activities, one epistemologically legitimate, the other illegitimate. One recognizes and describes the equivalent conditions of the world, however insignificant they might seem to be; another reorganizes, interprets, or ranks these facts. But by doing so this second operation negates the equivalence of the facts that it ranks, and can never make its claims persuasive. It passes judgment but cannot support this judgment with relevant discourse. So far, then, the young Wittgenstein seems to share the same epistemological space as Buber, even if not necessarily his assessment of it. Wittgenstein's accurate, objective, and relevant language is Buber's commotion. It is Michelstaedter's rhetoric and Kandinsky's materialism—all equally incapable of discovering value in a casual, accidental, equivalent world. The only thing that ultimately matters to the mind—namely, the question of what *to do* with these facts—is beyond the reach of its knowledge. And this includes the issue of the well-springs of human interest: "Of the will as the subject of the ethical," Wittgenstein warns, "we cannot speak" (Wittgenstein 1922: #6.423). If we did speak of the will we would simply be recasting this *source* of values as just another object among many, another element within the discourse that it presumably shapes. And the same can be said of Lukács's soul, of Michelstaedter's persuasion, of Buber's direction, and of Kandinsky's inner necessity. The deepest proclivities of the I cannot be fathomed by propositions.

This is not to say that ethics and aesthetics have no means of expression at all, but just that they cannot co-opt the language of knowledge. Notions of the desirable and the good do find their way into language. They act on it from the outside, as it were, in the manner of a Kantian "transcendental," informing patterns of speech even while being unable to become their object. We could also say this: It is not language that posits the desirable or the good; language is posited in them. "The inexpressible," as Wittgenstein writes in 1917, "is—inexpressibly—*contained* in what is expressed!" (Engelmann 1968: 6; translation revised). The beautiful and the good lie in nothing that language can say or conduct can follow; they are perspectives that are revealed in and by means of the shapes of language and conduct. They are treatments, perhaps even in a sense epistemological misuses, of descriptions, facts, or propositions.

In "The Teaching of the Tao" (1910) Buber distinguishes such treatments from the rule-governed rhetoric of science and law. These treatments amount to another type of speaking, a speaking indirectly, in tones of "concealment," in parables and myths, in words of "transition," which carry the absolute into the world of things and the world of things into the absolute (Buber 1910a: 42, 35). This other way of speaking is that speech of the Tao, or the Way, which Westerners call logos. Logos, says Buber, offers neither information about the "is" nor commandments of an "ought." It does something much more important: It transposes human life "into the transcendent," into the soil or horizon of human experience from which meaning grows. Logos does not explain itself. It cannot be represented. It "simply proclaims itself." And if language is knowledge, as Buber had claimed the previous year, then logos "is not knowing but being." "Man utters his words as the logos utters men" (Buber 1910a: 45, 49, 33, 52, 40).

Logos, then, is not meaning but the space of meaning, in whose context things let themselves be denoted and described. And this logos determines all uses of language.

This non-propositional space of language is related to that "highest judge of life" which Lukács calls form. Form, he writes in *Soul and Form*,

> is a judging force, an ethics; there is a value-judgment in everything that has been given form. Every kind of form-giving, every literary form, is a step in the hierarchy of life-possibilities: the all-decisive word has been spoken about a man and his fate when the decision is taken as to the form which his life-manifestations can assume and which the highest moments of his life demand. (Lukács 1910–11a: 173)

The "judgment" of form is not pronounced by positing facts or stipulating moral laws. It resides in a use of facts now transposed to an "imaginary" or "fictitious" space where they are no longer facts at all, but possible conditions of being. Ethics and aesthetics do not lie in the "content" of communicative behavior but in its form. Or, as Kandinsky would say, their special type of form entails a special type of content, one casting into doubt whether any content at all can be anything other than an effect of form.

But if this is so, and ethics and aesthetics can indeed find form in language, then why does Wittgenstein insist that they are unspeakable? "It is clear," he reemphasizes, "that ethics cannot be expressed" (Wittgenstein 1922: #6.421). It may be that he wishes to stress that one cannot assume that there is any necessary correlation between a moral teaching or an imaginative vision and the subject of which they speak. Every teaching or work of art is a fanciful sense of the facts. Its forms cannot be confused with the actual situations they treat (those historical, human situations which the young Lukács considered the most ineffable and formless realities of all). Wittgenstein intends to discourage the idealized use of ethics and aesthetics, the habits of dictating, as it were, in definitive and "propositional" terms, ethically or aesthetically appropriate behavior. No imaginative scenario can ever be presented as true. Any attempt to "justify" a particular view of affairs lacks its own justification; it speaks in the manner of an absolute, and thus absolutely arbitrarily, as something that cannot be proven by argumentation. "What rule are we using or referring to," asks Wittgenstein, "when we say: 'This is the correct way'?" (Wittgenstein 1966: 4).

This, once again, is the tragedy of the artist as well as the teacher. It is what Schoenberg himself acknowledged when he confessed that he could not teach but by example, and perhaps only by creating confusion. The very basis for the activity of the artist and the teacher is spiritual, linguistic bereavement. If they overlook the difference between what can and cannot be said, and prescribe an imaginative vision as though it were true, then all they offer is a misuse of language, false aesthetics, kitsch, a form that does not admit to its distance from things. And this is the danger of idealization.

To avoid this danger, ethics and aesthetics must begin in a recognition of the poverty from which they arise—a recognition of (1) how little is accomplished by grounding all knowledge in propositions and (2) how ungrounded is even the effort to transcend such propositions, or to picture an alternative state of affairs. "We feel," writes Wittgenstein on the first issue, "that even if *all possible* scientific questions be answered, the problems of life have still not been touched at all" (Wittgenstein 1922: #6.52). As for the second issue, Lukács notes that these "problems of life" cannot be touched on at all until their discursive space has been firmly distinguished from the space of science, information, morals, and law. Lukács's most remarkable attempt to delineate such a space takes place in 1911, in his "conversation and letter" called "On Poverty of Spirit."

SPIRITUAL POVERTY

Lukács writes his conversation in the months following the suicide of Irma Brandeis. "On Poverty of Spirit" is shaped as a letter from a certain Martha, the sister of a recent suicide (let us call her Irma), to the father of a close friend of Irma (let us call him Lukács). The letter tells the father of Lukács about a conversation between him and Martha shortly before he too followed the path of Irma. What reasons did Lukács have for ending his life? According to Martha's report he considered himself incapable of the goodness which could have saved Irma's life. Both suicides are thus caused by a failure of goodness, for had Lukács possessed it he would have spared two lives at once.

The interest of "On Poverty of Spirit" lies in its rigorous distinction between goodness in an absolute sense and intellectually, rhetorically, or socially based ethics (or action that is consonant with rules and models and signs). Lukács calls the latter ethics pure and simple, understanding it to entail a set of conceptions about what is appropriate to do in a given situation, usually by invoking a law or precedent by which to interpret a historical situation.

If Lukács feels responsible for Irma's suicide it is hardly because his ethics were not in order. He is not guilty of having been unwilling to respond to her appeals for help. Rather, he is guilty of not seeing through the signs in which the appeals were masked. Like many individuals with a strong sense of principle, he is a poor reader of concrete occurrence:

> According to every law of human morality I am guilty of nothing; on the contrary, I honestly carried out each one of my duties (he pronounced this word with great contempt). I did everything I could . . . she knew that there was nothing I would not have done had she only asked it of me. However, she requested nothing, and I saw and heard nothing. (Lukács 1911c: 372–373)

What makes Lukács guilty *before God* of Irma's death is that he was unable to communicate with her speechless soul. Had he been able to see into this woman he could have saved her from despair. Instead, he admits, "I had no ears for the voice of her silence . . . I adapted my behavior to the life-praising tone of her letters." Lukács is guilty of having followed the dictates of seemingly self-evident appearance, of having adapted his action to the shape of letters. Nothing would have changed if he had been in Irma's presence:

> I might have spied pain in her face and heard a new quivering in her voice. But what would I have learned from them? The understanding of the human heart is an interpretation of statements and signs, and who can say whether they are true or simulated? And one thing is clear: we interpret according to our own laws what occurs in the eternal unknownness of the other. (Lukács 1911c: 373)

The problem with methods for doing what is right is just that—they are methods and nothing more. They are dependent on rhetoric, on a system of signs standing in for souls and the communicative exchange that is enabled by these signs, a system in which one listens only for recognizable requests and responds only to audible calls (including the calls of duty and conscience, impersonal as any). The problem with ethics is that it is just a handbook. Its suggestions and regulations are products of speech-act theory. Hearing and responding to calls is not goodness; it is conformity of behavior to rules. If Lukács had possessed the independence of mind that comes with true goodness he would have understood something in Irma's situation which the rules could neither see nor say. "Had I been graced with goodness, her silence would have resounded far across the lands that separated us." Think back, he tells Martha, "on how the thoughts of others become manifest to Francis of Assisi. He does not guess at them. No. They become manifest to him. His knowledge is beyond signs and interpretation. He is good. In these moments he is the other" (Lukács 1911c: 373).

Does Martin Buber have Lukács's dialogue in mind when, one year after it appears in German, he, too, links goodness to silent understanding? In *Daniel* he writes that there are two ways of achieving the communion of souls that goodness entails: "decided acting" and "keeping silent"—just as Saint Francis kept silent when the Spanish Dominic said to him, "Brother, I would that your rule and mine were one" (Buber 1913a: 118–119). Such oneness cannot be willed, and it certainly cannot be the effect of a rule.[2] As "On Poverty of Spirit" understands it, goodness transcends the normative conventions of ethics. It registers messages that have no words. It is that "truly directed address" of Buber in whose every utterance "I 'mean' the person to whom I send it . . . this one unexchangeable person" (1913a: 47). Once again we are in the realm of logos, making such address more like music than speech. It can only be said "in deeds, not in words," and is to be recognized only "through its effect" (Buber 1913a: 58). Those graced with goodness, in Lukács and Buber, break down the barriers separating self from self. They possess "something like an understanding of humans which radiates, penetrating into everything, in which object and subject come to coincide: the good person no longer *interprets* the soul of the other, but reads in it as in his own; he *has become* the other" (Lukács 1911c: 375).

Thus does "On Poverty of Spirit" revise Lukács's earlier claim in "The Metaphysics of Tragedy" that humans are destined to solitude. The solitude presented there as an irremediable ontological condition now appears to be itself a product of rhetoric. Suicide is at bottom nothing else than an effect of communicative failure, the misappropriation of personal blame for the limits of linguistic expression. It is rhetoric that kills oneself and the other. One dies in language, or rather in

---

2. Lukács's influence on Buber remains largely unexplored. Most of what we know concerns the opposite influence, of Buber on Lukács. It is clear, for example, that Lukács had read Buber's *Ecstatic Confessions* by November, 1910. The following summer he comments on two other books of Buber, *Die Legende des Baal Schem* (1908) and *Die Geschichten des Rabbi Nachman* (1906). However, given echoes of Lukács's own work in Buber's *Daniel* of 1913, one begins to suspect that the influence was reciprocal. By February 1911 Buber had read Lukács's essay on Kierkegaard. By November of the same year Lukács had also sent him the German edition of *Soul and Form* in which the essay appears. Impressed by both, Buber responded to Lukács in some detail on the Kierkegaard essay. See their exchange of letters in Lukács, *Briefwechsel 1902–1920*, ed. Éva Karádi and Éva Fekete (Stuttgart: Metzler, 1982).

a misuse of language, a misuse that is communally sanctioned. Purporting to draw humans together, moral regulations only codify distance:

> Every ethics is formal: duty is a postulate, a form, and the more completed a form, the more it leads a life of its own, and the further away it falls from all immediacy. It is a bridge that divides us; a bridge over which we come and go and always arrive back at ourselves, without ever encountering each other. (Lukács 1911c: 374)

In their very abstraction these postulates and forms ignore the weaving dynamics of life, "its temporal fates, the unceasing differentiation of each of its parts" (Simmel 1918a: 25). The formality and universality of ethical laws stop us from stepping out to meet one another on unique and concrete terms. Ethics, writes Lukács, is "general and extraneous" to human beings, removing them from their living conditions. Goodness, instead, is a "return to real life," the life that resists its forms. "Living life is beyond forms, ordinary life is on this side of them, and goodness is the grace to shatter these forms [*die Güte ist das Begnadetsein: die Formen zerbrechen zu können*]" (Lukács 1911c: 375, 374). It is the same position taken by Kandinsky in the context of art. The broken and apparently anarchic forms of contemporary art, he had claimed, are the natural and inevitable consequences of a feeling for the good.

At this point Martha makes a bold objection to Lukács's argument. She claims that his notion of goodness is a frivolous one. While human solidarity may well be the objective of goodness, this does not mean that we can do without the signs that point us in its direction. It would be like turning to the end of a book without reading through its pages. Lukács is not overwhelmed by Martha's critique. His goodness, he answers, is an ethics of God, not of man. It is not the *effect* of ethical behavior but its cause—what makes it possible. What is frivolous, if anything, is the idea that one can be good simply by willing to be, or by obeying the letter of the law. This is not the frivolity, but the outright obtuseness of approaching the beginning by way of the end, of hoping to discover the foundation of ethics by enacting the gestures to which it leads. Goodness does not entail a psychological assessment of the consequences of this or that act. It is a "metapsychological" principle. If one judges it by its effects it is probably even "useless and has no cause." Good acts are "fruitless, confusing and without result." They only generate confusion in the understanding. And of all things with which they can be confused, the worst is a program for self-improvement. One is simply "not allowed . . . to want to be good" (Lukács 1911c: 374, 375, 378), for as Wittgenstein says, "if it took a theory to explain the nature of the ethical to someone, then the ethical would have no value at all." "You cannot lead people to the good; you can only lead them to a place. The good lies outside the space of facts (*Tatsachenraum*)" (Wittgenstein 1979: 116–117, 1977: 3).

Lukács is certainly willing to admit that a transcendent, pragmatically "useless" goodness shares little with the everyday principles we typically follow when deliberating what to do. And yet nothing but this "wild" and "adventurous" ideal accounts for the existence of such principles to begin with. Only *because* the good is so difficult to achieve do we formulate these principles at all. "If art could mold life, if goodness could be translated into act—then we would become gods" (Lukács 1911c: 377, 375). Put otherwise, the transcendent nature of the aims of both ethics and aesthetics is not a reason for reinterpreting the good and beautiful in practical terms. The aims of ethics and aesthetics should not be made pragmatic just because it takes a miracle to achieve them. On the contrary, the transcendence of the aims marks the boundaries within which we can actually, historically operate. "Justice," notes Michelstaedter, "the just person, the individual who is *in* the right, is a hyperbole." True virtue is a curve that approaches the straight line of justice without being able to reach it. Even as the distance separating a hyperbole from its axis gets smaller and smaller, so "the curve must prolong itself infinitely to make contact." And this means that good as a person may seem to be, "so infinite remains his duty toward justice" (Michelstaedter 1910: 77–79). Poverty remains the irremediable ground of justice. The only resolution one can make in the meantime is "to keep ourselves ready for our virtue" (Lukács 1911c: 383). "One purchases the right to life," in Michelstaedter's words, "not with limited work but with limitless activity." To expiate the guilt we possess by participating in the deficiency of being, we must embrace only one duty that overrides all others: "*to give everything and ask for nothing*" (Michelstaedter 1910: 78–79, 80).

Conceding to Martha that conventions for the good are all we can ever express, Lukács simply engages in the experiment of imagining what the good in itself might look like. Would it not entail a pure and impractical self-giving? A value at the source of all value? A direction without orientation? A logos underlying language?

While some might object that Lukács fails to heed Wittgenstein's strictures against predicating the good, he is perfectly well aware of the bind he is in. Like Michelstaedter's persuasion, his goodness remains indescribable. "It carries no signs, no indications that can be communicated, studied, or repeated" (Michelstaedter 1910: 104). "Incomprehensible and misunderstood, it emerges from life exactly like a solitary and great work of art" (Lukács 1911c: 375). This is the second time that Lukács likens the ethical realm to the aesthetic one, suggesting that each enacts a unique type of form that defies the limitations of communicative form. Each offers a solitary event that all available sign systems are destined to misunderstand. This, too, is why Lukács finds it easier to define goodness negatively—as the power to *shatter* such forms, as though this dissonant act might articulate the "living life" beyond them.

However perfect, persuasive, or original the form of a good act or work may be, its greatest distinction lies in something *else* that it reveals—something beneath, behind, or beyond its form. And this something is a tragic understanding: that form can never be generalized and always undermines the conventions it uses. Thus we reach Lukács's most profound description of form, more eloquently drawn than all recent theorizations of aesthetic negativity:

> Every written work, even if it is no more than a consonance of beautiful words, leads us to a great door—through which there is no passage. Every written work leads towards moments in which we can suddenly glimpse the dark abysses into whose depths we must fall one day. . . . Every written work is constructed round a question and progresses in such a way that it can suddenly stop at the edge of an abyss—suddenly, unexpectedly, yet with compelling force. And even if it leads us past luxuriant palm groves or fields of flowing white lilies, it will always lead to the edge of the great abyss, and can never stop anywhere else before it reaches its edge. This is the most profound meaning of form: to lead to a great moment of silence, to mold the directionless, precipitous, many-coloured stream of life as though all its haste were only for the sake of such moments [*die ziellos dahinschiefsende Buntheit des Lebens so zu gestalten, als eile sie nur um solcher Augenblicke willen*]. . . . A question, with life all round it; a silence, with a rustling, a noise, a music, a universal singing in front of, behind, and all around it: that is form. (Lukács 1910–11a: 113–114)

The greatest, most communicative forms arise there where one runs up against the limits of language. Words find their value where rhetoric fails. Goodness does the same in the face of morality. The silence at the heart of the artwork—the great "question" it addresses to the stream of life—is the unspeakability out of which it arises, or the knowledge that something is inevitably concealed in each one of its revelations. Form, in ethics and aesthetics, both damns and redeems itself. Its consonance is a product of dissonance, its miraculous tones are audible failures. Just as the I is the unspeakable edge of the empirical world, so goodness is the border of morals and logos the border of language. None offers an answer but only a question, with life all around it.

TRAGIC ACQUIESCENCE

According to Buber, Wittgenstein, and Lukács the higher wisdom of ethics and aesthetics involves formal recognition of the limitations of form, one implicitly announcing that no historical reality can be theoretically justified and no expression can retread the bridge that distances it from its intentions. Does such a wisdom have ethical implications of its own? Can any practical ethics, so to speak, be deduced from the undeducible nature of ethics? In one sense the answer is yes.

By recognizing the limitations of rhetoric we also agree to respect such limits. We no longer put language into the service of moral, metaphysical systems. By limiting language to a grammar of universal, conventional meaning, we accept the world as an appearance of its "correlative" or "commotional" media—as a value-less complexity of events defying whatever judgments one might wish to pass on them by means of these media. When the limits of my language are the limits of my world, I cannot conceive of reality outside of the finite, multiplicitous, accidental phenomena of which it is built. Reality is now presented to the understanding as a historically unfolding totality of concrete events—or nothing more or less than what it seems to be (which always changes). This "seeming" is the *only* reality, the only "divinity" of a godless world. "What is mystical," writes Wittgenstein, "is the feeling of the world as a limited whole" (1922: #6.45). What is mystical is the sense that the significance of experience is fully transcribed by language, that for all practical purposes things are indistinguishable from their forms of appearance, and that the highest respect one can show them is simply to note *how* they are. What is mystical, in other words, is not the sense of an extra-linguistic domain of truth. It is the givenness of speech itself, by which "the inexpressible is inexpressibly contained in what is expressed." And this is just another way of saying that experience is revealed by the words that we use (Cacciari 1982: 70–98, 1980: 19–32).

The limitations of rhetoric reorient our attention to the fortuitous,

rhetorical sum of natural/historical experience in which nothing has
any "inner identity" and everything is a function of its correlations. To
accept the exclusive reality of this rhetorical world is to acknowledge
that it does not incorporate those independent, universal or spiritual
values which we wish to discover within it. On the contrary, it militates against this process of idealization. All it shows is a type of "necessary" accidentality, creation and destruction in perpetuity, clarity and
darkness, emerging and passing away, rising and falling, wordless wishing and conventional speaking.

A similar view can be located in Michelstaedter. Once he recognizes
that experience contains no living correlatives for "eternity," "permanence," and "being," he finds himself in a world composed of rhetorical appearances. Everything that he tries to construct in the way
of knowledge or morality is predicated on this condition of ostensible
poverty, deficiency, and meaninglessness. To be persuaded is first to
tear apart the plot which weaves the accidentality of existence into a
coherent pattern (of being, possessing, and knowing). It is to acknowledge the fallacy of bringing the multiplicity of facts into moral or metaphysical order. Indeed, in Michelstaedter there is no being at all except
in the realm of words. We consider a situation real only when the terms
by which we describe it resound in other people's ears. Where these
terms find no resonance, as in the utterings of madmen (and also many
artists), their referent is not said to be. People inhabit a linguistic environment which "fabricates the sign of a self they do not possess, a
'knowledge' they presume to hold in their hand." Just as a child cries
in the darkness to give "a sign of himself," so adults turn to words
and beliefs to fill the "solitude of their empty soul" (Michelstaedter
1910: 99). Propositional knowledge seizes no being or subjectivity underneath our everyday activity; these ideas are themselves the shadows
of propositions.

Having torn apart the rhetorical plot, the hero of persuasion recognizes that "*Alle haben recht—niemand ist gerecht*: everyone is right—
but no one is *in* the right . . . each thing in the world is right to occur . . .
but no one is *just*" (*ogni cosa nel mondo ha ragione d'avvenire* [which
also means "everything has a reason for being," parodying arguments
for ontological necessity], *ma nessuno* è giusto) (Michelstaedter 1910:
77). While every occurrence is "right" by the mere fact that it occurs,
no person can stand outside the plot to evaluate it. Each has only the
spiritual poverty, the moral and intellectual insufficiency, of the re-

maining condition. And this is the emotional and intellectual pain of which one must be persuaded. The persuaded self is one who assumes *"the person of such pain"* (Michelstaedter 1910: 71). Only in this insufficiency can one find the *pleroma*, or plenitude of being. Superficial and meaningless presence is *all* the being there is.

The persuaded person "must experience insufficiency in himself and respect in others what they fail to respect in themselves; until attracted by his love, they take the form of the person that he loves in them: then the blind will see" (Michelstaedter 1910: 84). What the persuaded person loves in others is their own insufficiency, which they have repressed, their empty selves, the negative I belied by its masks. With Michelstaedter's hero of persuasion we are in the company of Schiele's Saint Sebastian, Schoenberg's martyrs and haunted faces, Kokoschka's and Nolde's Christ—figures all nailed to a cross. We are among "the beloved of the gods" who die early in Trakl and Rilke, the poor in spirit of Lukács and Buber. We are enveloped by the darkness of Berg and the silence of Webern. "O the blood that flows from the throat of the sinner, / The blue blossom; o the fiery tears / Wept into the night" (Trakl 1969: 117, 1988: 71).

It is not rhetoric alone that nails these figures to a cross, as though they were victims of a system that they fight in vain. What nails them to a cross is their *recognition* of the ubiquitous, constitutive structure of rhetoric, even in their own understandings of the world. It is their lucidity about the impossibility of transcendent knowledge. For these martyrs and speechless figures are not legislators, moralists, or metaphysicians; they are possessors of negative knowledge, who sense that rhetoric rules all modes of seeing. But this negative knowledge, Michelstaedter suggests, is precisely what restores the true nature of belief and sight. Attracted by the languageless love of such saints, he writes, people will recognize a fate they had never acknowledged. They too will see (and not only their blindness). They will see despite their blindness, embracing the hyperbolic way.

In Michelstaedter, then, "Know thyself!" does not mean "realize your individuality." It means

> react against the need to affirm your illusory individuality, have the honesty to negate your own violence, the courage to live the full pain of your insufficiency at every moment—in order to be able to affirm the person who incorporates the right, to communicate *individual value*. (Michelstaedter 1910: 85)

Of course, Michelstaedter is himself speaking hyperbolically, insofar as the communication of individual value is precisely what rhetoric does not permit. Yet, if the miracle were ever to occur, and a person were to find a way to affirm individual value, it would follow from a recognition of the impossibility of the same project. And it would restore the unjustified value of things in their sheer appearance, making one admit that they have no value but this. It would affirm the innocence of things in a world of guilt. Precisely the sense of what is *not* allowed in language and life would generate respect for the fact that each thing occurs "just so" and in no other way. And this is enough to convert pain into joy, nihilism into affirmation, sorrow into love of fate. Saying yes to the deficiency of being is the only way of being in the right.

It is also the only way to live, Michelstaedter adds. Like goodness in Lukács, "giving everything and asking for nothing" presents itself as a solution to the everyday suicide of linguistic and communicative failure. It is a response to those "frightening paths of death" that estrange the ego in a defensive world (Trakl 1969: 141) which fails to acknowledge its rhetorical nature. For ultimately it is nothing but fear of death that causes the struggle against insufficiency, the establishment of a "plot" in place of singular, polysemous events, maintained by a belief that whatever does not advance the story is evil, inexistent, or false. The intentions of persuasion are just the opposite: to put an end to this struggle against half of life, "to give no support to people's fear of death, but to remove this fear; to give them no illusory life and the means by which they keep demanding it, but to give them *life itself* here and now, in its entirety, so that they *will not demand*: this is the activity that tears violence away from its roots" (Michelstaedter 1910: 81). Violence results from demanding that things not be what they seem, but what the ego insists that they be.

Now if one objects that having life itself "here and now" is impossible, and that no living person has ever had more than some version of illusory life, then Michelstaedter replies: "the courage for the impossible is the light that dispels the fog." Precisely *because* illusions and desires cannot be abolished, value begins to accrue to the fleeting, fragile, and uncertain events that make up their substance. Precisely *because* one can never achieve one's ideal ends, all importance begins to reside in the means that one uses, in the ever-changing here and now. In the only persuasion that can be practically achieved, one gives oneself to experience completely, loving it not for what one hopes to receive in return, but "for what it *is*." Such giving is "*doing the impossible: giving is having.*" However small the object of one's attention, it is now a world unto itself. And so is the I in its presence. To reconcile oneself to the contingency and insufficiency of historical appearances means "to have, in the possession of the world, the possession of oneself—to *be one, oneself and the world*" (Michelstaedter 1910: 82).

Thus it is that persuasion "negates time and the will in all deficient time" (Michelstaedter 1910: 44). What is "deficient" about time is that it makes no place for our ideals. It excludes everything transcendent from the rhetorical and material facts of the present. "If by eternity is understood not endless temporal duration but timelessness," reflects Wittgenstein, "then he lives eternally who lives in the present" (1922: #6.4311). And if this present "has no value," remarks Michelstaedter, then "nothing has value" (1910: 69). But he might just as easily have said that *because* this present contains no value it assumes a value it never before had (Perniola 1989; Cacciari 1992a).

Acquiescing in a rhetorical world does not mean endorsing the reign of conventions, mores, and rules. It means submitting to a dissonant, conflictual condition in which one suffers a will to transcendence without being able to fulfill it. In acknowledging the autonomy of rhetoric we recognize that the world as a totality of facts is "independent of my will" (Wittgenstein 1922: #6.373). Art can never mold life itself, and the will cannot turn its historical experience into a destiny. My desires and ideals can never prevail over "what is the case." To acquiesce in rhetoric is thus to face up to the tragedy that arises when

> the drive for expression of what is innermost and most personal meets the given language of human beings: that battle of the irrational with the rational, which ends without victory or defeat, in a scrap of paper with writing on it, which to the seeing eye bears the seal of a great suffering. (Buber 1909: 9)

Buber's "scrap of paper" moves from the issue of an ethics of expressive limits to its applied aesthetics. It suggests that a work created in recognition of communicative limits will not picture a harmonious coincidence of intention and expression. It will not be a "classical" composition, subsuming an idea in an image or a content in a form. At best it will dramatize the condition of having *nothing* but form (rhetoric)— with no content preceding it and no intention predating its expression. In truth the "battle of the irrational with the rational" is not only the story of art in Buber's time, but the story of art in general, including

classical art—a story of formal self-hatred, and of rhetoric at odds with
itself. What distinguishes expressionist art is simply that it tells this story
more directly. It sees the battle as inherent to the enterprise in question,
where even the "contents" of ethics and aesthetics—their ideal, subjective, or transcendent objectives—are themselves rhetorical illusions,
arbitrary perspectives and misunderstandings. Expressionist art arises
when, "sighing, the fallen angel catches sight of his image" (Trakl
1969: 115). At that moment the seeming victim of rhetoric (the would-
be idealist oppressed by the deficiencies of language) appears as his
own self-murderer, deterred from grasping the sole realities of concrete
existence by his mistaken idealism, or by his reluctance to acknowledge the mere formalism of aesthetic activity. Such an Abel, writes Trakl
in 1909, is also Cain:

> From the deceptive emptiness of a mirror
> There slowly appears, as if from nowhere
> Out of horror and darkness a face: Cain!
>
> The velvet curtain rustles very quietly,
> The moon peers through the window as into emptiness,
> And I am alone with my murderer.
> (1969: 220)

Subjectivity and the desire for transcendence face up to their own
misguidance. But the recognition comes only after long service to an ingrained illusion, after a dirge on the deficiency of historical being and
unsuccessful efforts to discover some autonomous meaning beyond it.
Persuasion is thus the ultimate outcome of a cognitive development: The
first consequence of an awareness of communicative limits is an elegy
on the "soul-less" contingency of things; one laments the spiritual privation of being, its absence of coherence and justice. On further reflection this elegy seems to be caused by a particular perspective on this
meaningless presence, by a decision to *view* it as privation (or even as
a criterion for ethical decisions). The elegy comes to look like a self-
induced affliction, produced by a thirst of an I for something that cannot be attained. And this is why expressionistic ethics and aesthetics
are irremediably tragic. "We call a relationship tragic," writes Simmel,
"in contrast to merely sad or extrinsically destructive, when the destructive forces directed against some being spring forth from the deepest
levels of this very being, or when its destruction has been initiated in
itself" (Simmel 1911a: 43). Here the destructive forces—the oppressive
and "soul-less" aspect of purely objective becoming—have sprung from

the soul itself, from its quest for meanings not in concrete appearance, but in future possession, in theory and truth, in subjectivity and its "governing will." Thus Trakl admits: from the poet's own heart "gushes the self-spilled blood" (1969: 98). Where "the world is a sphynx," notes Adorno, "the artist is blinded Oedipus" (1985: 132). The guilt lies with oneself.

Only in the acceptance of this guilt do ethics and aesthetics arise. In guilt, writes Lukács,

> a person says "Yes" to everything that has happened to him; by feeling it to be his own action and his own guilt, he conquers it and forms his life, setting his tragedy—which has sprung from his guilt—as the frontier between his life and the All. (1910–11a: 165)

One forms one's life by sensing the deficiency to be an ineluctable feature of the human condition, and by speaking despite one's silence. One says yes to meaningless, "equi-valent" occurrences by embracing the shortcomings of language. Only when we recognize that a frontier eternally separates what we might wish to say from our means to say it—the "All" from our life, our persuasion from our rhetoric—do we even pose the question of *how* to speak or to act. Only then do we quit delegating our decisions to rules or reveling in the license of personal caprice. The true topic of language is now the *locus* of language—the nature and limits of meaning-formation, in thought and action. The question at stake is the irresolvable, complicitous conflict between the ineffably unique and the logorrheically clichéd, irresolvable in the sense that the frontier joins the two orders no less than it separates them; their functions are intertwined; they cannot operate independently. The frontier between one's life and the All marks all possible sites of self-and-world shaping. It marks the living, historical fate that art always echoes, announcing it to be the final topic of all scraps of paper.

Ethics and aesthetics have their say only at the point of this unifying divide—a say which can no longer pose as definitive or unequivocal in the manner of a law or a fact. It can only be an idiom of insecurity, an illuminating form of incomprehension. And the same goes for the audience of these special type of forms, forced by their equivocal uses of language to be interpreters of figures and letters. The experience of art is always "a polar one," making an image stand over and against the thing that it names "as the simulacrum the deed, as the possible the actual, as the ambiguous the simple" (Buber 1913b: 67, 1913a: 116–117). Autonomous as such images might initially appear to be, their deepest significance lies neither in what they "say" nor in some "world" to which they seem to refer. Rather, the significance lies in the formative process that the images enact. And this process transforms an image or a word which once named a being into "something that moves between beings" (Buber 1925: 63).

Ethical and artistic experience does not revolve around a word or an answer, but around a

> *tension* between word and answer; [around] the fact . . . that two men never mean the same things by the words that they use; that there is, therefore, no pure reply; that at each point of the conversation . . . understanding and misunderstanding are interwoven; from which comes then the interplay of openness and closedness, expression and reserve. (Buber 1925: 63)

What happens at the border between understanding and misunderstanding is a "detached" kind of imaging, one revealing, for example, an "unfathomable, significant secret in the lines and proportions of a familiar face" and unfolding a "spectacle of duality"—not the duality of morality or law, which never fathom the depths, but "the primal duality itself . . . the free polarity of the human spirit." In artistic and ethical activity there is no historical occurrence that "does not reveal its bottomless abyss, and all thinking threatens to shatter the stability of the knower" (Buber 1913a: 105, 102, 104, 89). It is the same "shattering" that Lukács discovers in the struggle to reconcile "life beyond forms" with life on this side of them. The limitations of rhetoric produce goodness and art as "upheavals" (Lukács 1911c: 377).

ECSTATIC CONFESSIONS

This account might make it seem that Lukács's goodness and Michelstaedter's persuasion envision an "ecstatic" type of experience that transcends the rule-governed fictions of everyday life. Ecstasy literally means a condition of spiritual transport in which one "stands outside of oneself" (from the Greek *ek-stasis*). Like Buber's direction, it breaks the circular self-interest of subjects closed in on themselves and places them beyond the "sign-begetting plurality of the I" (Buber 1909: 6). It silences the philopsychic voice "which tells one *you are*" (Michelstaedter 1910: 62). Ecstasy does not speak of subjects and objects or befores and afters, but of the unity of dispersive, historical presence. If living ordinarily means moving from one place or moment to another in a series that hovers between the no longer and the still to come, then "*the just man no longer lives*: he does not perpetuate himself, but satiates himself in the present" (Michelstaedter 1910: 80). Here the differentiated present comes into its own as the only true dimension of time, in that Dionysian experience which is exalted as much by the *Fragments* of Boine as the paintings of Nolde, Kandinsky, and Marc. "You will not take me out of the locked prison of the moment with idle chatter about the infinity of the eternal," writes Boine. "I am all in today and my name is *instant* . . . My name is *today,* and my path is called *lost* . . . Not the milestones of a straight road; just erratic masses and oases" (1915: 261–264; Fragments 43, 19, 25, 22). And this ecstasy is also at work in the conjunction of eros and *thanatos* in Trakl and Spielrein.

And yet, as much as these artists court ideas of ecstatic unification, we hardly find such equanimity in their lives or their work. Instead we find madness and suicide, asceticism, schizophrenia, and cries of irrepressible yearning. Indeed, ecstatic unification of I and world has always been more of a desideratum than an accomplishment in Europe. For most Westerners since Schopenhauer, it has described a vision of how life *might* be experienced if ever we could overcome rhetoric completely. Expressionist art expresses more of the tension than the unity of ecstatic experience. Where ecstasy is presented as mystical union or transport we have symbolism rather than expressionism.[3]

Michelstaedter, Lukács, Buber, and Wittgenstein are fully aware of the difficulty in attributing positive significance to ecstatic experience. For the Lukács of "On Spiritual Poverty" it is a gift of grace, visited only upon people of the rarest "caste," and certainly not the one to which he belongs (Lukács 1911c: 384–385). In his "definitive" philosophy of *I and Thou* (1923), Buber has openly rejected the mystical and monistic implications of his prewar meditations. He has become convinced that experience can never yield more than relationship, dialogue, tension, and distance. As for Michelstaedter, no ethic could be as impractical as the one he describes in *Persuasion and Rhetoric,*

---

3. Symbolist ecstasy can be sampled in Fernand Khnopff's "Memories of Burne-Jones" (1898). In front of a painting by the master, Khnopff recounts that he was enwrapped by a "living atmosphere of dream-love and of spiritualized fire, carried away to a happy intoxication of the soul, a dizziness that clutched the spirit and bore it high up, far, far away, too far to be any longer conscious of the brutal presence of the crowd, the mob of sightseers amid whom the body fought its way out again through the doors. The artist's dream, deliciously bewildering, had become the real; and at this moment it was the elbowing and struggling reality that seemed a dream, or rather a nightmare" (Khnopff 1898: 33–34). On the neoplatonic precedents of symbolist ecstasy see Dorra's note 32 in the same volume, pp. 321–322.

so impractical that its absolute "self-giving" can only be achieved in death. There is simply no life at all without the machinations of some "plot," without the gravitations of desire and the pull of the future, accompanied as they are by inevitable schemes of self-interest. Michelstaedter, Lukács, and Wittgenstein remain unable to join theory and practice. Their ethics as well as their aesthetics remain caught in between, examinations, if anything, of the distance between them. Lukács comes to abandon the ideal, unspeakable goodness of "On Spiritual Poverty," regrounding it after the war in the need for political engagement. Michelstaedter commits suicide, unwilling to bear the distance between what is and what could be. Wittgenstein cannot philosophize about ethics and aesthetics, but only about the conventional realms of "commotion." Schiele, Kokoschka, and Trakl, too, are more visibly distraught by the tragic configurations of human experience than affirmative of them.

Within a general European striving for ecstatic oneness between 1880 and 1914, the distinction of the expressionist generation lies not in offering formulas for achieving such unity, but in their reminders that this unity is *one and the same* as irremediably dispersive experience. The very unspeakability of the ecstatic condition (in Wittgenstein, Michelstaedter, and Lukács) already implies that it can never be conceived of as something other than everyday estrangement. It is only another way of experiencing the dissonance, or of finding some harmony within it. What remains of the expressionist ecstasy is thus the first fact informing its meaning: the condition of standing outside of oneself, of having no ground but in groundless experience, at the edge of a rhetoric that fails to center one's being. Put otherwise, what can never be eliminated from the expressionist ecstasy is the poverty underlying its plenitude, the "sufficiency" of its insufficiency, the experience of loving without possessing and of seeking without finding. That is why there are more martyrs in 1910 than revelers.

Expressionist ecstasy means acquiescence in a longing harbored in the experience of presence itself. It is a dynamic of eros, not the calculative exchange of anteros. As Lou Andreas-Salomé expresses it in *The Erotic* (Die Erotik, 1910), a work commissioned by Buber, eros is a living response to *thanatos,* a "creating, worshipping and joy" which acts as a glue to cosmic dispersion (1910: 30). In eros we step beyond our subjectivity, committing our attention to values over and above ourselves and rejoining the being to which we already belong. Lukács says something similar in the same year as Andreas-Salomé, but with an important addition. He excludes all oneness from the bonds this eros achieves: "Eros is in the middle; longing unites those who are unlike, but at the same time it destroys every hope of their becoming one; becoming one means finding one's way home [*Heimfinden*], and true longing has never had a home" (1910–11a: 92).

If ever there was a "pure state" of the soul—a primordial self beneath or beyond its rhetorical illusions—it is this ecstatic, erotic one. This is the poverty that the expressionists explore, abhoring it no less than they prize it. The question that then becomes emblematic (as though it furnished the link between one's life and the All) is the one earlier cited from Lukács: "Whom can I love in such a way that the object of my love will not stand in the way of my love? Who is strong enough, who can enclose everything in himself so that his love becomes absolute and stronger than anything else?" To love in such a fashion, he reflects, is "to try never to be proved right"—for the rightness of this love is already proved in itself (1910–11a: 34). It is *amor fati*, love of fate. To submit to the ecstatic, erotic condition, in the expressionist era, is to be reconciled to non-reconciliation.

INTRANSITIVE LOVE

Michelstaedter defends this non-reconciliation in the poem where he relinquishes the idea of possessing his beloved Argia Cassini. Why should he try, he wonders—if "I lost you completely / when, the day we first met, / you were not mine?" Michelstaedter spent this year of his life striving "to remove from [his] love all that was transitive." And that meant striving to make himself self-sufficient. Yet his striving was only that—an effort, not an actual achievement. Of all artists in 1910, only Rilke is truly able to find serenity in a condition so fraught with pain. If ecstasy means acquiescing in intransitive love (or in the fact that the transitivity of love is an ultimate, intransitive condition) then its most persuasive formulation lies in the second part of *The Notebooks of Malte Laurids Brigge*.

It first appears in a song that Malte hears sung by an anonymous woman (put to music, in 1910, by Anton Webern):

> Du, der ichs nicht sage, dass ich bei Nacht
> weinend liege,
> deren Wesen mich müde macht
> wie eine Wiege.
> Du, die mir nicht sagt, wenn sie wacht

meinetwillen:
wie, wenn wir diese Pracht
ohne zu stillen
in uns ertrügen?

Sieh dir die Liebenden an,
wenn erst das Bekennen begann,
wie bald sie lügen.

Du machst mich allein. Dich einzig kann ich vertauschen.
Eine Weile bist dus, dann wieder ist es das Rauschen
oder es ist ein Duft ohne Rest.
Ach, in den Armen hab ich sie alle verloren,
du nur, du wirst immer wieder geboren:
weil ich niemals dich anhielt, halt ich dich fest.

[You whom I don't tell that I lie awake
at night and weep,
whose being, like a cradle, makes
me tired and tender;
you who don't tell me when for my sake
you cannot sleep:
what if we endured this splendor
and let it ache
without relieving?

Look, when the lovers start
confiding the thoughts of their heart,
how soon they're deceiving.

You make me alone. You only I can exchange.
A while it is you, then a noise that seems strange,
or it is a fragrance without endeavor.
All whom I held in my arms did not remain,
only you are reborn again and again:
because I never held you, I hold you forever.]
(Rilke 1910: 208; translation in Kaufmann 1975: 235)

Malte hears this hymn to non-possession only after his months in Paris
have made him recognize how distant and dispersed the dimensions of
his own life have grown. At this moment all that he wishes to do is to
"learn the work of love," as though it were the only true discipline he
needs (1910: 121).

Malte embarks on his training by contemplating the great lovers of
history. All, he discovers, were lovers not of what is close at hand but
of love itself: women whose desire infinitely overreached the men to
whom they devoted their attention, exceptional figures who "had destroyed beforehand the words with which one might grasp them," de-

votees of God, artists whose longing found expression in song (1910: 120). Is there a "femininity" to this immense, unlimited love, as Rilke and his friend Andreas-Salomé suspect?[4] "In the woman's highest hour," she writes, "the man is always only Mary's carpenter beside a God" (Andreas-Salomé 1910: 45). Whether feminine or not, it is a man who here sings its praises, bringing the long series of reflections on negativity in the *Notebooks* to the point of equating ecstasy with loving in the absence of appropriation. Rilke, Andreas-Salomé, and Buber all agree: If there is a proper name for this type of experience it can only be God, "a direction . . . not an object of love," a withholding force which "quietly defers delight in order to let us . . . accomplish our whole heart." And accomplishing our heart means expecting nothing more from desire "than the endless road . . . in the suspension of heaven's gate" (Rilke 1910: 208, 209). Weak love dissipates itself in the object on which it fastens, canceling the ecstasy from which it springs. Strong love, on the contrary, is a permanent gravitation of the soul, loving in each object of attention a life that has not yet been, the fragments of a world that does not cohere.

What demeanor does such love imply? Hints can be found in Malte's retelling of the biblical parable of the Prodigal Son at the end of the *Notebooks*. In Malte's version, the Prodigal Son is the story of a person who left home because he *did not want* to be loved. At home, where everyone doted on him, he was oppressed by a feeling that "most things were already decided," decided rhetorically, that is, within a system of familiar and reciprocal interest. While one could certainly influence some details in this system of interest, in the main "one was the person for whom they took one here; the person for whom, out of his little past and their own wishes, they had long fashioned a life" (1910: 211).

No sooner does the Son leave his home than he begins to revel in the feeling that "the secret of that life of his, which never yet had been, spread out before him" (1910: 210). As much as he tries to suppress his love, however, he finds himself loving again in his solitude, "each

4. On the intellectual exchanges between Rilke and Andreas-Salomé, as well as her idea of the feminine narcissism at work in "objectless love," see Angela Livingstone, *Salomé: Her Life and Work* (Mount Kisco, N.Y.: Moyer Bell, 1984), 140–143; Biddy Martin, *Woman and Modernity: The (Life) Styles of Lou Andreas-Salomé* (Ithaca: Cornell University Press, 1991), 42–45; Ursula Welsch and Michaela Wiesner, *Lou Andreas-Salomé: Vom "Lebensgrund" zur Psychoanalyse* (Munich: Verlag Internationale Psychoanalyse, 1988), 161–213.

time with waste of his whole nature." Gradually he allows his love to
outgrow the things by which it is attracted,

> to penetrate the beloved object with the rays of his feeling, instead of con-
> suming it in them. And he was spoiled by the fascination of recognizing
> through the ever more transparent form of his beloved, the expanses it
> opened to his desire infinitely to possess. (1910: 212)

The Son is beginning to love ecstatically; the beloved is becoming a cipher of the absolute.

But, alas, the Son soon sees that his beloved does not love back in
the way she is loved. Suffering from the opaque sadness of embraces
that are not reciprocated, he takes up the life of a solitary shepherd. At
this moment he begins to feel "general, anonymous, like a slowly recov-
ering convalescent. He did not love, unless it were that he loved to
be." This is also the period when "he strode silently over the pastures
of the world" and explored his "long love to God, that silent, aimless
labor." His beloved has been supplanted by God. Did the Son perhaps
imagine that God, if no one else, would love him with the complete-
ness he sought? This, too, unfortunately, was not to be, for all the
Son encounters is His remoteness. The Son was like one "who hears a
glorious language" that he barely understands and feverishly conceives
plans "to write, to create, in it" (1910: 213–214).

Struggling to learn the grammar of this unknown language, the Son
finds momentous changes taking place within him:

> He almost forgot God over the hard work of drawing near to him. . . .
> Whatever of pleasure and pain were necessary lost their spicy by-taste and
> became pure and nourishing for him. From the roots of his being developed
> the sturdy, evergreen plant of a fertile joy. He became wholly engrossed in
> learning to master what constituted his inner life; he wanted to omit noth-
> ing, for he did not doubt that his love was in all this and growing. (1910:
> 215)

What the Prodigal Son gradually senses is that everything that constitutes his inner life, everything that is most truly his own, lies entirely outside him, in things "he had been unable to accomplish" and
he needed to gather together, in experiences he had not lived but "simply waited through." Memories of the past now appear as premoni-
tions, and "their counting as past made them almost future." To recuperate a life that had never been his, the Son makes one final turn in
his road: "He, the estranged, turned home" (1910: 215).

As he approaches his house he sees an aged face of recognition at the window. "Recognition?" wonders Malte. "Really only recognition?" No. It was something more: "Forgiveness. Forgiveness of what?—Love." The family forgives the Son for the love that made him leave—to pursue its direction. Transfigured into a general and anonymous creature, the Son also forgives his family for the love they thoughtlessly showered upon him. He ceases to rebel against a fate that was his from the start, seeing no personal offense within it. Thus ends the fable, and the *Notebooks* along with it, followed by one short, mysterious paragraph underscoring the new and ambivalent relationship between the Son and those to whom he has returned: "What did they know of him? He was now terribly difficult to love, and he felt that One alone was able for the task. But He was not yet willing" (Rilke 1910: 216). Whatever understanding the Son might reach with his family from this point on will only be based upon misunderstanding. Only One could cancel this problem, but He was not willing.

The Prodigal Son tells the tale of the peregrinations of non-philopsychic, non-anerotic love. It is also a parable of that *Heimfinden*—that finding one's home in longing—which Lukács thought impossible. Eros and ecstasy, in the *Notebooks,* mean finding one's home in estrangement, including the estrangement of the home. Does any particular "rhetoric" serve the Son's new "persuasion"? What "expressions" accompany this ecstatic new family relation? The *Notebooks* do not say. And yet one suspects that these forms of expression will hardly be different from the everyday terms of exchange already in effect before the Son left, even if they are not likely to be approached with the same understanding. At the point where the story ends, the Son is in the position of the young poet with whom Rilke corresponds throughout the years that he writes the *Notebooks*:

> Those who are near you are far away, you write, and this shows that the space around you is beginning to grow vast. And if what is near you is far away, then your vastness is already among the stars and is very great.

Here Rilke advises:

> be gentle with those who stay behind; be confident and calm in front of them and don't torment them with your doubts and don't frighten them with your faith or joy, which they wouldn't be able to comprehend . . . when you see them, love life in a form that is not your own. . . . Don't ask for any advice from them and don't expect any understanding; but believe in a love that is being stored up for you like an inheritance. . . . (Rilke 1903–08: 56–58)

But, to ask once more, what "practical aesthetics" accompanies the new ethics of misunderstanding discovered by the Prodigal Son? The closest Rilke comes to describing it (in 1910) is in a parable with which the second part of the *Notebooks,* here concluded, begins. A tale of young women transforming their love into art, it is a mirror-image of the legend with which the *Notebooks* end. And it suggests, quite simply, that homeless ethics finds its form in homeless aesthetics.

LADIES OF THE UNICORN: STRUCTIVE ART

The second part of the *Notebooks* opens with Malte reflecting on young women transfixed by the famous tapestries of "Lady with Unicorn" in Paris. They, too, like the Prodigal Son, have abandoned their homes, choosing to pursue their own directions. They, too, have rebelled against too much love, finding that it amounts to too little.

The fate of the young women who have left their homes is reflected in the tapestries themselves. In an epoch where "everything is disappearing out of houses," they no longer hang in the Renaissance chateau for which they were designed—to celebrate a marriage, and with it the foundation of a home. Instead they are in a museum. Their displacement is made starker by the nature of their subject: a lady of the court, harmoniously surrounded by both natural and supernatural phenomena. If anyone was ever at home in the world, it is she. But now, in the early twentieth century, the *Heimfinden* that the tapestries celebrate lives on only as an image of something lost. Across from this image stand its negative reflection: "young girls . . . who somewhere have gone away out of the houses that no longer keep anything" and who pass their time by copying these compositions onto pieces of paper (1910: 117).

Is it some particular aspect of these tapestries that captivates the girls' attention? Not really. "Only to draw," reflects Malte, "that is the main thing; for with this intent they one day left home, rather violently." They left home in order to draw. Had their families remained havens for religion, Malte suspects, allowing them to worship in tempo with others, they might never have left. But in this era families "can no longer approach God. . . . No, it is really better to draw, no matter what. In time some resemblance will appear" (Rilke 1910: 118).

What "resemblance" does Malte have in mind? Is it the formal resemblance between a sketch and its model? Or is it a more diffused type of resemblance, like the one between members of a family who worship together? Or is it a resemblance pervading all things in the universe, like the one pictured in the tapestries themselves—a reciprocal, all unifying love, which art, in the absence of religion, might try to recapture? Whatever the case, it is certain that these girls have had to suppress their own yearnings for love, their romantic outings and eventual weddings, in order to copy these pictures. What they find in the art, however, is a love that is greater for there, in the tapestries, an "endlessly ineffable, unalterable life . . . is radiantly opened up before them" (1910: 119).

Whatever resemblance might appear through these copies of the tapestries can only be the product of a radical difference—the difference, to begin with, between the lives of the women and the depicted lady. But it is also the difference between a lived, historical romance and its endlessly ineffable, unalterable life in art. Malte notes the same contrast between the great love of Gaspara Stampa or the Portuguese Nun and the paintings that make such love appear. Is it not a mystery, he wonders, that this transcendent love, which outgrows all objects on which it fastens, is recorded in portraits that look out at us in a gallery, "through a weeping which the painter caught because he did not know what it was" (1910: 119–120)? How was the painter able to make this weeping eloquent if he could not understand what it was? Was it precisely because he did *not* understand it? Nor do the young women know how to love; and because of that they draw it. As with the Prodigal Son, understanding takes place in misunderstanding.

The drawing of Rilke's young women represents a new art at a new moment in time; one abandoning the expressible, rhetorical familiarity of quotidian experience in search of an endlessly unalterable life. The quest itself is romantic, shared no less by symbolist art than expressionism. The expressionist difference, however, lies in the recognition, inherent to the formative process, that the quest cannot reach fulfillment. The at-homeness of the Renaissance work now has no historical or imaginative counterpart. At this period in history it can only be copied. Obstructed and suppressed by the era they inhabit, the love of these new artists must settle for likenesses of a totality they sense only negatively. And this forces them to struggle with the *medium* of likeness—the act of drawing—in the hope that eventually it might make resemblance appear. Consonance is now predicated on dissonance, unity on division, presence on absence. Art courts a communion that no longer exists.

At the very moment when all innerness has been estranged from

outerness, and all persuasion from its available rhetoric, art longs for
an ecstasy which only *another* type of art—perhaps a transcendent,
classical, or childlike one—can achieve. Is this not part of the motivation for the cultivated naiveté of expressionist art, not to mention its
polemic against naturalism and its thrust toward abstraction? In 1910,
the ecstatic unification can no longer find form in action or art. The
formative labor originates in a confession to the poverty in which it is
based; the labor is more visible than any result.

Not long after the publication of the *Notebooks* the paradoxical
nature of the expressionist project becomes apparent to many. "In expressionism," writes the art historian Wilhelm Hausenstein, "the claim
to the absolute has yielded merely the relative." What doomed the movement, argues Hausenstein, and he is speaking just nine years after 1910,
was its effort to wrest "form from deformation." Expressionism "embraced the universe. It strove to embrace God and the heavens. It
wanted more than it was capable of" (Hausenstein 1919–20: 479). It
was a grand, hyperbolic undertaking, insisting on a true and "non-
rhetorical" object, on a goodness exceeding all rules, on a direction defying all orientation. But what it succeeded in expressing was no more
than the hyperbole in which it was caught, like the seeker of virtue in
Lukács, or the hero of persuasion in Michelstaedter. Expressionism
recognized that art could arise only in the company of a divide that
separates it from its deepest intentions. It sought grace in a poverty of
means. Such art, claims Franz Roh in 1925, presents less of a product
than an act of production. It is not "work process effaced," but "work
process preserved" (Roh 1925: 493). In Rilke's own words at the very
beginnings of expressionism, the new art is "more than word and
image, more than metaphor and appearance"; it is a "becoming-thing
of its longings and anxieties" (Rilke 1902–07: 145).

One of the implications of the parable of the young women is that
even if dissonance and disjunctions can be harmonized in art, they
can never be eradicated from the process that gives it birth. Aesthetic
distance—which is effaced by the rhetorical correlation of word and
thing, but which is as necessary for contemplating forms as composing
them—lies at the heart of all possible persuasion. When experienced
in everyday life, this distance just as easily can produce madness or suicide as the creative explorations of art, both sensing the indivisibility
of "familiarity and strangeness, total enjoyment and total renuncia-
tion" (Buber 1913b: 67). Dissonance, in both, is a form of primordial
union. The art represented by the women's drawings can offer no un-

equivocal form for unequivocal content. Instead of synthesizing the polarities of human experience, this art "realizes" them, showing the recalcitrance of the media in which they are joined. This is another difference between expressionism and arts such as cubism, futurism, and dadaism. Still attached to a romantic metaphysics, expressionism does not celebrate the failures of conventional signification. It cannot quit aspiring to a work that can no longer be accomplished. It problematizes a project it still pursues. Artists like Campana, Kokoschka, Trakl, Kandinsky, Michelstaedter, and Schoenberg were willing neither to forgo the link between meaning and form, nor to strengthen it beyond reasonable measure, in the manner of symbolists. After moving to Los Angeles in the thirties, Schoenberg begins to distance himself from all avant-garde experiments in aesthetic technique. As he looks back on his art, it seems to him that the whole purpose of his own innovations had been precisely to recuperate what had been lost: a significant language, a formal necessity, a philosophical relevance to human invention. Indeed, this is why he developed serial composition in the twenties and later new methods of classical tonality, as though these alternative idioms might provide the formal necessity he sought. His music abhorred the casual and the arbitrary, the destitute and the unauthentic, the superficial and the irrelevant. It was precisely *because* he was so attached to the principle of harmony—and suffered rather than extoled his estrangement—that he gave voice to the dissonance that was his grief.

One final word on the philosophical implications of this dissonance. Among the cultural movements that preceded the Great War, notes Musil,

> there was something known as expressionism. Nobody could say just what it was, but the word suggests some kind of pressing-out; constructive visions, perhaps, but inasmuch as the contrast with traditional art revealed them as being destructive, too, we might simply call them structive, which commits one to nothing either way, and a structive conception of the world sounds fine enough. (Musil 1930–40: chap. 99)

Whatever constructive objectives such art might have, they follow from a type of destruction, and particularly of a preconstituted rhetoric of unity, coherence, and meaning. The simultaneity of this construction and destruction might thus be called "structive." In this structive process, artistic and ethical forms are neither icons of truth nor self-justifying adventures in imagination. Rather, they are analyses of given modes of knowledge and action. Musil's emphasis on vision and world-conception (*Weltauffassung*) in his description is reminiscent of what phenomenologists of his time called the "constitution" of the world: the process by which objective forms are constructed by means of the understanding. It is also reminiscent of the *Bewusstsein der Gesichte,* or consciousness of vision, which Kokoschka equates with the art of the portrait. Consciousness of vision, he explains, "is not a state in which one perceives or understands objects, but a situation in which consciousness experiences itself [*an dem es sich selbst erlebt*]" (Kokoschka 1912: 9). The consciousness that Kokoschka aims to enact in his art is not a subjective condition which precedes and is "expressed" by a painting, nor even a consciousness that later seems to be embodied by the forms of a composition. Rather, it is a dynamic activity, a process of formation that unfolds in the *course* of vision, whether the vision of the artist or that of the viewer. The portrait is simply the site of this cognitive shaping, its means, its place of occurrence. It focalizes that seeing in which both artist and audience participate and asks that it be experienced in and of itself.

The same holds for the works of Kandinsky, Michelstaedter, Campana, and Trakl, which do not offer definitive artistic images so much as occasions for an experience of art, for what Buber calls the "feeling of art" and Rilke the becoming–thing of longing or anxiety. Inherent to this feeling of art is the sense that one has, like the women before the Renaissance tapestries, that however persuasive or perfect artistic forms may be, they remain "withdrawn from and inaccessible to us" (Buber 1913b: 67). This insuperable distance informs rhetoric no less than the persuasion one seeks within it. The musician Hans Tiessen notes a similar function in the compositions of Schoenberg. They seek vision in an "absolute construction of the material," or in a "self-reflection on the material and its immanent functional possibilities" (Tiessen 1928: 40 and 43; see also Cacciari 1982, Crawford 1993, and Hailey 1993). They do not constitute vision so much as a seeking of vision. Before he discovers new paradigms by which to govern his musical constructions (i.e., the twelve-tone row), Schoenberg's reflection on the means of construction possesses the most urgent necessity. His atonal, expressionist compositions of 1908–1913 occur at the point when one formal method has broken down but no other has yet arisen. At the very moment when phenomenologists are tracing the rhetoric of worldviews to the "viewing" and "meaning-formation" out of which they arise, musical rhetoric is called back to the materials out of which it is built.

Rilke's homeless girls, Lukács's poor in soul, Michelstaedter's martyrs of persuasion—in short, all those who aim at significance in the absence of significance—acquiesce in the dissonance at the root of ethics and aesthetics. Their work is persuasive in lacking persuasion, in announcing that no form is free from misunderstanding and that each fails the communication it was designed to serve. This is the "great silence" the young Lukács detected at the bottom of art, as though it were the final and unspoken message of each effort at articulation. Offering not form but the forming of form, the process instead of the product, expressionist art redirects human attention to the ethic by which its activity is spurred. The ultimate expression of life no less than art is the "will to expression" that motivates both. In 1910 the understanding of history, subjectivity, and morality hinges entirely on this paradox of expression, to the point where Lukács finds it necessary to stress: "even the realized work is not worth anything as a work (as such it is completely objective and become independent of me), but [only] as an *act,* as *my* act." And, as though allowing for the formative problem to issue into the political and existentialist activism of the postwar years, he makes an important addition: "it is by my act alone that I will become an I" (Lukács 1909–11: 32). In 1910 this problem of becoming an I is a function of structive misunderstanding.

Afterword and
Aftermath

Expressionism, as this study describes it, had a short intellectual run. To begin with, many of its protagonists—Michelstaedter, Trakl, Schiele, Campana, Slataper, Marc, and Boine—were already dead or mad by 1918. But another, even more decisive intervention occurred with World War I. Between 1914 and 1918 everything that thinkers had been bemoaning in 1910—the deficiency of being, the failure of rational and ethical rhetoric, the tragedy of all efforts at self-determination, the battles of each against all—received such living confirmation that all prior, theoretical treatments of these issues could only pale. In the light of this unprecedented crisis in Europe, the ruminations of 1910 appeared merely to prefigure their own historical futility.

There were also internal reasons why the theoretical dynamics of 1910 were not destined to develop. Nothing much could be built upon them; they were not "useful" to the social, political, and economic needs of postwar countries. Michelstaedter's persuasion and Buber's direction offered no concrete directives for action, no functional models or systems, no idioms for practical behavior. They were utopian reflections on the homeless experience of a here and now. Lukács's goodness and Kandinsky's spirit were equally incapable of furnishing motivations to worldly behavior. They confused all distinctions between truth and error, the real and the apparent, the depths and the surface of things.

The European mind welcomes contradiction just so long as its terms can be resolved into a productive new position, a new form of consonance, as it were—a third "revelation" beyond the opposition of the original two. And this is precisely what does not happen with the dissonant arts of 1910. The contradictions they embody, to adapt the words of the Marxist Lukács, are devoid of "dynamic, developmental significance." The antagonisms simply "coexist, unresolved," allowing for no dialectical advancement (Lukács 1955: 482). The discoveries of 1910 establish no basis for social or intellectual progress. They mark merely the end of a certain way of thinking, and perhaps most loudly in their call for new beginnings. Michelstaedter's *Persuasion and Rhetoric* and Schoenberg's atonal harmonies, to take two examples, resolve only on this: to reject the very thirst for resolution. They are tenacious polemics against the world and its modes of self-understanding. To make matters worse, in their formal contortions these works *enact* the same dissonance that is their theme, supplying no solution to the tensions by which they are spurred. This is why Michelstaedter's suicide seems so coherent: a consequence of pushing contradictions to their deadly extreme. This is also why Schoenberg soon decides to abandon his expressionist atonalities. He could proceed no further along this path (Schoenberg 1926, 1941). What he needed was a new *method* of composition, discovered in the twelve-tone row, which could order the dissonances he had set free. The musical compositions of 1908–1913 destroyed one rhetoric without yielding another. The problem with free atonality, Schoenberg claimed, was that its dissonances still tended toward tonal harmony, even if they resisted the pull; and this suspension cried out for resolution.

As for the other figures of this study, Slataper and Marc lost their lives, with a large portion of their generation, in the war. Boine, always in poor health, died in 1917. Trakl and Campana struggled against the limits of comprehension straight through to the end (1915 in the first case, 1918 in the second, when Campana is interned in a mental asylum). Rilke has already outgrown the tense aesthetics of expressionism by the second part of the *Notebooks.* From 1911 to 1926, in the *Duino Elegies* and *Sonnets to Orpheus,* he carves out an interior, virtually posthumous space for poetic intuition on the margins of historical practice. Schiele pays the price for disregarding public opinion with imprisonment in 1912, and is inducted into the war in 1915. The chastening effect of both events makes him redirect his energies to new experiments in painting. Treating individuals and landscapes in the manner of still lifes, with intricate visual detail, his melancholy large canvases of 1917 and 1918 share little with his small, quick, bitter improvisations in pencil and watercolor from before the war. Kokoschka, too, outgrows his fiery youth, replacing his provocative and scandalous visions of 1910 with more subdued and subtle sorts of soulscape, including panoramas whose features are harmoniously interrelated.

Even Kandinsky gives up his intense, transitional style of the Munich years. At the onset of World War I he returns home to Russia, where he seeks common ground between his own aesthetic and the avant-garde movements of futurism, constructivism, and suprematism. He is not successful, unless, of course, one considers the extent to which *his own* style changes. Moving back to Germany in 1921, he joins the technical, analytic Bauhaus school in Weimar and seeks to give his spiritualistic leanings new practical functions. As the years go by, his art becomes increasingly programmatic, even dogmatic, bold in its figuration of geometric abstraction. Not suspended as once between two worlds, it loses its tentative nature. In his canvases of the twenties and thirties, flat and sharp shapes take precedence over effluent color, systematic arrangements over indomitable strife. Above all, the passionate and dynamic process in which his early abstractions compelled the viewer to participate (in Kandinsky's own version of "structive art," conscious of its own nature as becoming, of vision as a striving to see, and of understanding as an offshoot of misunderstanding) is replaced by a light, utopian mechanics.

In 1910 the greater part of the work of Buber, Lukács, and Wittgenstein still lies ahead of them. While the subject of the *Tractatus* as conceived between 1912 and 1914 is what can never be said in words, the embracing of this work by logical positivists builds Wittgenstein's fame as a philosopher of language. Even if he continues to exempt the most serious issues of life from its literal grasp, Wittgenstein ends his days as an ordinary language philosopher. By the twenties Buber is an existential theologian, interpreting all being as dialogue and that dialogue as fundamental to the Judaic tradition. Lukács converts to Marxism and denounces his earlier, more sensitive work, along with the modernist aesthetics to which it is tied, as a symptom of romantic capitalism. What might have come of the arts of 1910 had it not been for the shake-up of World War I is impossible to say; what is certain, however, is that they could not have continued much further along the lines they had taken.

Aspiring to be prophets of a more sophisticated consonance than any language could encompass, the artists and philosophers of 1910 became martyrs of the dissonance they themselves freed. The word *martyr* comes from the Greek *martirius*: a person who bears witness, who confesses to the nature of a particular situation. It was, in the early twentieth century, a "pathos of truth" that made some people prefer to perish from their findings than to compromise them. "To avoid no reef," declares Blumenberg, "one day that will be called 'heroic nihilism'" (1979: 22). One could also call it revolutionary nihilism, envisioning the prerequisites for change, imagining that solutions might be found in the fallout of testimony itself. That was the "harmony" implicit in the dissonance. Yet this martyrdom was not enough. An entire generation had to repeat it, even if rarely with the same level of awareness, believing, most often, that their war efforts were serving a grand cause. The Great War was a travesty of the unanchored idealism of 1910, a nihilism without heroic dimension, a dashing of oneself on the reef merely out of fear of the open sea.

It now appears that one of the things most fully understood in 1910 was misunderstanding—the vastness of its depth and promise. And it is this misunderstanding which made the future then seem so uncertain. "The world," writes Marc in the prologue to the projected second volume of the *Blue Rider,* "is giving birth to a new epoch. There is just one question: has the moment yet come for us to detach ourselves from the Old World? Are we ready for a *vita nuova?*" (quoted in Vezin 1992: 209). In this, the last tragic age of the West, few people were. If we look for "constructive" moments in the first decades of twentieth-century Europe, we are better advised to gaze past Marc to two developments on either side of the war's divide: the avant-garde energies unleashed in Paris in 1913 and the socialist revolution in Moscow, 1917. On these bases at least—in the relative independence of art from politics and of politics from art—things could still be built. Whether these two separate lines could ever be fully rejoined—and the dadaist events between them said no—is a question still with us today. "In France," Marc comments in 1910, "success follows on from the most daring experiments by the young, but for them taking risks derives from a tradition. With us, each risk is a desperate, chaotic experiment by a man who cannot master the language" (quoted in Vezin 1992: 104). The "tradition," in Paris and Moscow, was a conventional one. In the first case it consisted of a belief in the autonomy of art, in the second, of political activism. By contrast, the unmasterable language to which artists in Munich, Trieste, Vienna, and Budapest bore witness consisted of the imponderable means that were left once traditions and rhetoric appeared stripped of their cogency. This is why the idea of producing a "transvaluation of all values" through art or politics was just as dubious as it was necessary in 1910: The divorce between these two spheres of activity had already been felt. By contrast, the inspiration of much postwar art in Europe was still predicated on the series of oppositions whose relations the artists of 1910 had hoped to alter: practice vs. theory, "real" vs. "rhetorical" orders of action, conscious vs. unconscious knowledge, pragmatic vs. utopian ideals. After the war these oppositions appeared more fundamental and extensive than any possible art, even an art purporting to encompass them. They were ontologically constitutive structures, delimiting the very scope of aesthetics. And this vitiated all dreams of a "new life" in and by means of art alone.

The defeat of Germany left its expressionists clamoring to reconstruct their moral and political landscape, charged as degenerates by the Right and the Left alike. Most Austrians, including some of the most venturesome, secretly bemoaned the passing of the grand chaos their empire seemed so miraculously to contain. The revolutionary intentions of artists in Italy were co-opted by fascism. In the newly formed Soviet Union, the attempt to assimilate the avant-garde arts into the political order was not successful at all. By the 1930s, in most of Europe, the idea of a *vita nuova* through the agency of art was laid to rest.

What came of the four expressionist traits in this scenario? The idea of dissonance as a vehicle for ethical and artistic expression was lost precisely through the limitless possibilities of form that art was soon to arrogate to itself. It was lost when art conceived of itself as a realm of unfettered and unaccountable creation, whether its new topics were the fallen worlds of the everyday and the "inartistic" (Marcel Duchamp), the futility of its aspirations (dadaism), or the promise of spontaneous, unconscious revelation (surrealism and abstract expressionism). Where these topics encountered no strong countervailing tendencies in the conscious mind, art no longer grappled in the same way with the struggles out of which it once had grown. At best it *reflected* a dissonance outside it (through a process best traced by Adorno), in its historical context. It no longer thematized dissonance as something which might take the form of a privileged language, perhaps even because the very notion of a privileged language was definitively lost. Here Lukács and Wittgenstein proved prophetic: one could no longer invoke criteria for the "beautiful" and the "good." And this meant that other criteria came to take their place: imaginative conviction, visionary inspiration, the dictates of morality or will.

Before the Great War is out, German expressionists explicitly thrive on stridency, provocation, and imaginative violence. Yet the stridency tends to be formulaic. Disruptions of literary and pictorial syntax become commonplace, generating little tension among the elements so wrenched apart. One only has to contrast the lyrics of Trakl with those of many poets anthologized in Kurt Pinthus's *The Twilight of Humanity* (1919) to recognize the extent to which these poetic disruptions have grown ineloquent—and usually by seeking quite the opposite, or by imagining that eloquence can be achieved through the emotional immediacy of pure exclamations.

The musical situation in music is more complex. Here too, however, the dissonant aesthetic of 1910 is resolved through dodecaphonic composition, neoclassicism, and the efforts of *Gebrauchsmusik* ("music for use") to overcome the gaps between serious and light music. In each case dissonance is repositioned as a feature of larger and more complex contexts of resolution. It is less intrinsic than extrinsic to the search for moral/artistic harmony, a feature of the multilayered culture to which the musician brings such harmony. In its literalization of dissonance, expressionistic music comes to look like "the last attempt at self-justification undertaken by an individualism pushed to the point of absurdity" (Gutman 1929: 580).

In the light of these developments, what appears to be emancipatory in the arts of 1910 is not the larger, cultural scenario of dissonance that they help produce, even if this undoubtedly carries its own freedom; what appears to be emancipatory is the conflict between dissonance and consonance through which the scenario expands. Dissonance is not *what* is emancipated in the "emancipation of dissonance"; dissonance itself—the search for resolutions not found—bears the emancipatory charge. In other words, the phrase is to be read as a subjective rather than an objective genitive.

The second characteristic of 1910—that sense of a threatening and corrosive negativity at the very foundation of the vital process—is done in, as previously suggested, by the literal and material transformations it undergoes through the war. In the years following 1914–1918 it becomes impossible to reflect on negativity in the theoretical and metaphorical modes of 1910. The deficiency of being comes to mean primarily the destruction of millions of ordinary lives and secondarily the daily small deaths of social exploitation. There is also a warning, in this and the next great war, about the dangers of obsessions with negativity, for both of them relied on polemics against the "sick" and the "sinful," the degenerate and the infectious, the corrosive and the deadly. What good, if any, could come from lucubrations about the infinite ways life lets us down?

However, what probably did not register in the years following 1910 was the way in which the distance from these seeming abominations had already been shortened. It did not register because the gravitation toward a *coincidentia oppositorum* in 1910 did not yield a new conceptual language, which was not found until Heidegger culled the full implications of Simmel's essay on death in *Being and Time* (1927). There the traditional conception of death was rejected, replaced by one seeing mortality as the horizon of all decisive acts, as an immanent feature of life which delimited the very terms of choice. In the thirties and forties existentialist philosophers elaborated this notion further, explaining how liberty is always transcribed by its negative bounds.

But even these relations between absurdity and meaning, imprisonment and freedom, did not captivate the popular imagination, leading death to be again abstracted from the realms of theoretical awareness and consigned to the obtuseness of act: to concentration camps, to hospitals and mass murder, to the gerontological quarantine of states for retirement. When not courted directly, as in Nazism and Stalinism— not to mention dozens of genocidal platforms straight through to our time—the phenomenon of death was simply repressed. One thought one was eradicating death by abolishing its symptoms: depression and chronic unhappiness, useless metaphysical reflections, the wrinkles of flab and age—all matters of increasing taboo as the century progressed.

As for the question of soul, or rather the question of the articulation of soul, many postwar artists continued happily to assume that they were expressing deep and unique aspects of their personality in art. Ironically, this occurred during the same decades in which social and psychological theorists of every sort argued that, in a world of practical, commodified relationships such notions as self-knowledge and self-expression were hopelessly anachronistic. Our century has developed a more complex understanding than ever before of the *homo politicus,* of human enmeshment in ideological and economic apparatuses which makes the very project of self-determination chimerical. There has been no interior to express for quite some time, assuming that there ever was—but only things, endowed with their own, inherent logic. This turn from the internal to the external was already recognized in the twenties, when the literature of New Objectivity tried to offset the confessional impulses of expressionist aesthetics by reflecting on their sociohistorical underpinnings. It was also in the twenties that the prophetic and still untapped document of a post-subjective age was begun, and this by a man who had himself outgrown expressionism: Musil's *The Man Without Qualities*. Although expressionism had dramatized the end of subjectivity, our century has seen subjectivist ideologies chronically reborn as though such a death never occurred.

The ethical vocabulary that thinkers tried to weaken in 1910 was also strengthened in subsequent years. Dissonance, as Schoenberg described it in the *Theory of Harmony*, was essentially a more distant form of consonance, a less than obvious affinity between dissimilarities. To emancipate dissonance was ultimately to unmask the limitations of rigid, categorical thinking. Both during and after the war moral and ideological oppositions rather flourished as rarely before. Visions of what was required for both souls and nations became monolithically either/or. Forced consonance in Germany, Italy, and Russia—efforts, so to speak, at social unitarianism—responded to the ethnic and social dissonances that had helped cause the war.

To war-weary minds intent on rebuilding their projects, new forms of facile idealism were largely welcome: liberationist doctrines of libido, as central to the roaring twenties as to psychoanalysis; faith in the surreal and the unconscious; impassioned defenses of socialism no less than returns to Catholicism. The ultimate opposition again came down to the difference between "spiritual values" and pragmatism. But even this difference probably only covered over an interest the two factions shared: the desire for a functional system, for instruments by which to definitively cleave the good from the bad. The implicit hope of an ethics of misunderstanding was not fulfilled.

Where does this bring us today, in the decade that completes the century's frame? If the beginning of the century reaps the consequences of a tragically dichotomous intellectual history, the end seems to aspire to the opposite: the ideal of a resistance-free world, the multiplication of opportunities for limitless distraction, unending crusades for empowerment and ease. Do we share anything whatsoever with expressionists today? Is not our world the antithesis of theirs?

While artists in 1910 hoped their work would uncover a "truly living reality," today we see art as just another species of business, as a lucrative production of entertainment. Even when art has greater ambitions than this, it cannot easily dispense with parody, pastiche, or didactic morality. Today the difference between persuasion and rhetoric cannot even be thought. The "pathos of truth" has been replaced by the thirst for the happy ending. We want the answers without asking the questions, envisioning an abolition of all obstacles to desire through a consonance of wills or a Balkanization of interests and groups. Materialism, as the expressionists feared, has become the only sure measure of knowledge, and pragmatics the most reliable criterion of value. It is hardly an age for a thinker.

As for the self-searching promoted by the first decade of the century, select members of society are paid small fortunes to instruct us on how to go about it, promising us moral and emotional improvement into the bargain. More often than not, however, we recommend such analysis to others, inviting them to reflect on how *they* might be responsible for *our* shortcomings. But all irony aside, the ideological differences between the first and the last decades of the century are subtended by dozens of serious changes in the fabric of socioeconomic experience; they are also based on only one vision of contemporary popular culture, exemplified above all by the United States. In Europe the situation is somewhat different, though even there we find the same fear of fear, the same chimerical conjunctions of moral complacency and social intolerance, the same blend of cultural homogenization and cries for local autonomy. In the final analysis, dissonance is just as characteristic of our time as it was of the prewar years, even if it is not always as self-conscious. The last decade of the century is not simply the antithesis of the first; it is a mirror image, an inverted reflection. The social unrest following the recent collapse of the Eastern bloc repeats the political disintegration of the Habsburg, Czarist, and Ottoman empires, the independence of once colonized peoples resuming a process thwarted by the balanced world powers of 1918–1989. One can only hope that the events of post-1989 will do more than parody those spurring the Great War, where insecurity about one's place among others led to new tactics of self–assertion. The mobility, interdependence, and rapid transformation of classes, races, and nations at the end of the century makes the identity-discourse of the beginning now smack of falseness. It makes the dissonances we would like to emancipate today (or make consonant with a rule?) seem artificially recreated. One must hope that what we appropriate from the early twentieth century is not merely its naive, "expressive" intent, but also its negative knowledge. One ideal of 1910—to the effect that a sense of belonging might issue from precisely its lack, or that self-identification might be predicated on the crumbling of such counters of identification as groups and nations—might mitigate some opposite nostalgias.

In an article written for the *Voce* four years before the Great War, Slataper responded to the wishes of Italians to extend the borders of their country to encompass their brethren in Trieste and Trento. If one should aspire to anything, claimed Slataper, it was not to annexing the "Italian" parts of Austria-Hungary but rather to developing Italianity within them. Efforts to constitute identity, he thought, should precede the acceptance of such identity as a given. "We do not deny the importance of political borders," he wrote, "but we strongly feel that they do not contain the country." (Slataper, "L'irredentismo: Oggi," *La Voce*, December 12, 1910; quoted in Baroni 1975: 61). Before contemplating a takeover of those parts of the Habsburg empire where Italians existed, Slataper and other members of the *Voce* thought it necessary to note that others—for example the Slavs—were also there, in Trieste, and could not just be imagined away. And this is hardly the kind of patriotism one has come to expect from a member of a disenfranchised minority.

Michelstaedter gives the issue a more ethical edge:

> Non è la patria
> il comodo giaciglio
> per la cura e la noia e la stanchezza;
> ma nel suo petto, ma pel suo periglio
> chi ne voglia parlar
> deve crearla.—
>
> [One's country is not
> a comfortable bed
> for care and boredom and weariness;
> but within one's breast, and, at personal risk,
> whoever would speak about it
> must create it.—]
> (Michelstaedter 1987: 76)

Michelstaedter's poem is appropriately left untitled, for his homeland can have no name.

The antinationalistic positions of Slataper and Michelstaedter come close to defending what was later to be called the *Verjudung* (Judaization) of Europeans: a paradoxical condition of social and ideological dissonance in which positions could actually be assumed, where mortality, negativity, and loss were linked to morality, justice, and the very constitution of vision. In Nietzschean terms, one would say that *Übergang* relies on *Untergang*, overcoming on being overcome. A similar perspective informs the post-sentimental expressionism of Kandinsky and Schoenberg, favoring the arts of abstraction, recombination, and nonfiguration over those of representation and moralization.

It is also reflected in the "antirhetorical" styles of Triestine writers in Michelstaedter's generation. Steeped in a practical and mercantile tradition, Triestines were not easily seduced by the artistic currents that swept over Europe. "There is, in fact," writes Baroni, "not one great Triestine writer who, despite all the efforts of critics, can be assigned to one or another of the numerous literary 'families' of the twentieth century" (1975: 57). The dwellers of the free port of Trieste, like Levantine merchants in Izmir and Alexandria, were too rooted in multicultural exchange to define its "identities" by reference to theories. They resisted the rhetoric diminishing the differences between human beings as well as the one formulating absolutely distinguishing traits. Rather, they were more taken with the concrete complexities of the here and now. At the commercial crossroads of East and West, the inhabitants of Trieste were bound by productive, economic dependencies—obliged, as it were, to get along.

The spirit of Trieste was "as of the nature of the air" in Kandinsky's description, composed of foreign bodies. No doubt, the concept of individual identity was weakened by relativity; but it was also strengthened by relationship. Habitation meant cohabitation, belonging not being in power, majoritarianism mutual minoritarianism. Beneath all external conflict lay a deeper, internal conflict, which rhetoric and ideology try to hide. This is why we write, says Slataper in a letter "To Intelligent Young Italians" of 1909—not in order to express ourselves, but in order "to create internal clarity" (*La Voce*, August 26, 1909; quoted in Baroni 1975: 50).

Primary Sources

Most dates following authors' names refer to the year of the actual composition or first publication of a work. Some—not all—of the musical and pictorial works most relevant to this study are included among books, articles, and collections of poetry.

Adams, Henry
  1910   "A Letter to American Teachers of History." In *The Degradation of the Democratic Dogma*, 186–187. New York: Peter Smith, 1949.
Adler, Alfred
  1918   *The Practice and Theory of Individual Psychology.* Trans. P. Radin. 2d ed. rev. New York: Humanities Press, 1971.
Amendola, Giovanni
  1911   *La volontà è il bene: Etica e religione.* Rome: Lib. ed. rom.
Andreas-Salomé, Lou
  1910   *Die Erotik.* Die Gesellschaft: Sammlung Sozialpsychologischer Monographen, vol. 33. Ed. Martin Buber. Frankfurt am Main: Rütten & Loening.
Bahr, Hermann
  1916   *Expressionism.* Trans. R. T. Gribble. London: Frank Henderson, 1925.
Balázs, Béla
  1907   *Halálesztetika.* Budapest: Deutsch Zsigmond és Társa Könyvkereskedése.
Benn, Gottfried, ed.
  1955   *Lyrik des expressionistischen Jahrzehnts: Von dem Wegbereitern bis zum Dada.* Wiesbaden: Limes Verlag.

Berg, Alban
  1910   *Four Songs,* Opus 2.
Besant, Annie, and Charles W. Leadbeater
  1905   *Thought-Forms.* London and Banaras: Theosophical Publishing Society.
Boine, Giovanni
  1911a   "La ferita non chiusa." In Boine 1983, 384–395.
  1911b   "L'esperienza religiosa." In Boine 1971, 425–462.
  1913   *Il peccato.* In Boine 1983, 1–71.
  1915   *Frammenti.* In Boine 1983, 259–265.
  1971   *Il peccato e le altre opere.* Parma: Guanda.
  1983   *Il peccato, Plausi e botte, Frantumi, altri scritti.* Ed. Davide Puccini. Milan: Garzanti.
Buber, Martin
  1909   "Ecstasy and Confession." In *Ecstatic Confessions.* Ed. Martin Buber and Paul Mendes-Flohr. Trans. Esther Cameron. San Francisco: Harper & Row, 1985.
  1910a   "The Teaching of the Tao." In Buber 1974, 31–58.
  1910b   Debate with Simmel, Weber, Tönnies, and Troeltsch at the First Conference of the German Society for Sociology, October 21, 1910. *Verhandlungen des ersten deutschen Soziologentages: Von 19.–22. Oktober 1910 in Frankfurt am Main.* Schriften der Deutschen Gesellschaft für Soziologie, I. Serie, I. Band. Tübingen: Mohr, 1911. Reprint: Frankfurt am Main: Verlag Sauer & Auvermann KG, 1969, 192–214.
  1913a   *Daniel: Dialogues on Realization.* Trans. Maurice Friedman. New York: Holt, Rinehart and Winston, 1964.
  1913b   "The Space Problem of the Stage." In Buber 1974, 67–73.
  1923   *I and Thou.* 2d ed. Trans. Ronald Gregor Smith. New York: Charles Scribner's Sons, 1958.
  1925   "Drama and Theater: A Fragment." In Buber 1974, 63–66.
  1974   *Pointing the Way: Collected Essays.* Trans. and ed. Maurice Friedman. New York: Schocken Books.
  1993   *On Intersubjectivity and Cultural Creativity.* Ed. S. N. Eisenstadt. Chicago: University of Chicago Press.
Busoni, Ferruccio
  1907   *Sketch of a New Esthetic of Music.* Trans. Thomas Baker. New York: G. Schirmer, 1911.
  1957   *The Essence of Music and Other Papers.* Trans. Rosamond Ley. London: Rockliff.
  1987   *Selected Letters.* Trans., ed., and introd. Antony Beaumont. New York: Columbia University Press.
Campana, Dino
  1914   *Canti Orfici.* Ed. Fiorenza Ceragioli. Milan: Biblioteca Universale Rizzoli, 1989.
  1978   *Le mie lettere sono fatte per essere bruciate.* Ed. Gabriel Cacho Millet. Milan: All'Insegna del Pesce d'Oro.

Chamberlain, Houston Stewart
  1899   *Foundations of the Nineteenth Century*. Trans. John Lees. New
            York: H. Fertig, 1968.
Chipp, Herschel B., ed.
  1969   *Theories of Modern Art: A Source Book by Artists and Critics*.
            Berkeley: University of California Press.
Delaunay, Robert
  1909   *St. Séverin I*.
  1910–11   *Eiffel Tower*.
Dorra, Henri, ed.
  1994   *Symbolist Art Theories: A Critical Anthology*. Berkeley: Univer-
            sity of California Press.
Engelmann, Paul
  1968   *Letters from Ludwig Wittgenstein, With a Memoir*. Trans. L. Furt-
            müller and B. F. McGuinness. New York: Horizon Books.
Fechter, Paul
  1914   *Der Expressionismus*. Munich: R. Piper.
Freud, Sigmund
  1907   "The Sexual Enlightenment of Children." In Freud 1957–1978,
            vol. 9, 129–140.
  1910a   "The Origin and Development of Psychoanalysis." *American
            Journal of Psychology* 21, no. 2: 181–218.
  1910b   *Five Lectures on Psycho-Analysis*. In Freud 1957–1978, vol. 11,
            1–55.
  1910c   "Contributions to a Discussion of Suicide." In Freud 1957–
            1978, vol. 11, 231–232.
  1910d   "A Special Type of Choice of Object Made by Men (Contribu-
            tions to the Psychology of Love I)." In Freud 1989, 387–394.
  1912   "On the Universal Tendency to Debasement in the Sphere of
            Love (Contributions to the Psychology of Love II)." In Freud
            1989, 394–400.
  1915–17   *Introductory Lectures on Psycho-Analysis*. In Freud 1957–1978,
            vol. 15.
  1925   "An Autobiographical Study." In Freud 1989, 3–41.
  1957–78   *Standard Edition of the Works of Sigmund Freud*. Ed. James
            Strachey. London: The Hogarth Press and the Institute of
            Psycho-Analysis.
  1989   *The Freud Reader*. Ed. Peter Gay. New York and London: W. W.
            Norton & Co.
Gentile, Giovanni
  1910   "Il concetto della grammatica." In *Opere XLVII: Frammenti di
            estetica e di teoria della storia*, vol. 1, 117–129. Florence: Casa
            Editrice Le Lettere, 1992.
  1916   *The Theory of Mind as Pure Act*. Trans. H. Wildon Carr from
            3d ed., 1920. London: Macmillan and Co., 1922.
  1920   *Opere XXXVII: Discorsi di religione*. 4th ed. Ed. Fondazione
            Giovanni Gentile per gli Studi Filosofici. Florence: Sansoni, 1957.
  1922   Review of *La persuasione e la rettorica*. *La Critica* 20: 332–336.

Gerstl, Richard
  1905   *The Sisters.*
  1908   *Self-Portrait / Group Portrait (Schoenberg Family).*
Gordon, Mel, ed.
  1986   *Expressionist Texts.* New York: PAJ Publications.
Gutman, Hanns
  1929   "Music for Use." In Kaes, Jay, and Dimendberg, eds., 1994, 579–
              582.
Hart, Julius
  1901a   "Der neue Mensch." *Das Reich der Erfüllung: Flugschriften zur
              Begründung einer neuen Weltanschauung,* vol. 2. Ed. Heinrich
              Hart and Julius Hart, 14–28. Leipzig: Eugen Diederichs.
  1901b   "Von der Ueberwindung der Gegensätze." *Das Reich der Erfül-
              lung,* vol. 2, 29–44.
Hartmann, Eduard von
  1869   *Philosophy of the Unconscious.* Trans. William Chatterton Coup-
              land. London: K. Paul, Trench, Trubner, and Co., 1893.
Hausenstein, Wilhelm
  1919–20   "Art at this Moment." In Kaes, Jay, and Dimenberg, eds., 1994,
              479–482.
Husserl, Edmund
  1913   *Ideas: General Introduction to Pure Phenomenology.* Trans.
              W. R. Boyce Gibson. New York: Collier, 1962.
Jaspers, Karl
  1913   *Allgemeine Psychopathologie: Ein Leitfaden fur Ärzte und Psy-
              chologen.* Berlin and New York: Julius Springer, 1965.
Kaes, Anton, Martin Jay, and Edward Dimenberg, eds.
  1994   *The Weimar Republic Sourcebook.* Berkeley: University of Cali-
              fornia Press.
Kafka, Franz
  1912–13   *The Sons* (including *The Metamorphosis, The Judgment, The
              Stoker,* and "Letter to his Father"). Introd. Mark Anderson.
              New York: Schocken, 1989.
Kandinsky, Vasily [Wassily]
  1909   *Mountain / Improvisation 6.*
  1909–10   "Foreword to the Catalogue of the First Exhibition of the Neue
              Künstler-Vereinigung, Munich." In Kandinsky 1994, 53.
  1909–11   *On the Spiritual in Art.* In Kandinsky 1994, 120–219.
  1909–12   *Yellow Sound: A Stage Composition.* In Kandinsky 1994, 267–
              284.
  1910a   "From the Catalogue of the Second Exhibition of the Neue
              Künstler-Vereinigung Munich." In Kandinsky 1994, 82–83.
  1910b   "Content and Form." In Kandinsky 1994, 87–90.
  1910c   *Improvisation XI.*
  1910–11   "Wither the 'New' Art?" In Kandinsky 1994, 96–104.
  1910–13   *Untitled* (First Abstract Water Color).
  1912a   "On the Question of Form." In Kandinsky 1994, 235–257.

1912b   "On Stage Composition." In Kandinsky 1994, 257–265.
1913   "Reminiscences." In Kandinsky 1994, 357–382.
1914a   "Cologne Lecture." In Kandinsky 1994, 393–400.
1914b   Letters to Arthur J. Eddy. In Kandinsky 1994, 402–406.
1982   *Catalogue Raisonné of the Oil Paintings.* Ed. Hans K. Roethel and Jean K. Benjamin, vol. 1. Ithaca, N.Y.: Cornell University Press.
1992   *Watercolours.* Catalogue Raisonné. Ed. Vivian Endicott Barnett. Ithaca, N.Y.: Cornell University Press.
1994   *Complete Writings on Art.* Ed. Kenneth C. Lindsay and Peter Vergo. New York: Da Capo Press.

Kandinsky, Vasily, and Franz Marc, eds.
1912   *The Blaue Reiter Almanac.* New Documentary Edition. Ed. Klaus Lankheit. New York: Da Capo Press, 1974.

Kaufmann, Walter, ed.
1975   *Twenty-five German Poets: A Bilingual Collection.* Trans. Walter Kaufmann. New York: W. W. Norton & Co.

Khnopff, Fernand
1898   "Memories of Burne-Jones." *Symbolist Art Theories: A Critical Anthology.* Ed. Henri Dorra, 33–34. Berkeley: University of California Press.

Kirchner, Ernst Ludwig
1910   *Fränzi in Front of Carved Chair.*
1912   *Bareback Rider.*

Klages, Ludwig
1910   *The Science of Character.* Trans. W. H. Johnstons. Cambridge, Mass.: Sci-Art Publishers, 1932.

Kokoschka, Oskar
1907   *Murderer, Hope of Women.* In Henry I. Schvey, *Oskar Kokoschka: The Painter as Playwright,* 138–140. Detroit: Wayne State University Press, 1982.
1909   *Murderer, Hope of Women (Pietà) / Portrait of Ludwig von Janikowsky / Portrait of Auguste Forel.*
1910   *Portrait of Herwarth Walden / Portrait of the Architect Adolf Loos / Self-Portrait* (Poster for *Der Sturm*).
1912   "Von der Natur der Gesichte." In *Das Schriftliche Werk III: Aufsätze, Vorträge, Essays zur Zunst.* Ed. Heinz Spielmann, 9–12. Hamburg: Hans Christians, 1975. Two inaccurate translations of this lecture can be found in Miesel, ed., 1970, 98–101 and Chipp. ed., 1969, 170–174.
1974   *My Life.* Trans. David Britt. New York: Macmillan.
1994   *Works on Paper: The Early Years, 1897–1917.* Exh. cat. New York: Guggenheim Museum.

Kornfeld, Paul
1918   "Der beseelte und der psychologische Mensch." *Das junge Deutschland* 1: 1–13.

Landauer, Gustav
1907   *Die Revolution*. Die Gesellschaft: Sammlung Sozialpsychologis-
            cher Monographen, vol. 13. Ed. Martin Buber. Frankfurt am
            Main: Rütten & Loening.
1911   *Aufruf zum Sozialismus*. Ed. Heinz-Joachim Heydorn. Vienna:
            Europa Verlag, 1967.
Langbehn, Julius
1890   *Rembrandt als Erzieher*. Leipzig: C. L. Hirschfeld.
Lasker-Schüler, Else
1982   *Your Diamond Dreams Cut Open My Arteries*. Trans. Robert
            Newton. Chapel Hill: The University of North Carolina Press.
Le Queux, William
1906   *The Invasion of 1910*. London: Eveleigh Nash.
Lenin, Vladimir
1909   *Materialism and Empirio-criticism*. New York: International Pub-
            lishers, 1970.
Lista, Giovanni, ed.
1973   *Futurisme: Manifestes, proclamations, documents*. Lausanne:
            Éditions L'Age d'Homme.
Loos, Adolph
1910   Steiner House, Vienna.
1910–12   House on Michaelerplatz, Vienna.
Lukács, Georg
1908–11   *A modern dráma fejlödésének története*. 2 vols. Budapest:
            Franklin-Társulat, 1911.
1909–11   "Lukács György és Popper Leó levélváltásából, 1909–1911."
            Ed. Fekete Éva. *Valóság* 17, no. 9 (1974): 16–37.
1910   "Az utak elváltak." *Nyugat*, February 1, 1920, 190–193.
1910–11a   *Soul and Form*. Trans. Anna Bostock. Cambridge, Mass.: MIT
            Press, 1974. (*A lélek és a formák: Kísérletek*, Budapest: Frank-
            lin, 1910; a second, amplified edition, including the essay "The
            Metaphysics of Tragedy," was published in German in 1911 as
            Die Seele und die Formen.)
1910–11b   *Napló—Tagebuch (1910–1911)/Das Gericht (1913)*. Ed. Lend-
            vai L. Ferenc. Budapest. Akadémiai Kiadó, 1981.
1911a   "Zur Soziologie des modernen Dramas." *Archiv für Sozialwis-
            senschaft und Sozialpolitik* 38 (1914): 303–345 and 662–706.
            These ninety pages make up most of chapter 2, book 1 of the
            thousand-page Lukács 1908–11, which has not been translated
            into English.
1911b   *Il dramma moderno*. Trans. Luisa Coeta. Milan: SugarCo, 1976.
            A translation of chapters 1 and 2, book 1, of Lukács 1908–11.
1911c   "On Poverty of Spirit: A Conversation and a Letter." Trans.
            John T. Sanders. *The Philosophical Forum* 3, nos. 3–4 (Spring–
            Summer 1972): 371–385. ("A lelki szegénységröl. Egy levél és
            egy párbeszed," *A Szellem* [December, 1911]: 202–214. The essay

appeared in German as "Von der Armut am Geist. Ein Gespräch und ein Brief," *Neue Blätter* 2, nos. 5–6 [1912]: 67–92.)

1912–14 *Heidelberger Philosophie der Kunst (1912–14).* Darmstadt-Neuwied: Luchterhand, 1974. An abridged version of one of the essays in this volume, "Phänomenologische Skizze des schöpferischen und receptiven Verhaltens," has been translated by Glenn Odenbrett as "On the Phenomenology of the Creative Process," *The Philosophical Forum* 3, nos. 3–4 (Spring–Summer 1972): 314–325.

1913 *Esztétikai kultúra.* Budapest: Atheneum.

1916 *The Theory of the Novel: A Historico-philosophical Essay on the Forms of Great Epic Literature.* Trans. Anna Bostock. Cambridge, Mass.: The MIT Press, 1987.

1955 "The Ideology of Modernism." In *Twentieth-Century Literary Criticism: A Reader.* Ed. David Lodge, 474–488. London and New York: Longman, 1972.

1970 "Art and Objective Truth." In *Writer and Critic and Other Essays.* Ed. and trans. Arthur D. Kahn, 25–60. New York: Grosset & Dunlap.

1982 *Briefwechsel 1902–1920.* Ed. Éva Karádi and Éva Fekete. Stuttgart: Metzler.

Macke, August

1912 "Masks." In Kandinsky and Marc, eds., 1912, 83–89.

Macke, August, and Franz Marc

1964 *Briefwechsel.* Ed. Wolfgang Macke. Cologne: DuMont Schauberg.

Marc, Franz

1910a *Horse in a Landscape.*

1910b "Zur Ausstellung der 'Neuen Künstlervereinigung' bei Thannhauser." In Marc 1978, 126–128.

1911 *Blue Horse I / The Yellow Cow.*

1912a "The 'Savages' of Germany." In Kandinsky and Marc, eds., 1912, 61–64.

1912b *Tiger / Yellow Horses.*

1913 *Animal Destinies (The Trees Show Their Rings, the Animals Their Veins).*

1914 *Fighting Forms.*

1978 *Schriften.* Ed. Klaus Lankheit. Cologne: DuMont Buchverlag.

1985 *Briefe aus dem Feld.* Ed. Klaus Lankheit and Uwe Steffen. Munich and Zurich: Piper.

Marinetti, F. T.

1909 "Discorso ai Triestini." In *Teoria e invenzione Futurista.* Ed. Luciano De Maria, 247–253 and 584. Milan: Mondadori, 1983.

1910 "Futurist Speech to the English." In *Let's Murder the Moonshine: Selected Writings.* Ed. R. W. Flint. Trans. R. W. Flint and Arthur A. Coppotelli, 67–73. Los Angeles: Sun & Moon Press, 1991.

Matisse, Henri
    1900   *Male Model.*
    1908   "Notes d'un peintre." In *Écrits et propos sur l'art.* Ed. Domi-
                  nique Fourcade, 40–53. Paris: Hermann, 1972.
    1909–10 *Dance I* and *II.*
    1910   *Music.*
Mauthner, Fritz
    1910   *Wörterbuch der Philosophie: Neue Beiträge zu einer Kritik der*
                  Sprache. Munich: Georg Müller.
Meidner, Ludwig
    1912–13 *Apocalyptic Landscapes.*
Michelstaedter, Carlo
    1906–08 *Scritti scolastici.* Ed. Sergio Campailla. Gorizia: Istituto per gli
                  Incontri Mitteleuropei, 1976.
    1910   *La persuasione e la rettorica.* Ed. Sergio Campailla. Milan: Adel-
                  phi, 1982. First published posthumously in 1913.
    1922   *La persuasione e la rettorica.* Ed. Emilio Michelstaedter. Flor-
                  ence: Vallecchi.
    1958   *Opere.* Ed. Gaetano Chiavacci. Florence: Sansoni.
    1975   *Opera grafica e pittorica.* Ed. Sergio Campailla. Gorizia: Cam-
                  pestrini.
    1983   *Epistolario.* Ed. Sergio Campailla. Milan: Adelphi.
    1987   *Poesie.* Ed. Sergio Campailla. Milan: Adelphi.
    1988   *Dialogo della salute e altri dialoghi.* Ed. Sergio Campailla. Mi-
                  lan: Adelphi.
    1992   *L'immagine irraggiungibile: Dipinti e disegni.* Exh. cat. Ed.
                  Antonella Gallarotti. Introd. Daniela Bini. Gorizia: Instituto per
                  gli Studi Ebraici della Mitteleuropa / Edizioni della Laguna.
Miesel, Victor H., ed.
    1970   *Voices of German Expressionism.* Englewood Cliffs, N.J.:
                  Prentice-Hall.
Munch, Edvard
    1895   *Self-Portrait with a Cigarette/The Scream.*
    1895–1902 *Loving Woman (Madonna).*
    1902   *Sin.*
    1909   *Portrait of Dr. Daniel Jacobson.*
Musil, Robert
    1910–11 "The Perfecting of a Love." In *Five Women.* Trans. Eithne Wil-
                  kins and Ernst Kaiser, 123–177. Boston: Nonpareil Books, Da-
                  vid R. Godine, 1987.
    1911a   "The Obscene and Pathological in Art." In Musil 1990, 3–9.
    1911b   "Novellas." In Musil 1990, 9–10.
    1912   "Profile of a Program." In Musil 1990, 10–17.
    1930–40 *The Man Without Qualities.* Trans. Sophie Wilkins and Burton
                  Pike. 2 vols. New York: Alfred A. Knopf, 1995. References to
                  this work are by chapter number rather than page.

1990   *Precision and Soul: Essays and Addresses.* Ed. and trans. Burton
             Pike and David S. Luft. Chicago: The University of Chicago
             Press.
Nietzsche, Friedrich
1882   *The Gay Science.* Trans. Walter Kaufmann. New York: Vintage
             Books, 1974.
1883–85   *Thus Spoke Zarathustra.* In *The Portable Nietzsche.* Ed. and
             trans. Walter Kaufmann. New York: Viking Press, 1968.
1908   *Ecce Homo.* In *Basic Writings of Nietzsche.* Ed. and trans. Wal-
             ter Kaufmann. New York: Modern Library, 1968.
Nolde, Emil
1909   *The Last Supper / Apostle Head V / Wildly Dancing Children.*
1910   *The Dance Around the Golden Calf / Christ Among the Chil-
             dren.*
1911   *Masks.*
1911–12   *The Life of Christ.*
1912   *The Prophet.*
Nordau, Max
1892   *Degeneration.* Introd. George L. Mosse. Lincoln and London:
             University of Nebraska Press, 1993.
Ortega y Gasset, José
1914   *Meditaciones del Quijote.* Madrid: Revista de Occidente en
             Alianza Editorial, 1984.
Ouspensky, P. D.
1911   *Tertium Organum, the Third Canon of Thought: A Key to the
             Enigmas of the World.* Trans. Claude Bragdon and Nicholas
             Bessaraboff. 2d American ed. rev. New York: Alfred A. Knopf,
             1922.
Papini, Giovanni
1910   "Un suicidio metafisico." *Il Resto del Carlino,* November 5,
             1910, 3. Reprinted with the title "Carlo Michelstaedter" in
             Tutte le opere di Giovanni Papini: Filosofia e letteratura, 817–
             822. Milan: Mondadori, 1961.
1911   "Le speranze di un disperato." In Prezzolini, Gentile, and Schei-
             willer, eds., 1974, 107–108.
Pinthus, Kurt, ed.
1919   *Menschheitsdämmerung: Ein Dokument des Expressionismus.*
             Reinbek: Rowohlt, 1959.
Prezzolini, Giuseppe, ed.
1973   *Amendola e La Voce.* Florence: Sansoni.
Prezzolini, Giuseppe, Emilio Gentile, and Vanni Scheiwiller, eds.
1974   *La Voce 1908–1913: Cronaca, antologia e fortuna di una ri-
             vista.* Milan: Rusconi Editore.
Rank, Otto
1909   *The Myth of the Birth of the Hero.* Trans. F. Robbins and Smith
             Ely Jelliffe. New York: Johnson Reprint Corp., 1970.

Rilke, Rainer Maria
   1902–07   *Auguste Rodin*, Part I (1902) and Part II (1907). In *Sämtliche Werke*, vol. 5. Ed. Rilke-Archiv, Ernst Zinn, and Ruth Sieber-Rilke, 139–201, 203–216. Frankfurt am Main: Insel, 1965.
   1903–08   *Letters to a Young Poet.* Trans. Stephen Mitchell. Boston: Shambala, 1993.
   1910   *The Notebooks of Malte Laurids Brigge.* Trans. M. D. Herter Norton. New York: Capricorn Books, 1958. The original is cited from Rilke, *Sämtliche Werke*. Ed. Rilke-Archiv, Ernst Zinn, and Ruth Sieber-Rilke, vol. 6, 705–946. Frankfurt am Main: Insel, 1966.
   1911–23   *The Duino Elegies.* Trans. Stephen Garmey and Jay Wilson. New York: Harper Colophon, 1972.
   1950   *Briefe: Zweiter Band, 1914–1921.* Leipzig: Insel.
Romains, Jules
   1910   *Manuel de Déification.* Paris: Bibliothèque Internationale d'Édition E. Sanson et Compagnie.
Scheler, Max
   1913   *The Nature of Sympathy.* Trans. Peter Heath. Hamden, Conn.: Archon Books, 1973.
Schiele, Egon
   1910   *Nude Girl with Folded Arms (Gertrud Schiele) / Anarchist / Portrait of Dr. Erwin Graff / Portrait of the Painter Karl Zakovsek / Portrait Sketch of the Painter Max Oppenheimer (Mopp) / Portrait of Arthur Roessler / Portrait of Eduard Kosmack / Herbert Rainer / City on the Blue River (Dead City I) / Nude Self-Portrait, Grimacing / Self-Seers I / Female Nude.*
   1911   *The Prophet / Self-Portrait Masturbating.*
   1912   *The Old City I (Dead City V).*
   1913   *Coitus / Preacher.*
   1914   *Self-Portrait as St. Sebastian.*
   1915   *Seated Couple (Egon and Edith Schiele).*
   1917   *The Embrace (Lovers II).*
   1921   *Briefe und Prosa.* Ed. Arthur Roessler. Vienna: Richard Lányi.
   1983   *Tout l'oeuvre peint.* Ed. Gianfranco Malafarina. Trans. Gaston Duchet-Suchaux. Paris: Flammarion.
   1985   *I, Eternal Child: Paintings and Poems.* Trans. Anselm Hollo. New York: Grove Press.
   1990   *The Complete Works.* Catalogue raisonné. Ed. Jane Kallir. New York: Harry N. Abrams.
Schmitt, Carl
   1910   *Über Schuld und Schuldarten.* Breslau: Schletter.
Schoenberg, Arnold
   1907–08   *Second String Quartet,* Opus 10.
   1908   *Book of the Hanging Gardens,* Opus 15.
   1909   *Three Piano Pieces,* Opus 11 / *Five Orchestral Pieces,* Opus 16 / *Erwartung (Monodrama),* Opus 17.

1910a	"Frühe Aphorismen." *Die Musik* 9, no. 21: 159–163. Reprinted in Schoenberg, *Schöpferische Konfessionen*. Ed. Willi Reich, 12–16. Zürich: Peter Schifferli, 1964.
1910b	*The Red Gaze / Hands.*
1910–13	*Die glückliche Hand,* Opus 18.
1911a	*Theory of Harmony.* Trans. Roy E. Carter from 3d ed., 1922. Berkeley and Los Angeles: University of California Press, 1983.
1911b	"Problems in Teaching Art." In Schoenberg 1984, 365–369.
1911c	*Six Little Piano Pieces,* Opus 19 / *Self-Portrait.*
1912a	"The Relationship to the Text." In Schoenberg 1984, 141–145. Also in Kandinsky and Marc, eds., 1912, 90–102.
1912b	*Pierrot Lunaire,* Opus 21.
1912c	"Gustave Mahler: In Memoriam." In Schoenberg 1984, 447–448.
1926	"Opinion or Insight?" In Schoenberg 1984, 258–264.
1934–35	"Two Speeches on the Jewish Situation." In Schoenberg 1984, 501–505.
1938	"Malerische Einflüsse." *Journal of the Arnold Schoenberg Institute* 2, no. 3 (June 1978): 236–239.
1941	"Composition with Twelve Tones (1)." In Schoenberg 1984, 214–245.
1975	*The Piano Music.* Maurizio Pollini. Notes by Paolo Petazzi. Compact disc. Polydor 423–249–2.
1984	*Style and Idea: Selected Writings.* Ed. Leonard Stein. Trans. Leo Black. Berkeley and Los Angeles: University of California Press.
1988	*Self-Portrait: A Collection of Articles, Program Notes, and Letters by the Composer About His Own Works.* Ed. Nuria Schoenberg Nono. Pacific Palisades, Calif.: Belmont Music Publishers.
1991a	*Erwartung,* Opus 17. Michael Gielen, Phyllis Bryn-Julson, and the SWF-Sinfonie Orchester Baden-Baden. Compact disc. Intercord 860.915.
1991b	*Das bildnerische Werk / Paintings and Drawings.* Ed. Thomas Zaunschirm. Klagenfurt: Ritter. Includes essays by Zaunschirm ("Arnold Schoenberg the Painter," 13–97), Susanne Neuburger, ("Gazes, Visions and Images," 101–113), and John Russell (no title, 117–129).
1992	Foreword to the score of Webern's *Six Bagatelles for String Quartet,* Opus 9. Cited in Joachim Noller, "Webern/Gielen: Works for String Quartet." Compact disc. Sony SK 48059.

Schoenberg, Arnold, and Vasily Kandinsky

1984	*Letters, Pictures and Documents.* Ed. Jelena Hahl-Koch. Trans. John C. Crawford. London and Boston: Faber and Faber.

Schopenhauer, Arthur

1844	"The Metaphysics of the Love of the Sexes." In *The World as Will and Representation.* Trans. R. B. Haldane and J. Kemp, vol. 3, chap. 44. New York: AMS Press, 1977.

Serra, Renato
1915   *Esame di coscienza di un letterato.* Ed. G. de Robertis and
            L. Ambrosini. Milan: Fratelli Treves, 1919.
Simmel, Georg
1903   "The Metropolis and Mental Life." In *The Sociology of Georg
            Simmel.* Ed. and trans. Kurt H. Wolff, 409–424. New York:
            Macmillan, 1964.
1907   *Philosophy of Money.* Rev. ed. Ed. David Frisby. Trans. Tom
            Bottomore and David Frisby. London and New York: Rout-
            ledge, 1990.
1908   *Soziologie: Untersuchungen über die Formen der Vergesellschaf-
            tung.* 5th ed. Berlin: Duncker & Humblot, 1968. Trans. Kurt H.
            Wolff as Simmel 1964.
1910a   "Zur Metaphysik des Todes," an abridged version of which ap-
            pears in Simmel, *Brücke und Tür.* Ed. Michael Landmann, 29–
            36. Stuttgart: Koehler, 1957. Simmel later reworked this essay
            into "Tod und Unsterblichkeit" in Simmel 1918b, 99–153.
1910b   "Soziologie der Geselligkeit." *Verhandlungen des ersten deut-
            schen Soziologentages: Von 19.–22. Oktober 1910 in Frankfurt
            am Main.* Schriften der Deutschen Gesellschaft für Soziologie, I.
            Serie, I. Band. Tübingen: Mohr, 1911. Reprint: Frankfurt am
            Main: Verlag Sauer & Auvermann KG, 1969, 1–16.
1910c   *Hauptprobleme der Philosophie.* Leipzig: G. J. Göschen.
1911a   "On the Concept and Tragedy of Culture." In Simmel 1968,
            27–47.
1911b   *Philosophische Kultur: Gesammelte Essais.* Leipzig: W. Klink-
            hardt.
1918a   "The Conflict in Modern Culture." In Simmel 1968, 11–26.
1918b   *Lebensanschauung: Vier metaphysische Kapitel.* Munich and
            Leipzig: Von Duncker & Humblot.
1964   *The Sociology of Georg Simmel.* Ed. and trans. Kurt H. Wolff.
            New York: Macmillan.
1968   *The Conflict in Modern Culture and Other Essays.* Trans.
            K. Peter Etzkorn. New York: Teachers College Press.
1971   *On Individuality and Social Forms: Selected Writings.* Ed. Don-
            ald N. Levine. Chicago and London: University of Chicago Press.
Slataper, Scipio
1909   *Lettere triestine.* In *Scritti politici.* Ed. Giani Stuparich, 11–57.
            Milan: Mondadori, 1954.
1910–15   *Alle tre amiche: Lettere.* Ed. Giani Stuparich. Milan: Monda-
            dori, 1958.
1912a   *Il mio Carso.* Ed. Roberto Damiani. Trieste: Edizioni "Svevo,"
            1988.
1912b   *Ibsen.* Ed. R. Jacobbi. Florence: Nuova Vallecchi, 1977. Posthu-
            mously published in 1917.
1950   *Epistolario.* Ed. Giani Stuparich. Milan: Mondadori.
Soffici, Ardengo
1911   *Lemmonio Boreo.* Florence: Vallecchi, 1921.

Sorel, Georges
  1908   *Reflections on Violence.* Trans. T. E. Hulme and J. Roth. New York: Collier Books, 1974.
Spielrein, Sabina
  1909–12   *Diary (1909–1912).* In Carotenuto 1982, 3–44.
  1912   "Die Destrucktion als Ursache des Werdens." *Jahrbuch für psychoanalytische und psychopathologische Forschungen* 4: 465–503.
Steiner, Rudolf
  1910a   *Occult Science—An Outline.* Trans. George and Mary Adams. London: Rudolf Steiner Press, 1963.
  1910b   *Theosophie.* 5th ed. Leipzig: M. Altmann.
Stirner, Max
  1845   *The Ego and His Own.* Ed. John Carroll. New York: Harper & Row, 1971.
Stöhr, Adolf
  1909   *Der Begriff des Lebens.* Heidelberg: C. Winter.
  1910   *Lehrbuch der Logik in psychologisierender Darstellung.* Leipzig and Vienna: F. Deuticke.
Trakl, Georg
  1969   *Dichtungen und Briefe.* Ed. Walther Killy and Hans Szklenar. 2 vols. Salzburg: Otto Müller, 1969.
  1983   *Le poesie.* Trans. Vera degli Alberti and Eduard Innerkofler. Milan: Garzanti.
  1988   *Song of the West.* Trans. Robert Firmage. San Francisco: North Point Press.
Twain, Mark
  1910a   "The Turning Point of My Life." In Twain 1992, 929–938.
  1910b   *What is Man?* In Twain 1992, 731–804. The first publication of this work, in 1906, was anonymous.
  1992   *Collected Tales, Sketches, Speeches, and Essays 1891–1910.* Ed. Louis J. Budd. New York: The Library of America.
Unamuno, Miguel de
  1910   *Mi religion y otros ensayos breves.* Madrid: Espasa-Calpe, 1973.
  1913   *The Tragic Sense of Life.* Trans. J. E. Crawford Flitch. New York: Dover, 1954.
Vaihinger, Hans
  1911   *The Philosophy of "As If": A System of the Theoretical, Practical, and Religious Fictions of Mankind.* Trans. C. K. Ogden. New York: Harcourt Brace, 1924.
Waite, Arthur Edward
  1910   *Pictorial Key to the Tarot.* New York: Causeway Books, 1973 (an enlarged edition of Waite's *The Key to the Tarot* of the same year).
Wassermann, Jakob
  1908   *Caspar Hauser.* Trans. Cardine Newton. New York: H. Liveright, 1928.

Webern, Anton
    1909   *Five Movements for String Quartet,* Opus 5 / *Six Pieces for Large Orchestra,* Opus 6.
    1910   *Two Songs for Medium Voice and Eight Instruments on Poems by Rainer Maria Rilke,* Opus 8.
    1911–13 *Six Bagatelles for String Quartet,* Opus 9.
    1913   *Five Pieces for Orchestra,* Opus 10.
    1917–21 *Six Songs for Voice and Four Instruments on Poems by Georg Trakl,* Opus 14.

Weininger, Otto
    1903   *Sex and Character.* New York: AMS Press, 1975.
    1904   *Über die letzten Dinge.* 2d ed. rev. Vienna and Leipzig: W. Braumüller, 1907.

Wittgenstein, Ludwig
    1914–16 *Notebooks 1914–1916.* 2d ed. Ed. G. H. von Wright and G. E. M. Anscombe. Chicago: The University of Chicago Press, 1979.
    1922   *Tractatus Logico-Philosophicus.* London: Routledge & Kegan Paul, 1951. Textual references to the *Tractatus* are by proposition number rather than page.
    1966   *Lectures & Conversations on Aesthetics, Psychology and Religious Belief.* Compiled by Cyril Barrett from notes of Yorick Smythies, Rush Rhees, and James Taylor (from the year 1938). Berkeley: University of California Press.
    1977   *Vermischte Bemerkungen.* Ed. G. H. von Wright and trans. Peter Winch as *Culture and Value.* Chicago: The University of Chicago Press, 1988.
    1979   *Ludwig Wittgenstein and the Vienna Circle.* Conversations recorded by Friedrich Waismann. Ed. Brian McGuinness. Trans. Joachim Schulte and Brian McGuinness. New York: Barnes and Noble.

Woolf, Virginia
    1924   "Mr. Bennett and Mrs. Brown." In *Collected Essays,* vol. 1, 319–337. London: The Hogarth Press, 1966.

Worringer, Wilhelm
    1908   *Abstraction and Empathy.* New York: International Universities Press, 1958.
    1910   *Form Problems of the Gothic.* New York: G. E. Stechert & Co., 1920.
    1911   "Zur Entwicklungsgeschichte der modernen Malerei." *Der Sturm* 2, no. 75 (August): 597–598.

Secondary Sources

With a few exceptions, works whose full references are cited in footnotes are not listed here. For these consult the index.

Ackley, Clifford S., Timothy O. Benson, and Victor Carlson
    1995   *Nolde: The Painter's Prints.* Exh. cat. Boston: Museum of Fine
               Arts.
Adamson, Walter L.
    1993   *Avant-Garde Florence: From Modernism to Fascism.* Cambridge,
               Mass.: Harvard University Press.
Adorno, Theodor W.
    1985   *Philosophy of Modern Music.* Trans. Anne G. Mitchell and Wes-
               ley V. Blomster. New York: Continuum.
Altieri, Orietta
    1988   "La famiglia Michelstaedter e l'ebraismo goriziano." In *Dia-
               loghi intorno a Michelstaedter.* Ed. Sergio Campailla, 35–41.
               Gorizia: Biblioteca Statale Isontina.
Arangio-Ruiz, Vladimiro
    1922   "Per Carlo Michelstaedter." *Il Convegno: Rivista di letteratura
               di arte di idee e di libri* 7 (July): 343–363.
    1954   "Introduzione all'attualismo." In *Giovanni Gentile: La vita e il
               pensiero.* Fondazione Giovanni Gentile per gli studi Filosofici,
               vol. 7, 1–31. Florence: Sansoni.
Ascheim, Steven E.
    1994   *The Nietzsche Legacy in Germany 1890–1990.* Berkeley: Uni-
               versity of California Press.
Asor Rosa, Alberto
    1985   "La cultura a Firenze nel primo Novecento." In *Intellettuali di*

frontiera: Triestini a Firenze (1900–1950). Ed. Roberto Pertici, 39–53. Florence: Olschki.

Barilli, Renato, ed.
1990   *Espressionismo italiano 1910–20*. Milan: Fabbri.

Barnett, Vivian Endicott, and Armin Zweite
1992   *Kandinsky: Watercolors and Drawings*. Munich: Prestel.

Baron, Frank, ed.
1982   *Rilke and the Visual Arts*. Lawrence, Kans.: Coronado Press.

Baroni, Giorgio
1975   *Trieste e "La Voce."* Milan: Istituto Propaganda Libraria.

Behr, Shulamith, David Fanning, and Douglas Jarman, eds.
1993   *Expressionism Reassessed*. Manchester and New York: Manchester University Press.

Benson, Timothy O., ed.
1993   *Expressionist Utopias: Paradise, Metropolis, Architectural Fantasy*. Exh. cat. Los Angeles: Los Angeles County Museum.

Berman, Marshall
1982   *All That Is Solid Melts Into Air*. New York: Simon & Schuster.

Bertacchini, Renato
1980   "Autocoscienza di una scrittrice triestina: Confessioni e lettere a Slataper di Elody Oblath Stuparich." *Studium* 76, no. 6 (Nov.–Dec.): 762–769.

Bianco, Gabriella
1993   *La hermenéutica del devenir en Carlo Michelstaedter*. Buenos Aires: Torres Agüero.

Bini, Daniela
1988   "Carlo Michelstaedter: The Tragedy of Thought." *Differentia. Review of Italian Thought* 2: 185–194.
1992   *Carlo Michelstaedter and the Failure of Language*. Gainesville: University Press of Florida.

Blumenberg, Hans
1979   *Schiffbruch mit Zuschauer: Paradigma einer Daseinsmetapher*. Frankfurt am Main: Suhrkamp.

Boella, Laura
1977   *Il giovane Lukács: La formazione intellettuale e la filosofia politica, 1907–1928*. Bari: De Donato.

Botstein, Leon
1994   "Egon Schiele and Arnold Schoenberg: The Cultural Politics of Aesthetic Innovation in Vienna, 1890–1918." In *Egon Schiele: Art, Sexuality, and Viennese Modernism*. Ed. Patrick Werkner, 101–117. Palo Alto, Calif.: Society for the Promotion of Science and Scholarship.

Bradley, William S.
1986   *Emil Nolde and German Expressionism: A Prophet in His Own Land*. Ann Arbor: UMI Research Press.

Breicha, Otto
1991   *Richard Gerstl: Bilder zur Person*. Salzburg: Verlag Galerie Welz.

1993   *Gerstl und Schönberg: Eine Beziehung.* Salzburg: Verlag Galerie
            Welz.

Brion-Guerry, L., ed.
1971   *L'Année 1913: Les formes esthétiques de l'oeuvre d'art à la veille
            de la première guerre mondiale.* 2 vols. Paris: Klincksieck.

Bronner, Stephen Eric, and Douglas Kellner, eds.
1983   *Passion and Rebellion: The Expressionist Heritage.* South Had-
            ley, Mass.: J. F. Bergin.

Bürger, Peter
1984   *Theory of the Avant-Garde.* Trans. Michael Shaw. Minneapolis:
            University of Minnesota Press.

Butler, Christopher
1994   *Early Modernism: Literature, Music and Painting in Europe
            1900–1916.* Oxford: Clarendon Press.

Cacciari, Massimo
1978   "Intransitabili utopie." Afterword to Hugo von Hoffmansthal,
            La torre, 155–226. Milan: Adelphi.
1980   *Dallo Steinhof: Prospettive viennesi del primo Novecento.* Mi-
            lan: Adelphi.
1982   *Krisis: Saggio sulla crisi del pensiero negativo da Nietzsche a
            Wittgenstein.* 6th ed. Milan: Feltrinelli.
1983   "Metafisica della gioventù." Afterword to György Lukács, *Di-
            ario (1910–1911).* Ed. Gabriella Caramore, 69–134. Milan:
            Adelphi.
1992a   "Interprétation de Michelstaedter." In *DPAN: Méridiens de la
            décision dans la pensée contemporaine.* Trans. Michel Valensi,
            63–86. Combas: Éditions de l'Éclat. This essay first appeared in
            Italian in *Rivista di estetica* 22 (1986): 21–36.
1992b   "La lutte 'sur' Platon: Michelstaedter et Nietzsche." In *DPAN,*
            87–110.
1993   *Architecture and Nihilism: On the Philosophy of Modern Archi-
            tecture.* Trans. Stephen Sartarelli. New Haven: Yale University
            Press.

Campailla, Sergio
1973   *Pensiero e poesia di Carlo Michelstaedter.* Bologna: Pàtron.
1980a   "Espressionismo e filosofia della contestazione in Michelstaed-
            ter." In *Scrittori giuliani,* 103–131. Bologna: Pàtron.
1980b   "Psicologia del comico nei disegni di Michelstaedter." In *Scrit-
            tori giuliani,* 133–154.
1981   *A ferri corti con la vita.* Gorizia: Arti grafiche Campestrini.

Campailla, Sergio, ed.
1988   *Dialoghi intorno a Michelstaedter.* Gorizia: Biblioteca Statale
            Isontina.

Cardinal, Roger
1985   *Expressionism.* London: Paladin.

Carotenuto, Aldo
1982   *A Secret Symmetry: Sabina Spielrein Between Jung and Freud.*

Trans. Arno Pomerans, John Shepley, and Krishna Winston. New York: Pantheon Books.

Carravetta, Peter
1991   *Prefaces to the Diaphora: Rhetorics, Allegory, and the Interpretation of Postmodernity.* West Lafayette, Ind.: Purdue University Press.

Cary, Joseph
1993   *A Ghost in Trieste.* Chicago: University of Chicago Press.

Castillo, Debra A.
1986   "Georg Lukács: Forms of Longing." *Criticism* 28 (Winter): 89–104.

Cavaglion, Alberto
1982   *Otto Weininger in Italia.* Roma: Carucci.

Cerruti, Marco
1967   *Carlo Michelstaedter.* Milan: Mursia.

Chapple, Gerald, and Hans H. Schulte, eds.
1981   *The Turn of the Century: German Literature and Art, 1890–1915.* Bonn: Bouvier.

Cheetham, Mark
1991   *The Rhetoric of Purity: Essentialist Theory and the Advent of Abstract Painting.* Cambridge and New York: Cambridge University Press.

Chiarini, Paolo
1985   *L'espressionismo tedesco: Storia e struttura.* New edition. Rome: Laterza.

Chipp, Herschel B.
1981   "Self-Portraiture." In *The Human Image in German Expressionist Graphic Art from the Robert Gore Rifkind Foundation,* 16–24. Exh. cat. Berkeley: University Art Museum.

Clark, Martin
1984   *Modern Italy, 1871–1982.* London: Longman.

Clarke, I. F.
1966   *Voices Prophesying War 1763–1984.* London: Oxford University Press.

Colletti, Lucio
1973   *Marxism and Hegel.* Trans. Lawrence Garner. London: NLB.

Comini, Alessandra
1974   *Egon Schiele's Portraits.* Berkeley: University of California Press.
1994   "In Search of Schiele." In Kallir 1994, 17–37.

Comte, Philippe
1989   *Paul Klee.* New York: Mallard Press.

Congdon, Lee
1981   "The Tragic Sense of Life: Lukács's *The Soul and the Forms.*" In *Austrian Philosophy: Studies and Texts.* Ed. J. C. Nyíri, 43–74. Munich: Philosophia Verlag GmbH.
1983   *The Young Lukács.* Chapel Hill and London: The University of North Carolina Press.

Cook, Nicholas
1990   *Music, Imagination, and Culture*. Oxford and New York: Oxford University Press.
Cork, Richard
1994   *A Bitter Truth: Avant-Garde Art and the Great War*. New Haven: Yale University Press.
Crawford, John C., and Dorothy L. Crawford
1993   *Expressionism in Twentieth-Century Music*. Bloomington: Indiana University Press.
Dabrowski, Magdalena
1995   *Kandinsky: Compositions*. Exh. cat. New York: Museum of Modern Art.
David, Claude
1962   "Rilke et l'expressionisme." *Études Germaniques* 17, no. 2 (April–June): 144–157.
David, Michel
1966   *La psicoanalisi nella cultura italiana*. Turin: Boringhieri.
Derrida, Jacques
1993   *Aporias*. Trans. Thomas Dutoit. Stanford: Stanford University Press.
Dolei, Giuseppe
1978   *L'arte come espiazione imperfetta: Saggio su Trakl*. Stuttgart: Hans-Dieter Heinz.
Dube, Wolf-Dieter
1990   *The Expressionists*. Trans. Mary Whittall. London: Thames and Hudson.
Eksteins, Modris
1990   *Rites of Spring: The Great War and the Birth of the Modern Age*. New York: Doubleday.
Epstein, Isidore
1959   *Judaism: A Historical Presentation*. Harmondsworth: Penguin Books.
Falck, Robert
1982   "Emancipation of the Dissonance." *Journal of the Arnold Schoenberg Institute* 6, no. 1 (June): 106–111.
Fant, Åke
1986   "The Case of the Artist Hilma af Klint." In *The Spiritual in Art: Abstract Painting 1980–1985*. Ed. Maurice Tuchman, 155–164. New York: Abbeville Press and Los Angeles County Museum of Art.
Fiedler, Theodore
1972   "Georg Trakl's 'Abendland': Life as Tragedy." *Wahrheit und Sprache*. Ed. Wilm Peters and Paul Schimmelpfennig, 201–210. Göppingen: Alfred Kümmerle.
Fleisher, Robert
1989   "Dualism in the Music of Arnold Schoenberg." *Journal of the Arnold Schoenberg Institute* 12, no. 1 (June): 22–42.

Fortini, Franco
1985   "Contro la retorica del suicidio." In *Insistenze: Cinquanta scritti 1976–84*, 158–161. Milan: Garzanti.
Friesenbiller, Elfriede
1985   "Showing True Colors: Editorial Problem." Afterword to Egon Schiele, *I, Eternal Child: Paintings and Poems*. Trans. Anselm Hollo, 46–47. New York: Grove Press.
Frisby, David
1985   *Fragments of Modernity: Theories of Modernity in the Work of Simmel, Kracauer and Benjamin*. Cambridge: Polity Press.
Fussell, Paul
1977   *The Great War and Modern Memory*. Oxford and New York: Oxford University Press.
Gargani, Aldo
1985   *Lo stupore e il caso*. Rome: Laterza.
1986   *Linguaggio ed esperienza in Ludwig Wittgenstein*. Florence: Le Monnier.
Gay, Peter
1968   *Weimar Culture: The Outsider as Insider*. New York: Harper & Row.
Glaser, Hermann, ed.
1981   *The German Mind of the Nineteenth Century: A Literary and Historical Anthology*. New York: Continuum.
Gluck, Mary
1985   *Georg Lukács and His Generation, 1900–1918*. Cambridge, Mass.: Harvard University Press.
Goldmann, Heinrich
1957   *Katabasis: Eine tiefenpsychologische Studie zur Symbolik der Dichtungen Georg Trakls*. Salzburg: Otto Müller.
Gordon, Donald E.
1981   "Oskar Kokoschka and the Visionary Tradition." In Chapple and Schulte, eds., 1981, 23–52.
1987   *Expressionism: Art and Idea*. New Haven: Yale University Press.
Gravagnuolo, Benedetto
1982   *Adolf Loos: Theory and Works*. New York: Rizzoli.
Guenther, Peter
1977   *German Expressionism: Toward a New Humanism*. Exh. cat. Houston: Sarah Campbell Blaffer Gallery.
Haftmann, Werner
1966   *Painting in the Twentieth Century*. Trans. Ralph Manheim. New ed. New York: Praeger.
Hailey, Christopher
1993   "Musical Expressionism: The Search for Autonomy." In Behr, Fanning, and Jarman, eds., 1993, 103–111.
Hamann, Richard, and Jost Hermand
1977   *Expressionismus*. Frankfurt am Main: Fischer Taschenbuch.

Hamburger, Michael
1957   "Georg Trakl." In *Reason and Energy,* 239–271. London: Rout-
            ledge and Kegan Paul.
1970   "1912." In *Contraries: Studies in German Literature,* 263–290.
            New York: E. P. Dutton.
Hankoff, E. D., and Bernice Einsidler, eds.
1979   *Suicide: Theory and Clinical Aspects.* Littleton, Mass.: PGS Pub-
            lishing Co.
Harrison, Thomas
1991   "Carlo Michelstaedter and the Metaphysics of Will." *MLN* 106
            (December): 1012–1029.
1992   *Essayism: Conrad, Musil, and Pirandello.* Baltimore: The Johns
            Hopkins University Press.
Harrison, Thomas, ed.
1988   *Nietzsche in Italy.* Saratoga, Calif.: Anma Libri.
Heidegger, Martin
1927   *Being and Time.* Trans. John Macquarrie and Edward Robin-
            son. New York: Harper & Row, 1962.
1957   "A Recollection." In *Heidegger: The Man and the Thinker.* Ed.
            Thomas Sheehan, 21–22. Chicago: Precedent Publishing, 1987.
Heller, Agnes
1972   " 'Von der Armut am Geiste': A Dialogue by the Young Lukács."
            The Philosophical Forum 3, nos. 3–4: 360–370.
1983   "Georg Lukács and Irma Seidler." In Heller, ed., 1983, 27–62.
1992   "Death of the Subject?" In *Constructions of Self.* Ed. Georg
            Levine, 269–284. New Brunswick, N.J.: Rutgers University Press.
Heller, Agnes, ed.
1983   *Lukács Revalued.* Oxford: Basil Blackwell.
Heller, Erich
1975   *The Disinherited Mind: Essays in Modern German Thought.*
            New York: Harcourt Brace Jovanovich.
1981   "The Poet in the Age of Prose: Reflections on Hegel's *Aesthetics*
            and Rilke's *Duino Elegies.*" In Chapple and Schulte, eds., 1981,
            5–20.
Heller, Reinhold
1973   *Edvard Munch: The Scream.* New York: Viking.
Hermand, Jost
1991   *Beredte Töne: Musik im historischen Prozess.* Frankfurt am
            Main: Lang.
Hinton, Stephen
1993   "Defining Musical Expressionism: Schoenberg and Others." In
            Behr, Fanning, and Jarman, eds., 1993, 121–129.
Hofmann, Paul
1989   *Viennese: Splendor, Twilight, and Exile.* New York: Doubleday.
Hofmann, Werner
1986   "L'Émancipation des dissonances." *Gazette des Beaux-Arts* 6,
            no. 108 (December): 220–230.

Holmes, Joan E.
1982   "Rodin's *Prodigal Son* and Rilke's *Malte.*" In Baron, ed. 1982,
          19–25.
*The Human Image in German Expressionist Graphic Art from the Robert Gore
          Rifkind Foundation.* Exh. cat. Berkeley: University Art Mu-
          seum, 1981.
Janik, Allan
1985   *Essays on Wittgenstein and Weininger.* Amsterdam: Rodopi.
1990   " 'Ethik und Aesthetik sind Eins': Wittgenstein and Trakl." *Mod-
          ern Austrian Literature* 23, no. 2: 55–70.
Janik, Allan, and Stephen Toulmin
1973   *Wittgenstein's Vienna.* New York: Simon and Schuster.
Johnston, William
1972   *The Austrian Mind: An Intellectual and Social History 1848–
          1938.* Berkeley: University of California Press.
Kadarkay, Arpad
1991   *Georg Lukács: Life, Thought, and Politics.* Cambridge, Mass.:
          Basil Blackwell.
Kaes, Anton
1979   "The Expressionist Vision in Theater and Cinema." In Pickar
          and Webb, eds., 1979, 89–98.
Kallir, Jane
1981   *Austria's Expressionism.* Exh. cat. New York: Galerie St. Eti-
          enne & Rizzoli.
1984   *Arnold Schoenberg's Vienna.* Exh. cat. New York: Galerie
          St. Etienne and Rizzoli.
1992   *Richard Gerstl, Oskar Kokoschka.* Exh. cat. New York: Galerie
          St. Etienne.
1994   *Egon Schiele.* Exh. cat. New York: Harry N. Abrams.
Kamensky, Aleksandr
1989   *Chagall: The Russian Years 1907–1922.* New York: Rizzoli.
Kelly, John
1971   "Deux revues: 'Poetry and Drama' et 'The New Age.'" In Brion-
          Guerry, ed., 1971, 1007–1022.
Kern, Stephen
1983   *The Culture of Time and Space 1880–1918.* Cambridge, Mass.:
          Harvard University Press.
Kiralyfalvi, Béla
1975   *The Aesthetics of Georg Lukács.* Princeton: Princeton Univer-
          sity Press.
Kleefeld, Gunther
1985   *Das Gedicht als Sühne: Georg Trakls Dichtung und Krankheit:
          Eine psychoanalytische Studie.* Tübingen: Niemeyer.
Klein, Johannes
1969   "Georg Trakl." In *Expressionismus als Literatur: Gesammelte
          Studien.* Ed. Wolfgang Rothe, 374–397. Bern: Francke Verlag.

Knafo, Danielle
1993   *Egon Schiele, A Self in Creation: A Psychoanalytic Study of the Artist's Self-Portraits*. London: Associated University Presses.
Knapp, Gerhard P.
1979   *Die Literatur des deutschen Expressionismus*. Munich: C. H. Beck.
Kravitz, Ellen
1978   "Foreword: Schoenberg as Artist." *Journal of the Arnold Schoenberg Institute* 2, no. 3 (June): 163.
Kris, Ernst, and E. H. Gombrich
1967   "The Principles of Caricature." In *Psychoanalytic Explorations in Art*. Ed. Ernst Kris, 189–203. New York: Schocken.
LaCapra, Dominick
1983   *Rethinking Intellectual History: Texts, Contexts, Language*. Ithaca: Cornell University Press.
Lea, Henry A. "Musical Expressionism in Vienna." In Bronner and Kellner, eds., 1983, 315–331.
Leger, François
1989   *La Pensée de Georg Simmel: Contribution à l'histoire des idées en Allemagne au début du XXe siècle*. Paris: Kime.
Leopold, Rudolf
1973   *Egon Schiele: Paintings, Watercolors, Drawings*. Trans. Alexander Lieven. London: Phaidon.
Le Rider, Jacques
1982   *Le Cas Weininger: Racines de l'antiféminisme et de l'antisémitisme*. Paris: Presses Universitaires de France.
1993   *Modernity and Crises of Identity*. Trans. Rosemary Morris. New York: Continuum.
Lessing, Theodor
1930   *Jüdischer Selbsthass*. Berlin: Jüdischer Verlag.
Levine, Frederick S.
1979   *The Apocalyptic Vision: The Art of Franz Marc as German Expressionism*. New York: Harper & Row.
Lindenberger, Herbert
1958   "The Play of Opposites in Georg Trakl's Poetry." *German Life and Letters*. New Series, 11, no. 2: 192–204.
1971   *Georg Trakl*. New York: Twayne.
Long, Rose-Carol Washton
1980   *Kandinsky: The Development of an Abstract Style*. Oxford: Clarendon Press.
Luft, David S.
1980   *Robert Musil and the Crisis of European Culture 1880–1942*. Berkeley: University of California Press.
Macartney, Carlile Aylmer
1971   *The Habsburg Empire 1790–1918*. London: Weidenfeld and Nicolson.

Magris, Claudio
1983   Preface to Trakl 1983, vii–viii.
1991   *Un altro mare*. Milan: Garzanti.
Maier, Bruno
1981   "Lettere di Elody Oblath a Scipio Slataper." *Rassegna della letteratura italiana* 85, nos. 1–2 (Jan.–Aug.): 212–215.
Marcus, Judith, and Zoltan Tarr, eds.
1989   *Georg Lukács: Theory, Culture, and Politics*. New Brunswick, N.J.: Transaction.
Márkus, György
1983   "Life and the Soul: The Young Lukács and the Problem of Culture." In Heller, ed., 1983, 1–26.
Masur, Gerhard
1961   *Prophets of Yesterday: Studies in European Culture, 1890–1914*. New York: Harper & Row.
Mayer, Hans
1982   *Outsiders: A Study in Life and Letters*. Trans. Denis M. Sweet. Cambridge, Mass.: MIT Press.
Meerloo, Joost A. M.
1962   *Suicide and Mass Suicide*. New York: Grune and Stratton.
Mendes-Flohr, Paul
1984   "Fin de siècle Orientalism, the *Ostjude* and the Aesthetics of Jewish Self-Affirmation." In *Studies in Contemporary Jewish History, I*. Ed. J. Frankel, 96–139. Bloomington, Ind.: Indiana University Press.
1985   Introduction to Buber 1909.
1989   *From Mysticism to Dialogue: Martin Buber's Transformation of German Social Thought*. Detroit: Wayne State University Press.
Merz, Veronika
1982   "Die Gottesidee in Rilkes 'Aufzeichnungen des Malte Laurids Brigge.'" *Jahrbuch der Deutschen Schillergesellschaft* 26: 262–295.
Meyerowitz, Jan
1967   *Arnold Schönberg*. Berlin: Colloquium.
Miesel, Victor
1968   "The Term Expressionism in the Visual Arts." In *The Uses of History*. Ed. Hayden White, 135–151. Detroit: Wayne State University Press.
Mitsch, Erwin
1988   *The Art of Egon Schiele*. New York: Hudson Hills Press.
Mittner, Ladislao
1978   *Storia della letteratura tedesca* III vol. 2. Turin: Einaudi.
Mommsen, Wolfgang J., and Jürgen Osterhammel, eds.
1987   *Max Weber and His Contemporaries*. London: Allen & Unwin.
Mosse, George L.
1964   *The Crisis of German Ideology: Intellectual Origins of the Third Reich*. New York: Grosset & Dunlap.

1980   *Masses and Man: Nationalist and Fascist Perceptions of Reality.* New York: Howard Fertig.

Myers, Bernard S.
1957   *The German Expressionists: A Generation in Revolt.* New York: Praeger.

Nebehay, Christian M.
1979   *Egon Schiele, 1880–1918: Leben, Briefe, Gedichte.* Salzburg: Residenz.
1980   *Egon Schiele: Leben und Werk.* Salzburg: Residenz.

Neher, André
1981   *The Exile of the Word: From the Silence of the Bible to the Silence of Auschwitz.* Trans. David Masiel. Philadelphia: The Jewish Publication Society of America.

Neubauer, John
1991   *The Fin-de-Siècle Culture of Adolescence.* New Haven: Yale University Press.

Neumann, Erich
1979   "Georg Trakl: Person and the Myth." In *Creative Man: Five Essays.* Trans. Eugene Rolfe. Princeton: Princeton University Press.

Oxaal, Ivar, Michael Pollak, and Gerhard Botz, eds.
1987   *Jews, Antisemitism and Culture in Vienna.* London and New York: Routledge & Kegan Paul.

Palmier, Jean-Michel
1972   *Situation de Georg Trakl.* Paris: Éditions Pierre Belfond.
1979–80   *L'Expressionisme et les arts.* 2 vols. Paris: Payot.

Partsch, Susanna
1991   *Franz Marc, 1880–1916.* Trans. Karen Williams. Cologne: Benedikt Taschen.

Passuth, Christine
1971   "La revue 'Nyugat.'" In Brion-Guerry, ed., 1971, 1003–1006.

Pehnt, Wolfgang
1973   *Expressionist Architecture.* Trans. J. A. Underwood and Edith Küstner. New York: Praeger.

Perkins, Geoffrey
1974   *Contemporary Theory of Expressionism.* Bern: Herbert Lang.

Perle, George
1969   *Serial Composition and Atonality.* 2d ed. Berkeley: University of California Press.

Perloff, Marjorie
1986   *The Futurist Moment: Avant-garde, Avant Guerre, and the Language of Rupture.* Chicago: University of Chicago Press.
1992   "Toward a Wittgensteinian Poetics." *Contemporary Literature* 33 (Summer): 191–213.

Perniola, Mario
1989   "Beyond Postmodernism: Michelstaedter, Strong Feeling, the Present." *Differentia. Review of Italian Thought* 3–4: 39–50.
1991   "Enigmas of Italian Temperament." *Differentia. Review of Italian Thought* 5: 19–30.

Pertici, Roberto, ed.
1985   *Intellettuali di frontiera: Triestini a Firenze (1900–1950).* 2 vols. Florence: Olschki.

Petazzi, Paolo
1975   "Schoenberg: The Piano Music." Notes to Schoenberg 1975.

Pick, Daniel
1989   *Faces of Degeneration: A European Disorder, c. 1848–1918.* Cambridge: Cambridge University Press.
1993   *War Machine: The Rationalization of Slaughter in the Modern Age.* New Haven: Yale University Press.

Pickar, Gertrud Bauer, and Karl Eugene Webb, eds.
1979   *Expressionism Reconsidered: Relationships and Affinities.* Munich: W. Fink.

Pieri, Piero
1984   *La differenza ebraica: Ebraismo e grecità in Michelstaedter.* Bologna: Cappelli.
1989   *La scienza del tragico: Saggio su Carlo Michelstaedter.* Bologna: Cappelli.

Poggioli, Renato
1981   *The Theory of the Avant-garde.* Trans. Gerald Fitzgerald. Cambridge, Mass.: Belknap Press of Harvard University Press.

Poliakov, Léon
1977   *Histoire de l'antisémitisme, IV: L'europe suicidaire, 1870–1933.* Paris: Calmann-Lévy.

Pollak, Michael
1984   *Vienne 1900: Une identité blessée.* Paris: Gallimard.
1987   "Cultural Innovation and Social Identity in *fin-de-siècle* Vienna." In Oxaal, Pollak, and Botz, eds., 1987, 59–74.

Pullega, Paolo
1981   "Dai giardini di marzo al maggio operaio: L'espressionismo del giovane Lukács." Introduction to György Lukács, *Sulla povertà di spirito: Scritti (1907–1918),* 7–50. Bologna: Cappelli.
1983   *La comprensione estetica del mondo: Saggio sul giovane Lukács.* Bologna: Cappelli.

Raabe, Paul, ed.
1972   *Index Expressionismus: Bibliographie der Beiträge in den Zeitschriften und Jahrbüchern des literarischen Expressionismus, 1910–1925.* 18 vols. Nendeln, Lichtenstein: Kraus-Thomson.
1987   *Expressionismus: Der Kampf um eine literarische Bewegung.* Zurich: Arche.

Ranke, Joachim
1961   "Das Denken Carlo Michelstaedters: Ein Beitrage zur italienischen Existenzphilosophie." *Zeitschrift für philosophische Forschung* 1: 101–123.

Read, Herbert
1967   *Art and Alienation: The Role of the Artist in Society.* New York: Horizon.

Reed, Oreel P.
1977   *German Expressionist Art: The Robert Gore Rifkind Collection.*
        Exh. cat. Los Angeles: Frederick S. Wight Art Gallery, University
        of California.

Reif, Jo-Ann
1983   "Adrian Leverkühn, Arnold Schoenberg, Theodor Adorno: The-
        orists Real and Fictitious in Thomas Mann's *Doctor Faustus.*"
        Journal of the Arnold Schoenberg Institute 7, no. 1 (June): 102–
        112.

Rella, Franco
1981   *Il silenzio e le parole: Il pensiero nel tempo della crisi.* 3d ed.
        Milan: Feltrinelli.

Ringer, Alexander
1979   "Arnold Schoenberg and the Politics of Jewish Survival." *Jour-
        nal of the Arnold Schoenberg Institute* 3, no. 1 (March): 11–48.

Roethel, Hans, and Jean K. Benjamin
1979   *Kandinsky.* New York: Hudson Hills.

Roh, Franz
1925   "Post-Expressionist Schema." In Kaes, Jay, and Dimenberg, eds.,
        1994, 493.

Roh, Franz, and Juliane Roh
1969   *German Art in the 20th Century.* Trans. Cath Hutter. Ed. Julia
        Phelps. Greenwich, Conn.: New York Graphic Society.

Rosen, Charles
1975   *Arnold Schoenberg.* Princeton: Princeton University Press.

Rothe, Wolfgang
1977   *Der Expressionismus: Theologische, soziologische und anthro-
        pologische Aspekte einer Literatur.* Frankfurt: Klostermann.

Rothe, Wolfgang, ed.
1969   *Expressionismus als Literatur.* Berne and Munich: Francke
        Verlag.

Saas, Christa
1981   "Kandinsky und Trakl: Zum Vergleich der Abstraktion in der
        Modernen Kunst und Lyrik." In Chapple and Schulte, eds.,
        1981, 347–376.

Salter, Ronald
1980   "Georg Trakl und Egon Schiele: Aspeckte des österreichischen
        Expressionismus in Wort und Bild." *Österreichische Gegen-
        wart: Die moderne Literatur und ihr Verhältnis zur Tradition.*
        Ed. Wolfgang Paulsen, 59–79. Bern: Francke.

Schapiro, Meyer
1978   *Modern Art, 19th and 20th Centuries: Selected Papers.* New
        York: George Braziller.

Schneider, Ludwig
1967   *Zerbrochene Formen: Wort und Bild im Expressionismus.* Ham-
        burg: Hoffmann & Campe.

Scholz, Frances Mary
1982   "Rilke, Rodin and the Fragmented Man." In Baron, ed., 1982, 27–44.
Schorske, Carl E.
1981   *Fin-de-siècle Vienna: Politics and Culture*. New York: Random House.
Schreyer, Lothar
1948   *Expressionistisches Theater*. Hamburg: Toth.
Schröder, Klaus Albrecht
1993   *Richard Gerstl 1883–1908*. Exh. cat. Vienna: Kunstforum der Bank Austria.
Schröder, Klaus Albrecht, and Harald Szeemann, eds.
1988   *Egon Schiele und seine Zeit*. Munich: Prestel Verlag.
Schultze, Jürgen
1973   "Beobachtungen zum Thema 'Munch und der deutsche Expressionismus.'" In *Edvard Munch: Probleme—Forschungen—Thesen*. Ed. Henning Bock and Günter Busch, 147–160. Munich: Prestel.
Schweikert, Uwe
1982   "Georg Lukács: Briefe an Irma Seidler aus den Jahren 1908 bis 1911." *Neue Rundschau* 93, no. 1: 85–105.
Selz, Peter
1957   *German Expressionist Painting*. Berkeley: University of California Press.
Seton-Watson, Christopher
1967   *Italy from Liberalism to Fascism, 1870–1925*. London: Methuen.
Sharp, Francis Michael
1981   *The Poet's Madness: A Reading of Georg Trakl*. Ithaca: Cornell University Press.
Sheppard, Richard
1990   "Kandinsky's *Oeuvre* 1900–14: The *Avant-Garde* as Rear-Guard." *Word & Image* 6, no. 1 (Jan.–March): 41–67.
Shneidman, Edwin S.
1979   "An Overview: Personality, Motivation, and Behavior Theories." In *Suicide: Theory and Clinical Aspects*. Ed. L. D. Hankiff and Bernice Einsidler, 143–163. Littleton, Mass.: PSG Publishing.
Slonimsky, Nicolas
1971   *Music Since 1900*. 4th ed. New York: Charles Scribner's Sons.
Soergel, Albert, and Curt Hohoff
1963   *Dichtung und Dichter der Zeit: Vom Naturalismus bis zur Gegenwart*. Düsseldorf: Bagel.
Sokel, Walter H.
1959   *The Writer in Extremis: Expressionism in Twentieth-Century German Literature*. Stanford: Stanford University Press.
1980   "The Devolution of the Self in *The Notebooks of Malte Laurids Brigge*." In *Rilke: The Alchemy of Alienation*. Ed. Frank Baron,

Ernst S. Dick, and Warren R. Maurer, 171–190. Lawrence, Kans.: The Regents Press of Kansas.

Solomon, Robert C.
1988 *Continental Philosophy since 1750: The Rise and Fall of the Self.* Oxford: Oxford University Press.

Stern, Fritz
1963 *The Politics of Cultural Despair: A Study in the Rise of the Germanic Ideology.* Berkeley: University of California Press.

Strohschneider-Kohrs, Ingrid
1960 "Die Entwicklung der lyrischen Sprache in der Dichtung Georg Trakls." *Literaturwissenschaftliches Jahrbuch der Görresgesellschaft* 1: 211–226.

Stuparich, Giani
1950 *Scipio Slataper.* Milan: Mondadori.

Theunissen, Michael
1984 *The Other: Studies in the Ontology of Husserl, Sartre, and Buber.* Trans. Christopher Macann. Cambridge, Mass.: MIT Press.

Thürlemann, Felix
1986 *Kandinsky über Kandinsky: Der Kunstler als Interpret eigener Werke.* Berne: Benteli.

Tiessen, Heinz
1928 *Zur Geschichte der jüngsten Musik, 1913–1928.* Mainz: Melos.

Tilgher, Adriano
1922 "Carlo Michelstaedter." *La Stampa,* December 23, 1922, 3. Reprinted in *Filosofi e moralisti del Novecento,* 295–304. Roma: Liberia di Scienze e Lettere, 1932.

Tilghman, B. R.
1991 *Wittgenstein, Ethics and Aesthetics: The View from Eternity.* Albany: State University of New York Press.

Tuchman, Maurice
1986 "Hidden Meanings in Abstract Art." In Tuchman, ed., 1986, 17–61.

Tuchman, Maurice, ed.
1986 *The Spiritual in Art: Abstract Painting 1980–1985.* New York: Abbeville Press and Los Angeles County Museum of Art.

Turchetta, Gianni
1990 *Dino Campana: Biografia di un poeta.* Milan: Marcos y Marcos.

Vergo, Peter
1975 *Art in Vienna 1898–1918.* London: Phaidon.
1980 "Music and Abstract Painting: Kandinsky, Goethe and Schöenberg." In *Towards a New Art: Essays on the Background to Abstract Art, 1910–20,* 41–63. London: Tate Gallery.

Vezin, Annette, and Luc Vezin
1992 *Kandinsky and Der Blaue Reiter.* Trans. Judith Hayward. Paris: Pierre Terrail.

Vietta, Silvio, and Hans-Georg Kemper
1985 *Expressionismus.* 3d ed. Munich: Fink.

Vogt, Paul
  1980   *The Blue Rider.* Trans. Joachim Neugroschel. Woodbury, N.Y.:
              Barron's.
Waite, Geoffrey C. W.
  1981   "Worringer's *Abstraction and Empathy*: Remarks on Its Recep-
              tion and on the Rhetoric of Criticism." In Chapple and Schulte,
              eds., 1981, 197–224.
Webber, Andrew
  1990   *Sexuality and the Sense of Self in the Works of Georg Trakl and
              Robert Musil.* London: Modern Humanities Research Institute.
Weingartner, Rudolf H.
  1959   "Form and Content in Simmel's Philosophy of Life." In *Georg
              Simmel: A Collection of Essays.* Ed. Kurt H. Wolff, 33–60. Co-
              lumbus: The Ohio State University Press.
Weiss, Peg
  1979   *Kandinsky in Munich: The Formative Jugendstil Years.* Prince-
              ton: Princeton University Press.
Werenskiold, Marit
  1984   *The Concept of Expressionism: Origin and Metamorphoses.*
              Trans. Ronald Walford. Oslo and New York: Universitetsfor-
              laget and Columbia University Press.
Werkner, Patrick
  1993   *Austrian Expressionism: The Formative Years.* Palo Alto, Calif.:
              Society for the Promotion of Science and Scholarship.
Werkner, Patrick, ed.
  1994   *Egon Schiele: Art, Sexuality, and Viennese Modernism.* Palo Alto,
              Calif.: Society for the Promotion of Science and Scholarship.
White, Hayden
  1987   *The Content of the Form: Narrative Discourse and Historical
              Representation.* Baltimore: The Johns Hopkins University Press.
Whitford, Frank
  1981   *Egon Schiele.* London: Thames and Hudson.
Willett, John
  1970   *Expressionism.* New York: McGraw Hill.
Williams, C. E.
  1974   *The Broken Eagle: The Politics of Austrian Literature from Em-
              pire to Anschluss.* London: Paul Elek.
Williams, Eric, ed.
  1991   *The Dark Flutes of Fall: Critical Essays on Georg Trakl.* Colum-
              bia, S.C.: Camden House.
Winteler, Paula Michelstaedter
  1973   "Appunti per una biografia di Carlo Michelstaedter." Appendix
              to Campailla 1973, 145–164.
Wohl, Robert
  1979   *The Generation of 1914.* Cambridge, Mass.: Harvard University
              Press.

Wörner, Karl H.
  1970   *Die Musik in der Geistesgeschichte: Studien zur Situation der
             Jahre um 1910.* Bonn: Bouvier.
Wuorinen, Charles
  1975   Introduction to Schoenberg, *Pierrot Lunaire, Op. 21.* Compact
             disc. Elektra Nonesuch 9-79237-2.
Zitta, Victor
  1964   *Georg Lukács' Marxism, Alienation, Dialectics, Revolution: A
             Study in Utopia and Ideology.* The Hague: M. Nijhoff.
Zweite, Armin, ed.
  1982   *Kandinsky und München: Begegnungen und Wandlungen 1896–
             1914.* Munich: Prestel.

Index

Designer: UC Press Staff
Compositor: Prestige Typography
Text: 10/13 Sabon
Display: Sabon
Printer: Thomson-Shore, Inc.
Binder: Thomson-Shore, Inc.